MW01205444

The American Puritans Series

CHRIST
THE FOUNTAIN OF LIFE

John Cotton

Edited by
Nate Pickowicz

With
John Manning

ENTREATING FAVOR

Christ the Fountain of Life
Copyright 2017 by Nathan Pickowicz
All rights reserved. No part of this book may be reproduced in any form without written permission from the author.

Publishing imprint:
Entreating Favor Books
P.O. Box 163
Gilmanton Iron Works, New Hampshire 03837

This volume is an edited and modernized version of a work by John Cotton (1584-1652), which is in public domain: *Christ the Fountaine of Life* or, *Sundry Choyce Sermons on the first Chapter of the first Epistle of St. John* (1651).

Cover design: Stephen Melniszyn, Stephen Melniszyn Designs, Tulsa, Oklahoma
Interior layout and design: John Manning

ISBN: 978-0-9832946-4-1

This volume is dedicated to

Dr. Digby L. James

for his thirty years of devotion to the work of John Cotton

THE AMERICAN PURITANS SERIES

Over the last fifty years there has been a renewed interest in the Puritans. In past generations, works by the English Divines sat dusty and derided, but soon found new life through the efforts of D. Martyn Lloyd-Jones, Iain H. Murray and the Banner of Truth Trust, and J.I. Packer. Today, many of the once-forgotten Puritans are household names in the Christian community—men like William Perkins, Richard Sibbes, Thomas Watson, Samuel Rutherford, Richard Baxter, John Owen, John Bunyan, Matthew Henry, and others.

However, during the Great Migration (1630-1640), not a few Puritan leaders fled persecution and made their way across the Atlantic Ocean, and settled in the American Colonies. These early American Christian leaders were not only pillars in the church, but also acted as spiritual and intellectual fathers to a great nation. But many of these faithful pastors are relatively unknown, their work is barely read, and their publications have long been out of print.

The American Puritans Series exists to reintroduce the work of the first Christian leaders to a modern audience. Each reprint will consist of the author's original work, yet gently edited and modernized for the ease of the reader. By the grace of God, this series will help rekindle a love for the writings of the Puritans whose theology was built on the biblical doctrines of the Reformation. May a whole new generation see Christ afresh through the work of our spiritual ancestors.

Nate Pickowicz
Series Editor

Editor's Introduction

O ne of the greatest Christian leaders ever to cross the Atlantic Ocean to the New World was John Cotton (1584-1652). In England, he had a faithful and influential ministry that blessed thousands, making him one of the leading Puritans of his day. But the persecution of Protestants by King Charles I drove many to flee the continent—including the Reverend Cotton.

Upon his arrival to the Bay Colony in 1633, Cotton was joyfully embraced by New Englanders, and thus resumed his ministry in the growing town of Boston.[1] John Winthrop, the governor of Massachusetts, would rely heavily on John Cotton for his wisdom and spiritual counsel as he made fateful decisions in the early days of the burgeoning colony. In the area of ecclesiology, Cotton would write extensively on the development and implementation of

---

[1] John Norton notes, "By the English settlers, it was first called Tremount, or Trimountain, from its three hills. After the removal of Mr. Cotton, it received the name of Boston, from the place of his former residence in England." *Memoir of John Cotton*. (Perkins & Marvin: Boston, 1834), 4.

Congregationalism, whereby even Puritan giants such as John Owen and Thomas Goodwin gleaned from his work. Cotton's writings would stand as the backbone of the New England Way for decades to come.

This present volume, *Christ the Fountain of Life*, was originally the product of Rev. Cotton's teaching ministry in England. Prior to immigrating to New England, he preached through First John. However, it would not be until 1651 that he would compile eleven sermons from 1 John 5:12 and five sermons on the subsequent verses into one volume. On the value of the work, Puritan scholar Dr. Charles Hambrick-Stowe writes, "*Christ the Fountain of Life* expresses Puritanism's evangelical and pastoral impulses as plainly as any of the widely used devotional manuals published in London and Boston during the seventeenth century."[2]

It has been over three centuries since this book has been in print, though a facsimile reprint was published by Arno Press (New York) in 1972. However, in recent years, Dr. Digby L. James of Quinta Press has undertaken the monumental task of transcribing and replicating the complete works of John Cotton. The church universal would be tremendously blessed should Dr. James' work find its way into print.

---

[2] Charles E. Hambrick-Stowe, "Christ the Fountain of Life by John Cotton (1584-1652)" in Kelly M. Kapic and Randall C. Gleason, eds. *The Devoted Life: An Invitation to the Puritan Classics.* (Downers Grove, IL: InterVarsity, 2004), 78.

This present inaugural release of *Christ the Fountain of Life* in the American Puritans Series has been gently edited for the ease of the modern reader. A few of the updates include:

- **Language and spelling.** The Old English text has been adapted to fit modern vernacular, as well as spelling.

- **Added Chapter Titles and Paragraph Headings.** The titles have been extracted from verbiage in the text, while in many cases, paragraph headings were borrowed from marginal notes printed in Cotton's original manuscript.

- **Re-formatting.** Many of the longer paragraphs have been broken up for the sake of ease in reading. Additionally, verse quotations and references have been updated to fit modern standards.

- **Bible translation.** The majority of Puritans used the Geneva Bible. For the sake of uniformity in modernizing the text, while the original translation was not changed, the verbiage has simply been updated.

- **Corrections made.** In the original 1651 printing by Robert Ibbitson, some mistakes were made. Most of them had to do with Scripture references. Nearly fifty of these references have thus been corrected.

- **Adjustments to Punctuation and Capitalization.** Minor changes in punctuation have been made (seventeenth century grammar was troublesome by our modern standards!) for the sake of an easier read, though much was left in hopes of keeping the author's original voice intact.

It is my great hope that this reprint will bless the reader, and aid in rekindling a love for John Cotton and the American Puritans, namely the trailblazing saints of early New England. If there is any lack to be found in this current volume, it is surely due to my own efforts, and not the original author.

Soli Deo Gloria!

Nate Pickowicz

Gilmanton Iron Works, 2017

Table of Contents

PART I

THE WAYS WE HAVE CHRIST

HAVING CHRIST BY WAY OF WORSHIP

He that has the Son has life, and he that has not the Son has not life.
(1 John 5:12)

These words contain part of the record that God bore of His Son, to whom this eternal life is communicated, and that is to all such as to whom the Son is communicated; amplified by the contrary, "He that has not the Son has not life."

Doctrine: *According to, or upon our having, or not having of Christ, depends our having or not having of life.*

The note is of special weight in our Christian experience, and therefore let us take so much the more care in opening of it: "He that finds Me (which is all one with, 'he that has Me') he has life" (Prov. 8:35), "but he that is estranged from Me, he loves death" (v. 36). So that, find Christ, and find life. Find Him not, but be estranged from Him, and find death. Also, Ephesians 2:12, "In times past you were without Christ being aliens from the commonwealth of Israel, strangers from the covenant of promise, having no hope, and without God in the world." And

Ephesians 4:18–19, where he speaks of some that were alienated from the life of God; but in verses 20-21, "You have not so learned Christ, if so be you have been taught by Him as the truth is in Jesus."

For further clearing of this point, let me show you first the reasons upon which it depends, and then the uses of it.

REASON 1: CREATURES ARE BROKEN CISTERNS WITHOUT CHRIST

The first reason arises from the insufficiency of all the body of the creature to give us life without Christ: "It is not possible that the blood of bulls and goats should cleanse the conscience from sin" (Heb. 10:1–4). They are not a valuable recompense to God for the transgressions we have done by our transgressions. We had deserved death, for which the death of the beasts cannot make recompense.

And besides, should we die for our sins ourselves, our death would not free us from the punishment, for we are not able to overcome death, but should forever sink under it. If there had been a law that could have given us life, then we might have lived by it. But there is no such law as can give us spiritual life. David speaks in the name of Christ in Psalm 22:29. It is the speech of our Savior, or of David in His name: "No man can keep alive his own soul." It is beyond the power of the creature to keep alive his own soul, no not so much as natural life. See Psalm 49:7, "No man can give a ransom for the soul of his brother." No man is able to ransom or redeem his own life or another's. Yes, (which is much) Adam, in innocence, was taught to look for the preservation of his innocent nature out of himself, for to that end did God give him the tree of life (Gen. 2:9). The tree of life grows not in Adam, but in the Garden. Now he that was to eat of the tree, called the tree of life, he was taught from thence that the maintenance and continuance of that life which he then lived (a life of grace and glory) was not to be expected from his own strength, but from something from outside of himself. The tree of life was a type of the Lord Jesus Christ, the second person in the Trinity. Now, if Adam could not keep alive his own soul but by that tree, how much less Adam—fallen and corrupted—being now become unable to keep that law which in innocence he might have kept?

But more clearly see the grounds of this insufficiency in the creature to help itself.

The first is taken from the preciousness of the price of our redemption—the costliness of it. The matter of our justification is the price of our redemption, and without justification, no spiritual life at all. Now, the price of our redemption is our justification. The form of that justification is God's accepting of it and imputing it to us. But the matter of it is the price of our redemption, and that is the root of all our spiritual life. The price of our redemption given to God is accepted of Him, and by Him given to us. Psalm 49:8 reads, "Precious is the redemption of souls." It is far beyond the power of the creature that which may be fit matter to give to God by way of satisfaction for a soul that is very precious, and this was only the obedience of Christ to the death. He by suffering death for us, and rising from the dead, declared Himself mightily to be the Son of God, and He by His obedience to the death, offered to God the price of our redemption: "He gave Himself a ransom for many" (Mark 10:45). And this shows that it had been impossible for any under the Son of God to have given a sufficient price for our redemption. Neither man nor angels could do it. But He, in giving a sufficient price for us, did thereby mightily declare Himself to be the Son of God. He, only by His death, is the matter of our justification, and His rising is our life. The Father Himself, it could not stand with His justice to give a price for our redemption, He being the person offended. But the Son, taking upon Him our nature, that nature which had offended God, He by this means made atonement between the Father and us. And in making atonement declared Himself mightily to be the Son of God. None but He alone was able to tender to God such a recompense as might be a satisfaction for our sins.

Secondly, this is ground why there is no sufficiency in the creature to give us the life of our justification; so it is also taken from the root of our sanctification and consolation. For they spring both from one fountain, and that is the Spirit of God's grace. We see, in John 16:7, that He is the "Comforter," that is, our Sanctifier, and this "springs in us to everlasting life" (John 4:14). Now, He that can give a spirit of sanctification and consolation is only the Lord Jesus Christ; unless He go away and send the Comforter to us, He never comes. If you would know who it is that can give this water of life, you shall read John 4:10; that it is only the Lord Jesus. He it is only that goes to the Father and sends His Spirit of grace into our hearts. Unless He go to heaven, and send it down from heaven to us, it is not given. So that, He being the root of the Spirit of consolation, and of sanctification, all this life of consolation & sanctification springing from the Spirit as from a fountain, and Christ being He that "sets open this fountain" (Zech. 13:1). Therefore, it is that there is an insufficiency in the creature to shed abroad such a thing as this into our hearts. When he was to give a reason of the spirit of tongues, he fetches it from the resurrection of Christ, that He, by His ascending into heaven, "did shed abroad this word which you now see and hear" (Acts 2:33); so that by His death He gave to God, not only the price of our redemption, but prevailed with the Father to bestow upon Him the Spirit to give where, and to whom He will.

And for a third ground, why eternal life cannot be given by any but by Christ, is taken from the invincible difficulty of the passage to eternal life, from the hand of death and the grave, there is no redemption: "What man is he that can deliver his soul from the hand of the grave" (Ps. 89:48)? And if the soul be severed from the body, no man can quicken his own soul; that is beyond the power and reach of the creature. Death is the passage to eternal life, and this passage is of invincible difficulty for a man to die, and then to translate himself from death to life. It is far beyond the capacity of the creature, and therefore says our Savior, "I am the resurrection and the life" (John 11:25). And He speaks of it formally and properly, as if He should say, "Being risen from the dead Myself, I rise Myself, and therefore raise up others also." So that, if you look at the invincible difficulty of it, you shall see that it is only the Lord Jesus that can give eternal life. It is a sign of a hypocrite when with Simon Magus we think this gift may be bought with money.

REASON 2: FOR THE FATHER'S GOOD PLEASURE

It is taken from the good pleasure of the Father, whom it has pleased that "in Christ all fullness of life should dwell" (Col. 1:19). "And when He which is our life shall appear, we shall appear with Him" (Col. 3:4). And therefore, since God has concluded, and shut up all the springs of life in Christ, and out of Christ there is nothing but death, the good pleasure of the Father has determined this point that He having given us this eternal life in His Son, there is no deriving life from any fountain, but only from the Son.

Use: If upon our having or not having of Christ depends our having or not having of life, then from hence you see an evident ground of trial of every one of our estates. Whether we be alive or dead, would any man know whether he have, or not have life; consider then whether you have, or not have Christ.

And from hence you may discern *three grounds* of trial to discern whether we have Christ or not.

HOW TO DISCERN IF WE HAVE CHRIST

First, consider what it is to have a Christ. Secondly, what it is to have the Son. Thirdly, what signs there be of life; and hereby we shall have direction, whether we have Christ or not, and by this, we may inform ourselves aright in this particular. This point contains in it the pith and marrow of Christianity, so far as any comfort of it may redound to us.

First, then let us consider what signs the Holy Ghost has given us of our having of Christ. We are said to have Christ four ways[1] in Scripture.

First, by the honor, or service, or *worship* of Him.

Secondly, in some sense we are said to have Christ by *purchase*.

Thirdly, by way of *covenant*.

---

[1] These four ways will be explored over the course of Sermons 1-3.

Fourthly, by way of *free acceptance*, when God offers Him.

First, a man is said to have God, or to have Christ, that *worships* Him, and the very worshipping of Him is the having of Him. So you read in Exodus 20:3: "You shall have no other gods but Me." It is the express words of the commandment, and by having of God there, He means thus much, "You shall worship no other gods but me." In essence, "Worship Me, and you have Me; worship any other, and you have another god, and not Me." So, have the Lord Jesus Christ by worshipping of Him; and you have Him fully. "He is the Lord your God, and worship you Him" (Ps. 45:10–11); implying that, as God has set over His Son to us, to be our Lord, so we must receive, accept, and worship Him. This is that which Moses and the people of Israel sung, "He is my God, and is become my salvation. He is my God, and He is my father's God, and therefore I will exalt Him" (Ex. 15:2). So that, to set up and exalt God in our hearts and lives, and to worship Him, is all one. This sets up the Lord, to worship Him, is to be our God.

Now a little better to understand this point, that you may conceive what this worship of Christ is; you are to conceive that worship is performed to Christ, in *mind*, in *heart*, in *life*, both in our *obedience* that we perform, in our *life*, in *suffering*, and *patience* which we yield to God in our lives, by all this we worship Christ, and so have Him.

THE FIRST PART OF THE WORSHIP OF CHRIST: IN THE MIND AND JUDGMENT

We then indeed worship Christ when we have Him in high estimation. The worship and honor that we owe to Christ is to have Him in high esteem. In the Song of Solomon 5:10, "She," the Spouse there may well call Him "her beloved;" Christ is my Christ when He is to me the "chiefest of ten thousand." And, "Who among the sons of the mighty can be likened to the Lord" (Ps. 89:6)? And Exodus 15:11, "Who is a God like unto You?" When the soul of a man does esteem of Christ above all other things in the world, when there is nothing that the soul so prizes as the Lord Jesus Christ, then the soul has Him. And herein lies the difference between spiritual and earthly things: you have a high esteem of an earthly thing, and yet have it not; a man may highly prize a good bargain, and yet have it not. But no man sets a high price upon Christ, but he that has Him. Spiritual things we wholly neglect until we have them, and when we have them, then there is nothing with us comparable to them. Until a man have his portion in the Word of God, it is but a thing of small value to him. And so, the Spirit of God's grace and the blood of Christ, until a man have it, it is but a light vain thing to him. Yes, till he have the Lord Jesus Himself, no spiritual thing is of any value with him. But so soon as ever the heart begins to prize Jesus Christ as the chiefest of all the blessings that ever God bestowed upon the sons of men, and if the soul think that had he but his part in Christ, he were the happiest man in the world! In thus prizing Him, he worships Him; and in worshipping Him, he has Him.

Now, you must conceive that all worship stands in advancing another with the debasing of ourselves; we humble ourselves that we may advance another. Now, if our debasement to them be such as is not compatible to a creature as when we subject our heart and spirits to them, this is divine honor. Now that soul that exalts the Lord Jesus Christ as the highest in his own esteem, he debases himself to the dust in his spirit before Him. It is the speech of John the Baptist (speaking of the Lord Jesus Christ), "He that comes after me is preferred before me, whose shoe latchet I am not worthy to loose" (John 1:27). This is a true worshipping of Christ, when in comparison of Christ, he thinks himself unworthy to loose His shoe latchet. No mortal man but he may be worthy to loose any man's shoe latchet, if he be but worthy to live; but this is the honor and worship of Christ that when your soul looks upon Christ, He is so highly to be preferred before him, as that he thinks himself not worthy to untie His shoe.

Now, when a man is framed to these thoughts in his mind, as that he looks at Christ as the chiefest of all the blessings of God, as the greatest mercy that ever could befall a poor soul; and in respect of Christ, he looks at himself as an unworthy creature most unworthy of Christ, most unworthy to come in His presence, and much more unworthy to be made partaker of so glorious a match as the Lord Jesus is, or to have his part in His body and blood, the very worship of Christ is, in truth, the having of Christ. If we have such a singular esteem of Him, we may be sure we could never have thus prized Him, but that He first prized us.

Christians Worship Christ in Their Minds

For further opening this worship of Christ in our minds, because it is of singular importance, and may help and stay a poor Christian, when his heart may be most dead, and all other things fail him, yet this high esteem of Christ in his mind is never wanting to an honest hearted Christian, but he ever has occasion to look at Christ as most glorious, and at himself in comparison of Christ, as unworthy to loose His shoe latchet.

Let us therefore consider a little further of it. You may read the like gracious disposition in Moses. He so prizes Christ, that everything belonging to Christ seems honorable to him, "he esteemed the very reproaches of Christ above all the treasures of Egypt" (Heb. 11:26), and those are less than a shoe latchet, in untying a shoe latchet, there is neither shame nor pain. But for a man to be reproached for Christ, if anything be base and dishonorable, sure it is that. For a man that was taken to be the son of Pharaoh's daughter, and for him not to be ashamed of the people of God, nor of being reproached with them; yes, so far from being ashamed, as to think it "greater riches than the treasures of Egypt." He was sure gone far in his esteem of Christ, that man truly worships Christ that honors the reproaches of Christ above all other things.

But yet there is something more in it than this in this worship of Christ in our minds. We honor or worship Christ in our minds when we make Him the chiefest, and esteem nothing more worthy to be known than to know the Lord Jesus Christ. "This is life eternal to know You the only true God, and Jesus Christ whom You have sent" (John 17:3). Now, when the soul esteems nothing more worth the knowing than Jesus Christ, this is an honoring of Him. "I determined not to know anything among you save Christ and Him crucified" (1 Cor. 2:2). And in Philippians 3:7–10, he looks at "all things as loss, and dross, and dung that he might be found in Christ, not having his own righteousness, but might know the power and virtue of His resurrection." This is that which the Apostle did prize in his judgment as more honorable and comfortable than anything under the sun, and this was an evident sign that Paul had Christ.

For this is an ordinary experiment in nature. No man has any blessing, but he would know the worth of it. If a man have "a farm or a yoke of oxen, he will prove them" (Luke 14:19). A man will know beforehand if he can, but when he has it then he will prove it. And truly, so is it with every one that has the Lord Jesus—he is desirous to prove Christ. He would know by experience what the virtue and power of His death is, how it pardons his sin, and mortifies his corruptions, and he would know the power of His resurrection—strengthening and quickening grace in Him. And the power of Christ's ascension, ascending into the presence of His Father, and sitting at the right hand of God to rule all creatures in heaven and in earth; for the church's good, and subduing our enemies, and bringing us to glory in the end. A man that has Jesus Christ, he is inquisitive to know all the virtue that is in Christ, and he thinks in his mind, there is nothing better worth the knowings than to know and feel the virtue and power of Christ Jesus in his heart. And this is the first part of the worship of Christ, though we be yet doubtful whether we have Christ or not. Yet it is an evidence to the soul that you have Him, because you do worship Him, and so highly prize Him in your mind. And if you could but know Him, and your part in Him, this is the chiefest comfort you can pitch your mind upon. Certainly He is your beloved, since He is to you the chiefest of ten thousand.

THE SECOND PART OF THE WORSHIP OF CHRIST: IN THE WILL AND AFFECTIONS

Secondly, a man worships Christ, not only by an act of his mind, but a man has Christ likewise when he has Him in the deep affection of his heart; when he deeply affects

Him in his heart as his chiefest good. The former was an act of the judgment and understanding; this belongs to the heart, will, and affections. "Whom have I in heaven but You, or in earth in comparison of You" (Ps. 73:25) and "my soul pants or breathes after You my God" (Ps. 42:1, 2). He was then a banished man from the congregation, and it was a weary sad time to him. His soul panted like a chased deer for the rivers of water. His soul was "athirst for God! Oh when shall I come, and appear before Him?" This is such a longing desire, when a man wants Christ. As that it is called, "hunger and thirst" (Matt. 5:6), such a desire as cannot be satisfied, but with meeting with that which the soul does hunger and thirst for. Give a hungry man a house full of gold, and he is hungry still, but give him meat and then you satisfy him. So in this case, the soul that hungers after Christ, give him profit and pleasure, and you give him nothing, but his soul is fit to perish for want of Christ.

This is a deep worship we put upon Christ, and in so affecting Him, we have Him. When the soul has the Lord Jesus, the highest and chiefest cause of rejoicing it has is only its having of Christ (Gal. 6:14). If he have his part in Christ, that is his crown and his portion. He counts it a goodly portion; his lot is fallen into a pleasant place. If we have Him for our portion, we have enough, therein the soul is fully satisfied. And if we have lost Him, we chiefly mourn for that, our chiefest care is to get Him; and we mourn most bitterly for want of Him (Zech. 12:10). And we make it our desire chiefly to have Him, and then we truly have Him when we so set Him up in our hearts. We may affect many earthly blessings and want them, as gold and silver, and friends, and health, and yet want them all. But no man desires Christ thus, but he has Him. I mean if he desire Him as his chiefest good, the having of any blessing does not so rejoice his heart, nor the want of it so afflict him, such a soul has Christ.

Objection: *But the church in Songs 3:1, she wanted Christ, and yet earnestly desired Him, therefore a soul may have a strong desire to Christ, and yet be without Him, how can she be said not to find Christ, and yet to have Him?*

Answer: She could neither have loved Him nor have sought Him, nor have so known the worth of Him, if He had not loved her first (cf. 1 John 4:19). And if she in some measure had not had Him; but when she says she found Him not, the meaning is, not in that feeling and comfort, not in that measure she sought for, not in that life and power, her soul desired; she sought Him by night in a dark time, but though she wanted the comfort of Christ in His Ordinances. As she then desired, yet she had Christ, and had true fellowship with Him, else she could never have so loved Him. For she says she sought Him whom her soul loved, and this is indeed so much the more truer worship of Him when it is so hearty. In our judgments, we prize Him as the chiefest blessing in heaven and in earth, and in our hearts we so affect Him, and cleave unto Him.

So now, on the contrary, let the same heart look into itself, and in comparison of Christ, he not only in his judgment barely esteems of himself, but in our affections we look at ourselves as loathsome in comparison of Christ. This you shall find to be true, the more the heart does inwardly love Christ, the less we do love ourselves. So, when God revealed Himself to Job, he cried out, "I am vile," and then he abhors himself, and repents in dust and ashes (Job 40:4). There is no soul that has any high esteem of God, or any strong affection to Him; but the more highly and deeply he affects Him, the more he disaffects himself and loathes himself. As unmeet to come into the presence of the Lord, when as Isaiah saw the glory of the Lord sitting upon the cherubims, he cried out, "Woe is me! I am undone, for I am a man of unclean lips" (Isa. 6:5-6)! This shall you ever find to be the frame of the spirit of a Christian: the more deeply he affects Christ, the more inwardly he loathes himself. He looks at himself as fit rather to be swallowed up of judgement than capable of any mercy, not only grieve for his sin against Christ or not only the more fear his sin, or the more be ashamed of his sin, by how much the more he sees the glory of Christ; but he so much the more loathes himself, as one clean out of heart. He abhors himself as an unclean and abominable thing, that if he could go out of himself, and be severed from his own soul, he would never own himself more. And therefore, Christ puts *self-denial* for a principal part of His worship (Luke 9:23). This very denial of ourselves is a worship of Christ, hereby we so affect Christ, that we are quite out of conceit and love of ourselves. And so loath ourselves for our sins, as they make us unmeet to be joined to so glorious a head as Christ, and then indeed we have Him.

THE THIRD PART OF THE WORSHIP OF CHRIST: UNIVERSAL OBEDIENCE

A third part of this worship of Him is in our life. And in our life, we worship Him by obedience in doing His will, and by patience in suffering His will, or anything comfortably for His sake. Hearty obedience is a true and sincere and real sign of this worship of Christ, and true sincere obedience to Him is a true having of Him.

This is first, when a man has such respect to all the commandments of God, as that there is none of them but he greatly delights in it. "Then shall I not be ashamed, when I have respect to all Your commandments" (Ps. 119:6). He looks at them all with such respect, as the commandments of a great God; he respects them all as God's commandments. When as a man is willing to take up every commandment of Christ, he submits to them all every one.

And which is more, as he has respect to all God's commandments, so he has respect to all God's commandments in all his ways. There is a double universality of obedience, and they both hold forth this truth. It brings into subjection every thought and imagination to the will of Christ (2 Cor. 10:9). Now, this is a marvelous subjection that a man is not to dare to allow himself insomuch as a thought unless it be in a way of obedience to the will and word of God. Unless a thought be suitable to the will of Christ and allowable to the word of Christ, he dare not accept it. When a man has such a professed subjection to Christ that, as he respects every commandment of God, so he would not be at his own choice, insomuch as in any one thought, and this is such a solid and complete worship of Christ as that a greater honor cannot be done to Him. "Him only shall you serve" (Matt. 4:10). He will not allow himself in one evil thought, much less will he allow himself to speak evil words, or least of all, to do this or that evil in the sight of God. So that, this is the worship of Him, when we subject all the passages of our heart and life to His will, "we serve the Lord and not man" (Col. 3:23–24). We do not anything in our callings, but we do it in obedience to Christ, and according to the rules of Christ, and for the glory of Christ. And this is the service we do to Christ, not a passage in our whole life, but we desire to have respect to all God's commandments, and this is a right and true having of Him.

Worshiping God by Suffering His Will

And as it is thus for our obedience in doing His will, so is it for our patience in suffering His will. There is a glorious worship given to Christ in patience when, as if so be it be the will of God to call us to suffer, we lay our hands upon our mouths and sit down, and quiet ourselves in this, that it is the will of Christ it should be so. And being for the glory of His name, in the defense of His truth, and from His own hand, it endears us not. We sit down quietly under the hand of Christ as knowing whose hand it is that is upon us. It is a worship of Christ and we debase ourselves to worship Him, when we acknowledge that it is no matter what becomes of us so the will of God be done. This is true worship of Christ.

It was a good testimony of Eli's sincerity when he heard of the woeful judgment that God would inflict upon his household. When Samuel had made an end of expressing the whole judgment, he said, "It is the Lord, let Him do what seems Him good in His own eyes" (1 Sam. 3:18). Wherein he fitly expressed the point in hand, "It is the Lord, let Him therefore do what He will," we have the Lord for our Lord, and He is a Lord to us, when we give him leave to rule us, "the Lord has given, and the Lord has taken away, blessed be His name" (Job 1:20, 21). This shows the subjection of Job's will to God. If He see it good to take all away, as He sometime saw it good to give it all, this patient submission of the heart to God is an undoubted argument that we have the Lord for our God. Had we not Him for our God, the heart of man would so grudge at this and that evil which befalls us, and would bitterly fall upon instruments, and weary heaven and earth with our moans and cries. "But I held my peace and said nothing, for You Lord have done it" (Ps. 39:9). A sign we have Him for our Lord is when, in all His providences, we acknowledge His good hand in it. And He is our Lord if we can so sit down and not murmur nor grudge against Him.

According to that you read Lamentations 3:28-29, the church complaining of her misery, he tells you the frame of her spirit in such a temper the soul now "sits alone and keeps silence." He has "learned to bear God's yoke," he is yoked to the will of God; to His commandments, to His providence, and he "puts his mouth in the dust if there may be any hope." He is content to lie down under the hand of God, grudges not at it, but in quietness and silence of heart, bears God's yoke. And God is then the God of our salvation when we "keep silence before Him" (Ps. 62:1). This is a solemn worship of God when in the midst of trouble, we can quietly sit down; when the soul can say, "I will bear the indignation of the Lord" (Mic. 7:8, 9). When we see the Lord's hand in all the punishments and judgements that befall us, and we bear it willingly, this is solemnly to worship Him. And to be wrought upon as clay in the hand of the Potter, and in thus doing we have Him.

And if the case should be, that we should come to suffer for the name of Christ, it is so far off from being matter of murmuring to a Christian man, as that he suffers not only patiently, but joyfully, and if "any man suffer for the name of Christ as a Christian, let him glorify God on that behalf, for the Spirit of glory and of God shall rest upon him" (1 Pet. 4:14). When a man thus worships God, patiently submitting himself to Him, and gives up himself in His way to be quieted by Him, this is a true worshipping of Christ. And whoever thus worships Him, has Him. Though we cannot yet tell whether we have faith or not, whether repentance or not, whether any true love to God or not. Yet if we can find this in us, that in our hearts, we thus worship the Lord Jesus, so highly prize Him as the "chiefest of ten thousand." In so doing, we worship Christ and in worshipping Him, we have Him. But on the other side, if we so look at Christ as we can prefer ten thousand other things before Him, and can sit down quietly without Him; if we look at Christ as a refuse commodity, not worth the cheapening, and we look at ourselves as the great Omegas of the world, and we would not have our names blemished with seeking after Christ, but have greater business than that to look after, and we will be our own carvers; if so, then we do not worship Christ, and then we have Him not, and so no redemption by Him.

Having Christ by Purchase

He that has the Son has life, and he that has not the Son has not life.
(1 John 5:12)

Because in Scripture phrase, there are more ways of having Christ requisite for the knowledge of every soul, I thought it therefore not amiss to open those other ways by which in Scripture we are said to have Christ.

As therefore we have Him first by *worshipping* of Him, so secondly we have Him *by purchase*. This way of having Christ is expressed to us partly in the parable of the merchant man, "who when he had found a pearl of precious price, he sold all that he had and bought it" (Matt. 13:46). That is one way of having Christ—to purchase Him, to buy Him. You have the like also held out in Isaiah 55:1–2, "every one that is athirst, come and buy without money or without price." Wherein the Holy Ghost calls upon us to receive the Lord Jesus Christ as revealed in His Ordinances, and He makes a solemn proclamation to all, to come to "these waters and buy without money." Without money, why without money? or how without money? It is true, should a man offer his house full of treasure for Christ, it would be despised (Songs 8:7), and when Simon Magus offered to buy the gifts of the Holy Ghost for money, it was rejected with a curse (Acts 8:18–20). And if the gift of the Holy Ghost cannot be bought for money, how can the Lord Jesus Christ be bought for money?

And yet this much I say, that many times without laying out of money, He cannot be had. Without parting with money, we cannot get Him. The case so stands that sometimes, the holding fast a man's money lets go the Lord Jesus Christ. You have a famous example in the young man in Matthew 19:21-24, where our Savior shows how hard a thing it is for a rich man to enter into the Kingdom of Heaven, because it is hard for a rich man to part with all that he has when God calls for it at his hands, so that without money sometimes Christ cannot be had. And yet, for money He cannot be had, it was upon the point of money that the Lord Jesus parted with the Pharisees in Luke 16:11–12, "If you be unfaithful with mammon of iniquity, who will trust you with true treasure?" If you use not outward things well, who will give you saving grace in Jesus Christ? So that, sometimes for want of spending of money in a right way, many a man loses the Lord Jesus. So that, though Christ cannot be had for money, yet sometimes without expense of money He cannot be had.

Three Cases of Paying a High Cost for Christ

For opening of this point, there are three cases in which money must be laid out, or else Christ cannot be had, and in refusing to lay out money, we refuse life in Him.

First, when the Lord by some special command requires it, as was the case of the young man in the Gospel; there was a special commandment given to him, not given to every man, nor to every rich man, nor scarce any man in ordinary course nowadays, yet then given to him. And now, to stick for money, and rather lose eternal life than his goods, in such a case as this, he loses his life in Christ. And upon the same point, or the like, broke Ananias and Sapphira. It was the common resolution of the church of God in that age to sell all that they had, and to give to the poor, and to live after the same rate that other men did, a like proportion to every man; and to distribute faithfully to every man as every man had need, and as the apostles saw cause. And when they come and keep back part of the price for which their possessions was sold, you see how bitter a curse from the presence of the Lord fell upon them. They were cut off from the congregation of God's people. And it is much to be feared, cut off from the Lord Jesus Christ, and from all hope of eternal life, and to stand as a terrible example to the whole church of God, to show what a dangerous thing it is to stand upon terms with Christ, and not to part with money for Him. They could not have fellowship with the people of God unless they parted with all they had, and live upon the common distribution. But this case is not always.

But secondly, there is another time, namely, when in case of persecution the market of Christ goes at so high a rate that a man cannot have Christ with any comfort in his soul, or peace to his conscience, or purity of heart or life, unless he hazard all his estate, or a good part of it. In buying and selling of a precious commodity, a good chapman will have it whatever it cost him. So Christ is sometimes at a higher, and sometimes at a lower rate, but whatever He costs him, he will have Him. It is spoken in commendation of the Hebrews, that "they suffered joyfully the spoiling of their goods" (Heb. 10:34), to show you that sometimes it comes to that pass that unless a man be content to part with all his goods, he cannot have the recompense of reward—the Lord Jesus Christ to his soul—and therefore, the servants of God have been content to lose all that they had, and willing to resign up all for the maintaining the integrity of their spirits, and the purity of their hearts and lives in the presence of God, and then let all go, they can "suffer the spoil of all joyfully."

Third, it is in case that by God's providence you be cast to live such congregations, where you cannot have the Ordinances of God but at a great charge, as it is the case of many places, that unless they be at charge for the ministry of the gospel it cannot be had. Then we must communicate freely that way, then "be not deceived, God is not mocked, for what a man sows that shall he also reap" (Gal. 6:6–8). Where the Apostle does encourage men at such a time as this, when the gospel cannot be had but at great charge, then lay out liberally for the gospel of Christ, and he calls it "a sowing to the Spirit." As a man that lays out his money for an earthly commodity, for a good bargain, he reaps corruption. So he that sows of the Spirit, shall of the Spirit reap life everlasting. When a man lays out his money unto spiritual ends to obtain the free passage of the Ordinances of Christ, to enjoy the liberty of the gospel, he thereby sows to the Spirit, and shall of the Spirit reap life everlasting. For this is the blessing promised unto it, such as so sow, "shall of the Spirit reap life everlasting." So that when a man out of a good and honest heart, and a hungering desire after God's Ordinances shall be willing to be at charge for them, he has this promise made to him, and it shall be fulfilled, "he shall of be Spirit reap life everlasting." But yet, when a man has laid out his money for this end, if he then think his money is worthy of Christ, he gets Him not. But this is the first way of having Christ by way of purchase; a seasonable laying out our money for Him as God requires it.

PURCHASE CHRIST BY PARTING WITH ALL THAT KEEPS HIM FROM US

Secondly, Christ is to be purchased, not so much by money, as chiefly this purchase must be made by parting with all those many and strong lusts, and corruptions, and sinful rebellions of heart, by which we keep off Christ from coming into our hearts. This is that which the prophet Isaiah directs us to: "Let the wicked forsake his way, and the unrighteous man his thoughts, *etc.*" (Isa. 55:7). Where he tells us what we must give for Christ, for sin is neither money nor money's worth; but he makes a good bargain that parts with his sins, though he should get no Christ for his parting with them. He speaks of the first and principal part of the life of a Christian man, the life of his justification that springs from pardon of sin. Let a man forsake those sins and lusts that he has been most carried captive with. Let a wicked man forgo his thoughts and ways, both his secret and open sins, and let him then turn to God, and He will abundantly pardon; then God will receive him graciously to the justification of life.

This is the thing that we must do. This was the point upon which sundry of them that have been hopeful for religion have broken off from Christ, and Christ from them; they have forsook Him, and He left them. Jehu stuck upon this very point, he would go a great way, but where it comes (as he thinks) to hazard his title to the crown, then he will set up the golden calves. When he saw that all must be parted with, rather than forgo that without which he could not maintain his kingdom, he would rather lose Christ than venture the loss of that. "He regarded not to walk in all the commandments of the Lord" (2 Kings 10:29, 31), and then, as he cut short with God in reformation, and did not fulfil to walk after the Lord. Therefore, God cut Jehu short of all the hopes of grace that ever he might have attained (v. 32), so that if we cut at a scanting with God, and will part with some lusts and corruptions, but not with others, then will God cut you short of all your hopes of eternal life.

And it was upon the same terms that Herod fell short of Christ (Mark 6:14-29; Luke 3:19ff.). He had done many things according to John's ministry, but when God would cut him short of Herodias, his darling lust, that nothing might lie between God and him; but now might become fit for Christ because he would not cut himself short of Herodias, and cut short his reformation there. Then this was added to all his other sins, he shut up John in prison and afterward cut off his head also. So that when there is any sin, whether honor or pleasure or any comfort in this life that men will not be content to cut themselves sort of, it is the way to utter ruin; God will not be abundantly ready to pardon such.

And so was it with Demas, when the love of money did so prevail with his heart after he had been much esteemed of the apostles, and mentioned honorably in their writings. Yet in the end, it is said of him, "He has forsaken me, and loved this present world" (2 Tim. 4:10). Love of the world had so prevailed with him that he fell off from Paul, and from the Lord, whose servant Paul was, and from fellowship in the gospel, and so did not find Christ. This rule is universally to be followed, and the care of it not to be neglected in any case that our sins are to be put out of our hearts and hands as ever we look to find Christ, and life in Him.

Notable is that expression recorded in Judges 10:10-16, the people come and cry to the Lord to deliver them out of the hands of their enemies. But they had got to themselves other gods, and now He would deliver them no more. When the people heard that God would not deliver them, and could find no acceptance from Him so long as they continued in such a sin, they thereupon go and put away all their idols, and leaves not one to be seen among them. And when God sees that they had put them away, the text says, "that His soul was grieved for their misery," and His bowels rolled within Him for them, and He delivered them.

So that, when men are willing to forego their honorable sins, their sweet and delightful sins, their profitable sins, and those wherewith they have been most captivated—and He knows one may as well pull their hearts out of their bellies, as some sins out of them—but when He sees men are willing to forego their most darling delightful sins, willing to break off all impediments that stand between God and them, the soul of God is grieved in such a case, and it pities Him how that such a soul should be without Him. And then it will not be long ere God stirs them up means of deliverance, and He Himself will reveal Himself unto them.

Notable is that speech in Hosea 14:3, 8, when they take words to themselves, and promise to leave all their evil ways, whereby they sin against God, they make this request to God, that "He would take away their iniquities from them." And least God should answer them, but be you doing something in the meantime; they profess that, for their own parts, they will set about the doing of their iniquities away, and they say, "Ashur shall not save us, and we will have no more to do with them." Wherein he shows you that God looks not that only His people shall pray Him to take away their iniquities, for we may pray so long enough, and not find it done. But when we desire God to do it, and set our hearts and hands to it, and now with heart and hand say, "Ashur shall not save us, nor will we say any more to the works of our hands, you are our gods." Then says God in verse 4: "I will heal their backslidings and will love them freely, *etc.*" God is then abundantly ready to pardon when men forsake their own ways and thoughts, and throw away the sins that hang about them. God will say of such a people, "I will heal them, and love them freely, mine anger is turned away from them." And you may presume when God's anger is turned away, it is by and through Christ, or else there is no healing. And therefore, in verse 8, Ephraim says, "What have I to do any more with idols?" The heart of a Christian, or of a nation, shall openly acknowledge that they will have no more fellowship with these abominations. And then says God, "I have heard him, and observed him."

God hears us, and understands what we say, and observes us well, and offers to be a covert to us from the storm. When we begin solemnly to abandon such evils, then He hears us, and answers us according to the desire of our hearts. You have many a soul that cries to God, take away our iniquity, and many petitions we put up to God to that purpose; and that sometimes with many bitter moans, but God hears it not. We pour out our complaints in vain, and He regards it not. But when we come to God, and desire Him not only to take them from us, but begin to consider our own ways and iniquities, and to put them from us, out of our hearts and hands, and we will no more take such bad ways, as heretofore we have done; we will no more ride upon horses, nor run to foreign princes for succor; then God hears, and grants graciously whatever His poor people beg at His hands, and answers it according to all the desire of their hearts; then the Lord presently gives us the Lord Jesus Christ, and life and healing in Him; and this is the second way of having Christ by purchase.

PRIZING CHRIST ABOVE THE ORDINANCES

Thirdly, God sometimes requires that we should part with all His holy Ordinances in some cases, part with all confidence in them, and from staying our hearts upon them. We may soon lose Christ, and lose His protection, and His fatherly compassion towards us, if in the use of the blessed Ordinances of God, we be not willing so far to sit loose from them, as not to look for life in the Word, or Sacraments, or communion with God's servants. But to look for it all in Christ, not that God would have us cast His Ordinances behind our backs, but therein to seek Him. Yes, "to seek His face evermore," and not to be barred from them, He would have a child of God to count it his greatest misery (Ps. 27:4; 42:3, 4). Though God would have us to make account that "one day in God's court is better than a thousand elsewhere" (Ps. 84:10), yet God still has regard to this, that He would not have us to trust "in the temple of the Lord." Because to do so is to trust "in lying words" (Jer. 7:3, 4). Hold close to the Ordinances, and by no means part with them if you can have them in any purity, and peace to your consciences, but rather part with princes' palaces than with them.

But while you enjoy them, trust not in them, nor think not to stand upon this, that you are blessed in regard of them. But look at them all as loss, and dross, and dung—"that you may win Christ." Look not so wishly at the privileges of the Ordinances. Trust not in the outward letter of them (Phil. 3:6, 7, 8). This is that which keeps off many a poor soul from coming on to grace. He lives in no open gross sin, and in the midst of the Ordinances of God, Christ is preached amongst them, and therefore they conclude that at the last day Christ will receive them, and yet this will then deceive them (Matt. 7:22, 23). Some iniquity rested still in their hands, for which He will bid them depart from Him as "workers of iniquity;" they it may be, had some of them been themselves ministers, and had done much good in the name of Christ, and "called upon Him, 'Lord, Lord,'" and yet but hypocrites; which shows you that it is not the liberty of God's Ordinances, and the dispensation of them that can secure us; and therefore trust not in them, trust not in this, that you are diligent hearers, or that you can pray powerfully. Trust not in this, though you were preachers of the Word of God, but trust on Him only for life and salvation, and He will never deceive you.

And as at all times we are to sit loose from the Ordinances in respect of our trust and confidence, so sometimes we must be content to forego the Ordinances of God for Christ's sake. If we cannot enjoy the liberty of the Ordinances, but with sin against our souls, in this case the Ordinances of God are to be neglected and omitted. If he cannot have them with innocency and purity to his soul, he must let them go. All the good priests that were wont to minister before the Lord in the Synagogue throughout the ten tribes, when they could not enjoy their places, but worship the calves (though the calves were very like the cherubims), when they could not do their service to God, but they must serve such images as God had not set up there. Thereupon all the honest and true-hearted priests left their places, and would no more minister there, rather than be compelled to minister at

Dan and Bethel (2 Chron. 11:14). Jeroboam cast them out because they would not do so, and they were content to be cast out, and sold their livings, and went up to Jerusalem.

To show you that sometimes when Christ cannot be had, but we must forgo the very Ordinances of God, because we cannot have the Ordinances without impure mixtures of human invention; then let them go rather than defile our own hearts and hands with sin against God. And so, Songs 1:7–8, "Tell me where you dwell, and feed your flocks at noon." After the separation was made between Israel and Judah, when the Mother Church of Israel was angry with the Church of Judah, and cast her off; "tell me where you lie and feed your flocks, *etc.*" How should I go to the golden calves at Dan and Bethel and worship there where God had never put His Name to be worshipped? Why, Christ answers them, "If you know not, O you the fairest among women" (as all such Christians are the fairest among women), "If you know not where I rest, go forth by the foot-steps of the flocks, and by the shepherds tents, and feed there." Have they not removed their tents to Jerusalem? Why go after them, and feed with them? This was fulfilled in 2 Chronicles 11:16, the people left all, and went up to feed themselves there, "by the tents of the shepherds." This is another part of our purchase of Christ (which God forbid it should be our case), but if it should come to that pass, rather forego the Ordinances of God, which were of His own setting and planting, as were the ministry in the Synagogues. And they were to be divided all the kingdom over; and the "priests' lips should preserve knowledge, and we should seek the law at his mouth" (Mal. 2:7–8). Therefore, that being a holy Ordinance of God, they would by no means part with the free passage of any one of God's Ordinances, which sometimes they did enjoy, but when they could not enjoy them in the purity thereof, but must be cast off from being priests, unless they will do all, then they were content to be cast out from all fellowship with the church, and leave their estates and forego all rather than enjoy the liberty of some other with sinful defilement. And though it might be thought their own, over much, over readiness to cast off themselves, yet notwithstanding the Holy Ghost excuses it, they did not cast off themselves, but the text says, "Jeroboam cast them out," if they will not minister upon such terms, then it is he that casts them out, and that was the sin chiefly, whereby "he made Israel to sin."

And therefore when you come to the Ordinances, and though you find Christ there, yet trust not upon them unless you trust upon Christ, and seek Him to give you a meeting there; you have trusted but upon lying words, you went out full, and come empty home. You hear much, and profit little; and all that you learn you put into a broken bag, into cracked memories, and all because you did so trust upon the means. And truly in this case this shall you often find to be true, you come full of hopeful expectation to the congregation, but return very empty home, or full of bitterness in your souls. And all was because you "trusted in lying words," in words that could not profit; you trusted in the parts of Christians, in the Sacraments, Word, and Prayer. But "what is Paul, and what is Apollo, one of them may plant, another may water," but neither of both can give the increase (1 Cor. 3:5, 6). "He that plants, and he that waters is nothing." Therefore chiefly have respect to Christ, look not at Paul, nor at Apollo, nor at any, though you had men equal with them for gifts had you such, yet if you put trust and confidence in them, you will lose all the blessings that you desire and hope to find in them.

And therefore so come to the Ordinances, as that you trust not in the means; pray to Christ to bless the Ordinances to you, and entreat Him to cleanse your hearts and hands from those evils that are in His sight, and come trusting on Him, not on any strength in the means, but on His blessing upon the means. And then He will be found of you, if you thus seek Him in truth. But if they cannot be had but with danger to you, to lose the peace of your consciences, then be content to sit loose to the Word and Sacraments, and from Christian communication. Then, in this case, give this price also for Christ. For we come not to the Ordinances for the Ordinances' sake, but for Christ's sake to find Him there, but rather than willingly put forth our hands to any sin; rather, lose the Ordinances then lose Christ.

Giving Up Gifts of Grace to Buy Christ

Fourthly, there is yet something more than all this, a further price to pay, if we mean to purchase Christ. And that is that we part with all our good parts, and all the good common gifts of grace, which are found sometimes in good nature, and sometimes in the children of the Church. We must part with them all that we may win Christ. "If any man among you seem to be wise in this world, let him become a fool that he may be wise" (1 Cor. 3:18). Whoever would be a wise man (as a wise man he cannot be, if he have not his part in Christ), he must lay aside his serious and sad deliberation, and communication with flesh and blood, and all things in the way of God that he thinks will be prejudicial. If any man be so wise, as to see this and that danger in a Christian course, let him become a fool, else he shall never become a Christian. If a man will be content to forsake all for Christ, he must first be a fool, and be content to be counted a fool, and hear every carnal man to count him a fool.

And I speak not only of carnal and civil wisdom that that only is to be denied in this case. But common graces, which many times chokes all the hypocrites in the bosom of the Church; they are commonly choked upon this point, upon these things they trust, and do therefore verily believe, that this and that interest, God has in them, and they in God; because they have received such and such gifts from Him, and this is the case formerly mentioned. In Matthew 7:22–23, they pleaded their spiritual gifts, though common gifts, and such as may be found in "workers of iniquity," they "prayed to God" a common gift; and they "prophesied in His name," they had prophetical gifts; some measure of the spirit of ministry, and they were able to "cast out devils in Christ's name."

Now when as men do trust upon these, and settle themselves upon such a change, truly, hereby they lose that power in Christ which else they might have had. It's a wonder to see what a change prophetical gifts will work in a man. In 1 Samuel 10:10–12, Saul had a spirit of prophesy came upon him, and the people wondered at it, it works a strange change in a man, and so in the next chapter (vv. 19, 23), he prophesied till he came at such a place, so that you shall see a man that is trained up in any good order, though sometimes given to loose company. When once God begins to pour into him any spiritual gift to enlighten his mind, and to enlarge his affection, that he begins to have some love to, and some joy in the Word, and some sorrow in hearing of the Word, and some comfort in meditation. It's a wonder to see what a change this will work in the spirit. He forthwith begins to abandon his loose courses, and sets himself to a more strict course, then he begins to see his acquisite learning is but a small matter to edification. He prizes his spiritual gifts, and he is able now to do much.

And when a man's heart is thus changed by prophetical gifts, it works in a man such confidence in his soul that he thinks all the Congregation shall perish before he can perish. And if ministers may be thus deceived by common gifts and graces, how much more may their poor hearers be deceived when they by hearing the Word find such comfort, and illumination, and enlargements, that they thereby find a great change wrought in them. And yet if ministers may be so much deceived in presuming vainly of their good estate, which was not so, then much more common Christians.

Should any man presume at Felix his trembling (Acts 24:25), at Jehu's zeal (2 Kings 10:16), at Ahab's humiliation (1 Kings 21:28-29), at Herod's joy in hearing? You know what became of all these, these be graces of God, though but common graces, and if the prophets were deceived, may not these be deceived also that have neither Christ nor any part in Him. And therefore a man that would be sure not to go without Christ, nor without life in him; he must not trust in any spiritual gift he has received though his mind be enlightened, sometimes to fear, sometimes to joy, to humiliation, to enlargement, to zealous reformation, yet rest in none of these. For these you may have and yet want Christ, and life in

Him. Common graces may and will deceive you. A man may have all these, and yet not prize Christ as his chiefest good. He may have all these, and yet not worship Him.

Notwithstanding all these, there may be some iniquity in their hands for which cause God will not show mercy on them. See and observe if in the midst of all these you do not work some iniquity; they were workers of iniquity always at the best (Matt. 7:23), you may be workers of iniquity, notwithstanding all these. And therefore consider if there be not some vein of pride and hypocrisy, and covetousness that cleaves fast to your hearts which you allow yourselves in, which if you do, these very gifts will be your shipwreck, your anchor will break, and your ship will be carried away, and you fall down in destruction. But see that your hearts be clean, and see that there be not an ill thought or way that you allow yourselves in. And if so, then your heart will lay hold upon God, and you will prize Christ, and then it is a sign those gifts you have are not in hypocrisy. For in a hypocrite, they are always found with some sin, which if a man do not willfully shut his eyes against he may see. For our Savior speaks of such a sin in them, as the rest of the people of God may know them to be counterfeits, from verse 15 to 23: "You shall know them by this, do men gather grapes of thorns, or figs of thistles?" Have not they their ill haunts, but put away these from you, if you mean to have Christ.

HAVING CHRIST IN JUSTIFICATION AND SANCTIFICATION

Fifthly, if we would have Christ and life in Him, we may have Him in justification, but not in growth of sanctification. If you part not with confidence in the saving graces of God's Spirit, you must not look to be justified by them. For if you do you will discover them not to be sanctified graces, nor the fruits of them, the fruits of saving grace, "Christ shall profit you nothing, if you look to be saved by the righteousness of the Law" (Gal. 5:3, 4). If therefore we think that for these graces' sake, God accepts us, truly we lose the things that we have wrought, and for all that we have received, we have no part nor portion in the Lord Jesus Christ.

Neither Abraham nor David had whereon to boast (Rom. 4:4, 18), "But blessed is the man to whom the Lord imputes no sin, and in whose spirit there is no guile." Therein stands our blessedness, when the Lord imputes not sin to us, but if we look to be justified either by the gifts of grace we have received or by the works and acts of grace that we have performed, we shall certainly fall short. Paul knew nothing wherein he had dealt unfaithfully, and yet was he not thereby justified, "but He that justifies me is the Lord" (1 Cor. 4:4). And therefore, if you trust upon a gift and thereby to be justified and accepted, you declare your graces to be but common, and such as are but found among hypocrites. And in this, the Papists have cause to groan under the burden that lies upon their religion. They, by looking for salvation and acceptance by common graces, do plainly show that Christ profits them nothing.

And further, as you are not to trust upon them for justification, so neither are you to trust upon them for the life of your sanctification. For though they be truly parts of sanctification, faith, hope, love, patience, humility, and every other grace of God which flows from our fellowship with the death of Christ, because there are parts of our sanctification, you may look at them as precious talents received from God. Yet if you trust in these: in preaching, or praying, or edifying yourselves, or families, or neighbors, and that in the strength of these you shall do valiantly, and bring mighty things to pass, and be a fruitful Christian, you have truth of grace, sound hearted saving grace, and you doubt not, but God will carry you an end in a comfortable Christian course. If so, you will find this to be true, that you will want Christ in the quickening and enlarging, and thriving power of the life of your sanctification.

It cannot be but that where saving grace is, there is Christ; but you may have Christ and yet have but a dead Christ of him. He may be so dead in your spirit that you shall cry out, "O what a dead heart, and a dead spirit have I, and yet I doubt not but Christ is in my heart." True, it may be you have received Him, but Christ can tell how to lie dead, and to work but little there where saving grace is laid up. And therefore the life of Christ is not a life of grace, but a life of faith. I live not by all my zeal and humility, and gifts of grace, for I might have all these, and make but dead work of them all. How then? "By the faith of the Son of God" (Gal. 2:20). It is one of the chiefest points that concerns our Christian practice, and therefore I pray you consider it. The life of Christianity is not a life of wisdom and graces, but of faith. If you would have Christ live in you, and live so that He may show His life in you, you must then live by faith; that is, not only look for your justification by faith in Christ, but look for your sanctification and consolation from Christ by faith, that if you go about any duty, go not about it in the strength of grace received, preach not, or pray not in the strength of your knowledge, and love, and zeal, and humility, but go about them all in faith in Jesus Christ; that is, by coming to Him, and being inwardly sensible, that unless He put new life into us, and make new work in our souls, we may have but a dead business of it, all the graces of God's Spirit in us but dead. And herein it is wonder to see sometimes how God's servants are straightened, all for want of the life of faith in their souls. If God cut short with us, it is because we do not live in Christ but in the spirit of grace, and think to walk by the strength of grace received, we lose by it, and spend of the stock of grace. And therefore remember that speech in Isaiah 40:30, 31, "They that wait on the Lord shall renew their strength." To show you your duty, it is a borrowed speech from young men going out to war. They go out in the name of the Lord of Hosts, as David went out against Goliath (1 Sam. 17).

If we wait upon the Lord, and be sensible of our own insufficiency and unworthiness of doing any Christian duty, and not depend upon our own sufficiency, then we shall find God lifting us up far beyond all our own apprehensions and gifts. God will put a new life into us, and in this case even the weakest gifts of God's servants are sometimes much enlarged, and the same Christians gifts far more enlarged at some time above what they are at another, only by waiting upon the Lord, and that puts life into our duties. Therefore if you would find Christ to be the life of your sanctification, then you must put away all confidence in saving graces. They are not able to make you bring forth any one lively fruit of sanctification, I mean in your own estimation; and you will have little comfort in it. There is in this case much difference between one Christian and another, and between the same Christian and himself, at one time and another, according to his waiting on the Lord for the renewal of his strength. Therefore trust not in any grace, if you do, you will want it when you stand in most need of it.

Having Christ by Covenant & by Free Acceptance

He that has the Son has life, and he that has not the Son has not life.
(1 John 5:12)

Having Christ By Covenant

We now come to speak of the third way of having Christ, and that is *by way of covenant*. We read: "I will give you for a covenant of the people, to establish the earth, to cause to inherit the desolate heritages" (Isa. 49:8). "Gather My saints together unto Me, those that have made a covenant with Me by sacrifice" (Ps. 50:5); so that, would you know to whom God is a God, and to whom it may be said, "He is my God"? Any of us that have made a covenant with God by sacrifice; no man has Him unless by way of covenant. For all these ways, though diverse in explication, yet all coincident to this having of Christ.

And such as have made a covenant with God by sacrifice, they are His people. Of them it is said, "I am your God," according to the tenor of the covenant. "Behold, I make a covenant with you this day, to be a God unto you, and to your seed" (Gen. 17:7). God becomes a God to me, and to my seed by way of covenant (Deut. 29:10-13); both your children of understanding, and your little ones of no understanding. You are all here before God this day to enter into a covenant with Him, to keep His commandments forever. "You and yours enter into a covenant with God, and this is the way of having Him for our God. This day you have avouched the Lord to be your God, and He has avouched you to be His people" (Deut. 26:17, 18). Junias translates the word, "You have required by way of covenant, and He has promised that He will be your God." In the original it is, "He has made you to speak, you have made God to speak this." As men that make promises one to another, so that when people give up themselves to be the Lord's and offer themselves up to Him. And when God requires it of us, we yield ourselves to Him, and desire God to be a God to us. Then He is our God, and we are His people by way of covenant. "They gave themselves first to the Lord, and then unto us by the will of God" (2 Cor. 8:5). When we have bestowed ourselves upon God, He is not wanting to receive us to be His people.

Now for further opening of this, it was said this covenant was made with God by way of sacrifice (Ps. 50:5, 7), that was according to the sacrifice which the people of God did solemnly offer before God, of which you read in Exodus 24:3-8. Moses told the people the words of the

Lord, and the people answered with one voice and said, "All the words which the Lord has said, we will hear it, and do it." They promise themselves to be an obedient people to God, whatever He commands them, that will they hear, and that will they do.

And on the other side, Moses took the blood of the sacrifice, and sprinkled it upon the people, and by this means they did pass into covenant with God. It implies thus much, when we come to make a covenant with God, we profess ourselves as guilty of death, and therefore look up to Christ, desiring that His death might be imputed to us. And we thereupon offer ourselves, souls and bodies, to be obedient to God to the death. Only we require this back again of God, that as we give up ourselves a sacrifice to Him, so that the Lord Jesus Christ might be imputed unto us; and the blood of Christ, and the life of Christ might be communicated to us. His life of righteousness, and holiness, and of eternal glory, all that life that is in Christ might become ours, this does God require of them, and this is to make a covenant with God by way of sacrifice. For the burnt offering (v. 5) was a type of Christ, the meat offering was a type of the peoples giving up themselves to God. And this is to make a covenant by sacrifice: we confess we deserve death, but for time to come, we desire to give up ourselves to do and suffer His will, only we desire that the blood of Christ might be sprinkled upon our souls that we might live in His sight.

Now those that have thus made a covenant with God, He calls them His people and saints. Thus you see what it is, and wherein this covenant stands. Sometimes some branch of this is expressed in other covenants: God promises to Abraham that He will be a God to him; that is, He will not only be a good Father to him, nor only a good Master, or Tutor, nor only a good King, nor a good Physician; but whatsoever is good that is in God, and it is but a drop, but a spark of the well-spring of life in Him.

All the goodness that is dispersed in the creature flows from Him. There is goodness in a good father, or magistrate, or minister, or friend. But when God undertakes to be a God to us, He promises to be to us whatsoever is good in the creature: a good Father, a good Friend, a good Physician. Whatever is good for soul and body, He will be all in all to us, and that partly in His own person, and partly in so ordering matters that all those things wherein His goodness is communicated, He will so dispose them, that we shall see a goodness of God in them all. We shall see the presence and goodness of God in all the blessings we partake in this world. He will be whatsoever is needful for us in every kind, and though any means should fail, yet God will not fail us. This do we desire of God when we desire Him to be our God. God is a heap and fountain of goodness, and He undertakes so to be to us.

Now as we expect this from God that He would be a God to us, so we desire also and offer ourselves back again to God to be obedient to His will, and to wait upon Him for all that which He has promised us; to expect it, and to wait for it. And when we undertake to be obedient to Him—not that we promise it in our own names and for our own parts, but in the behalf of every soul that belongs to us, as we desire a blessing upon all that belongs to us—so we offer up ourselves to God, and our wives and children, and servants, and kindred, and acquaintance, and all that are under our reach, either by way of subordination, or co-ordination, so far as in our power we may reach, either by commandment or counsel. We do as much as in us lies promise to God that we and our households will serve the Lord, as in Joshua 24:15, "he and his household." That is, his children and servants, and all that are bought with money, they will all serve the Lord. This they offer to God as a father in a family; he and his, so much as he is able, will prevail with them to keep God's commandments. And God will be a God to them all: a Father, and Master, a Magistrate and Minister, Husband, Friend, and Physician and all, and whatsoever is good, thus you see how God comes to be ours by way of covenant.

GOD'S THREE-FOLD COVENANT

For further clearing of this point, there is a three-fold covenant wherein God does bind Himself to His people, and we back again to Him, according as there is among the reasonable creatures.

The first is, *between prince and people*. So the high priest made a covenant between him and between all the people, and between the king that they should be the Lord's people. And such a covenant there is usually in all well governed commonwealths unless the king comes in by way of conquest and tyranny. But in well settled commonwealths, there is a covenant and oath between Prince and People.

Second, there is *a covenant between man and wife*, of which it is said in Proverbs 2:17, "Which forsakes the guide of her youth, and forgets the covenant of her God." These are all called the covenant of God; He is a party in the covenant ever.

Thirdly, another is an oath or a covenant of God to pass *between friend and friend*; such was the covenant between Jonathan and David in 1 Samuel 20:16. Now there is a certain covenant between God and His people in all these. That look what a king requires of his people, or the people of a king, the very same does God require of His people and the people of God. That offers Himself to be a God to His people; that is, a Governor, a Provider for, and a Protector of His people, to fight their battles for them, and to guide and rule them in peace and justice. And the people undertake to be obedient to His laws to whatever He declares to be the counsel of His will.

Again, there is *a covenant of marriage* between God and His people (Jer. 3:14). So as the wife promises to be to her husband alone (Hos. 3:3, 4), so the Church of God promises that she will be for God alone, and God will be for us alone; and we embrace the seed of His Word and grace in our hearts, and bring forth fruit to God alone.

And there is also *a covenant of friendship* between God and us, "a covenant of salt" (2 Chron. 13:5). A covenant of salt is to be fed with the same salt, as it were, to eat many a bushel of salt together, that is a covenant of friendship. "Did not you give the land to the seed of Abraham your friend forever?" (2 Chron. 20:7)—therein he fitly expresses the nature of a covenant of salt by friendship forever. Salt eaten together expresses familiarity and durableness. Now God expresses Himself thus, to enter into a covenant with His people. He takes Abraham as a friend forever, and Abraham takes God as his friend forever. And this league of friendship implies not only preservation of affection, but it requires a kind of secret communication one to another, and a doing one for another. God grants our petitions for us as a friend, and we do His commandments as a friend out of the integrity of our hearts: "You are My friends if you do whatsoever I command you" (John 15:14); "I know that Abraham will command his household to fear Me" (Gen. 18:19). And therefore, in verses 17 and 18, He says, "How shall I hide from Abraham the thing that I am about to do?"—it was concerning a secret counsel of God. Now when God undertakes to be our friend, He undertakes to communicate sundry of His counsels to us, "His secrets are to them that fear Him" (Ps. 25:14).

Many secret passages shall their hearts be made privy to, that others shall never be acquainted with. He will acquaint us with His secret purpose about a people, sometimes in prayer, sometimes in humiliation, sometimes one way, and sometimes another. So as you may see He walks towards us in a covenant of friendship; and so He will play a friends part, He will counsel us for the best. He will tell us, this and that is the best course for us to take, "Him shall he teach" (Ps. 25:12). He will come and tell us what He would have us to do (see Ps. 32:8). Sometimes by His Word and sometimes by His providence; and when we look up to Him as to a friend, He will do a friend's part. And on the other side, for our part we shall never take any business in hand, but we shall sadly and seriously communicate all our affairs with God, and think ourselves bound to do it, not to dare to rush upon anything but upon consultation first with the Lord, and acquainting Him with such and such things. "We know not what to do, but our eyes are unto you (2 Chron. 20:12).

So we offer up ourselves to be ready at His commandment to do whatsoever He shall counsel us to do. Let Him but make our way plain before us, and we will hear Him in whatsoever He requires of us. Be it what it will be, if God lay it before us, we will do it. See Psalm 119:1-5: "Teach me Your statutes, and I will keep it even to the end." Observe then, whether we have Christ for our Christ by way of covenant. Did there ever pass such a conveyance between Christ and you, to God the Father, about Him and your souls, that if God should look upon you, and consider your case, your just and due desert is everlasting destruction? And therefore you account yourselves unworthy of any mercy from God, but yet notwithstanding if He will be but pleased to accept the death of Christ for you, and to be-sprinkle you with the blessings of His grace, you will give up yourselves to an acceptable service of Him all your days? And will be ready to do His will? And that He shall be to you as a King and Governor? Have you ever passed over to Him your preservation, and protection, and provision?

And look what affection is between husband and wife. Has there been the like affection in your souls towards the Lord Jesus Christ? Have you a strong and hearty desire to meet Him in the bed of loves, whenever you come to the congregation, and desire you to have the seeds of His grace shed abroad in your hearts, and bring forth the fruits of grace to Him, and desire that you may be for Him, and for none other, and you desire to acquaint Him with all your counsels and secrets, and desire to do nothing but as He shall counsel and direct you?

And have you therefore been willing to give up yourselves, you and yours to be ruled by Christ; and is it the grief of your souls if any of your children, and servants shall not stoop to God, and if you use the best means to draw them on to goodness? Truly, then you have Christ for your Christ, because you have Him by way of covenant.

When God gives us hearts thus to agree with Him, He always prevents us, He is ever before us, then Christ you have, and in Him you have life. But if on the contrary, we never come before God in acknowledgement that death was our portion, and desired the blood of Christ to be applied to us, not in an overture of speech, but when it comes to the point, what will you do? Will you accept Him as your friend, and as your husband, and will you expect all good things from Him? And you will not dare to venture upon any course or way further than the light and sincerity of the Word gives liberty? And if you never came to this, nor was it ever your care whether your household served God or not, though they sin against God, and swear and lie, yet all this is nothing to you.

But it is all one with you, then there wants a covenant between God and you, and then if you have Him not by covenant, you have Him not at all. He that has Him anyway has Him every way, though it be not so clearly seen every way. If you have Him, then you have friends and enemies in common. If it be not so with you that you observe not the counsels of God, but you will be at a loose end, and do what you think good in your own eyes, then there is no covenant between God and you, and then you have not Christ, and then no life, much less in abundance.

Objection: *But you say, Who is there that so looks to himself, his wife, and children, and servants, so to his own heart and others, as that they are so wholly conformable to God's will in all that He counsels and commands, and who so expects such blessings, but that they take from God many things in ill part, and oft times sit down murmuring and discontent?*

Answer: Even they that make a covenant with God, they often break covenant with Him. And so often as you entertain any thought in your mind, wherein you have not consulted with God, and do anything further than you have warrant from God, so often have you broken covenant. So often as there is any passage in our lives for which we had not warrant from the mouth of God, and wrought it by the strength of His grace, and eye of His providence, so far have we broke covenant with Him. But yet notwithstanding this breach of covenant, here stands their help. And this is their comfort that God has given Christ for a covenant (Isa. 49:8). So that He will make good our breach of covenant on His own part.

And Hebrews 7:22, He becomes a surety for our parts. God needs no surety for His part, but we need one. So that if we have Christ for our surety, then this is required of us, that knowing we have broken covenant with God, we ought to blush, and to be ashamed of it. See Ezra 9:6-12 and Daniel 9:5-20; they confess they have broken covenant with God, and thereupon they sit down blushing, and weeping, and rending their garments, that they should enter into such a solemn covenant with God, and hope to receive so many mercies from Him.

And yet so unfaithfully to break covenant with Him when we see that we have transgressed and forgotten the covenant of God, and break the counsels of God, we or ours. It is for us in such a case to do as those people did in Ezra and Nehemiah who broke covenant with God; to go and blush before Him, that we should deal so unworthily with that God, that has made such a perpetual covenant of faith with us, that will be all that is good to us, and has not been wanting to do all for us. And we notwithstanding, who undertook solemnly that we and our children, and servants should walk after God, and we would teach them to do what is good in God's sight, and yet we do not take care that they do so; and for other of our friends whom we might be helpful to, we wholly neglect them. We ought to shame ourselves for this breach of covenant, else we cannot say that we make a true covenant with God, and charge ourselves for being so false unto God, and then some good may come of it.

When the people had broken covenant with God, and God was very angry, and would have no more to do with them (Exodus 32). But chapter 33, the people put off their best clothes and came before Him, and humbled themselves in His presence, and put off their best clothes, and entreated God to be reconciled unto them, and then He again renews His covenant with them.

To show you how God is wont to express Himself to His people when we have broken covenant with Him, God will say, He will not look at us any more, He will never protect us more, He will neither meddle nor make with us, but will expose us to all evil. Now if hereupon we return and bewail our breach of covenant with God, how little good we have done and how little serviceable we are, He is then wont to let us see that His covenant was never so far broken, but He can tell how to be good to us for the Lord Jesus Christ's sake. And this is a third way of having of Christ.

HAVING CHRIST BY FREE ACCEPTANCE

A fourth way is a way *of free acceptance*. We have Christ by receiving Him. That is the last way whereby Christ is said to be conveyed to us, "to as many as received Him, to them He gave power to be called the sons of God" (John 1:12). That is the life of a Christian to become a son of God, and God is the Father not of the dead but of the living. So that, here is a receiving of Christ by faith, whereby we become the sons of God. So that if you would know whether you have Christ or not, whether or not, do you receive Him? Receive Him by faith, and that goes through all the former, but something different.

Amongst interpreters, this receiving of Christ is many ways taken. Some say it is to receive Him as a King and a Savior. And it is not in vain, but under correction. It does not fitly interpret the notion of the Word. But the substance of the thing delivered by the Holy Ghost, if I do not mistake it, the phrase expresses thus much: "As many as receive Him into their hearts as into a house or temple, and it will hold according to the comparison used by the Holy Ghost. 'He came unto His own,' into the Temple, or House of God, and thither He came as into His own proper place, He came unto his own." You are to conceive he speaks not only of Christ's coming among them in the tabernacle of flesh and blood for of that in verse 1, but the whole chapter is a history and declaration of Christ, partly before the world was. And in their giving light to all in the Creation, and after the Fall when the world was grown dark. Then He was the "true light that enlightened every one that was in the world." Now He was in the world, and the world was made by Him, but the world knew Him not. And He came to His own people in His Ordinances, and they apprehended Him not; but as many as received Him of old, to them He gave power to be called the sons of God.

But for further opening of this phrase, read John 19:27: "He took her home to his own house." It is in the original the same word with that in John 1:11, in "to His own home." He came unto His own home or house, unto His own Temple and people, and they received Him not, but neglected His Ordinances, neglected to seek Christ in the Temple. But as many as did there seek Him and look toward Him, He gave them power to be called the sons of God. So that, to receive Christ according to the meaning of this place is to receive Him into our hearts as into His proper house. And He comes there as a Master and these receive Him as into a temple, then we have Him by receiving Him into a house or home. Now you are "the temples of the living God" (2 Cor. 6:16); "I will dwell in you, and you shall receive Me."

CHRIST RECEIVED AS INTO A TEMPLE THREE WAYS

Now, how do we receive Christ into our hearts as into a Temple? There be three things by which we receive Christ as into a Temple:

The First Way of Receiving Christ

First, when we do prepare a way for Christ to come in to us, as it is said of John, he prepared the way for Christ that so He might suddenly come into His Temple (Mal. 3:1). And Isaiah speaking of the same Messenger, he says, "Every mountain shall be brought low, and every valley filled up; crooked ways be made straight, and rough ways made smooth" (Isa. 40:3, 4). And this is the preparation we must make for Christ to come into us.

You have sometime heard this fully spoken to, that is, when the high mountains of our great spirits, and lofty looks, are brought so low, that we are content to be nothing in our own eyes, that we have all we have in Christ, and are able to bring nothing to Him, and are willing that He should take all from us, whatever He would have us to part with. And when we are willing to be whatsoever He would have us to be, and that He should do with us what is good in His own eyes; then these high mountains being brought low, we are made fit for Christ to come into us, we must have no crooked ways of our own. If we have any imagination of our own left in us, that we will part with such and such lusts. But yet are loath to be disposed of in all things as God will have us, then there is no room for God, He will not climb for it. But if we smooth the way for Him, then He will come into our hearts.

But besides this, there is to be filled up every low valley, and that holds forth two things. Every valley shall be filled, that is, first, every base heart shall lift up itself to the high things of God. For he speaks of valleys first, as if there were such a low dejectedness in the creature, as made it unfit for Christ. God requires that every base heart should be exalted to the minding of high and heavenly things, lifted up far above these low things that cannot reach the ways of God. These gates must stand open and be lifted up, "that the King of glory may come in" (Ps. 24:7-10). And He means the gates of our hearts, and He calls them "the gates of eternity." They are our hearts and souls.

Stand not pouring upon earthly things here below, but lift up your heads higher, look for a God, and for a Kingdom. Stand not peddling about these earthly things as if you had nothing else to look after. Your hearts lie too low for Christ to come into, but if you would lie level with Him, then lift up your mind to heavenly things. Let the bent of your heart be for pardon of sin, and for everlasting life. Be of a level frame of spirit to the Kingdom of Heaven, and then Christ will come into you.

And as it implies that the heart must not be too low for Christ through baseness of spirit and an earthly mind, so it may be too low through despair, and through excessive sorrow for sin, he may be cast so low down in dejection of spirit that his heart lies too low for Christ, not able to lay hold on God's favor to him in Christ. Thinks the promises belongs not to him, it is well and happy for them that can lay hold upon them. But for his part there are none of these promises reach him. Did you ever know any in my case find mercy? Now the heart lies something too low, this man's heart is not base, he looks at Christ as the most honorable thing in the world. He sets his heart upon the blood of Christ, and would be glad with all his heart that he had his part in it. But he is dejected, and lies too low, fit to despair. And therefore in this case a Christian must be thus far exalted as to be made level with Christ, to believe there is hope in Israel touching his estate. Christ has had mercy upon many in such a case, and He will do so to us if we seek Him in the way of His Ordinances. And if therefore we resolve to seek Him, and put our mouths in the dust, expecting salvation to be revealed by Him, and follow Him in His Ordinances, and never have fellowship with the unfruitful works of darkness, and will still continue to seek Him, then we begin to be something level with Christ.

But you say, "There is such a crookedness in my heart, and unevenness, that Christ cannot come in." Truly, that must be made straight. Princes are not wont to go down back lanes, but down plain ways. So Christ, as He would have His way neither too high, nor too low, so He would not go round about, but would have the way to lie plain before Him. The judgement, and heart, and affection, lie in such sort of evenness as simply to aim at the glory of God in his way, and therein to be ruled by the Word of God, and then is the heart of a man in a good frame. If there be nothing in a man's heart, but he is willing to be guided in it by the straight rule of God's Word, and he aims directly at the glory of God, and the coming of His Kingdom, and the doing of His will. Then is all a man's crooked ways laid aside, and the heart lies so level that Christ will suddenly come into His Temple, these crooked windings of a spirit of hypocrisy are made straight when he is brought low. Yet he may have much hypocrisy in him, pretend to be more than he is. He may be doing good duties more to be seen of men, than that God should observe him. Therefore when God has brought us to this, that we are desirous of grace, rather in truth than in outward show, or if in show, but that we might do others good thereby, and singly aim at God's glory in it, and desire and endeavor to walk by the straight rule of the Word of God. Then are our hearts cleansed in some measure from the crooked windings of hypocrisy, which might hinder the free passage of Christ into the soul.

And yet there is another winding in a man's heart, though in some truth the duties be done. Yet there is many times an aptness in us to cover and to wind about our own sins, and to make them less than they be, and this is a wicked course (cf. Ps. 125:4, 5). And therefore God would have us deal most plainly with Him, that in the singleness of our hearts, when it may stand with the glory of God, and the confusion of our own faces, we will not be wanting to lay open our hearts before Him. There be such windings as will not profit us when we deal plainly and confess what we have done, and come to be thus open hearted to God, then is Christ ready to come suddenly into His Temple. When we have brought down our high spirits, and raised up our too low, bare and dejected spirit; and laid all level before Him, then there remains no more, but for Christ to come suddenly into His Temple.

But yet besides all this, when all this is done, yet there may be still a great measure of a rough, and harsh, and sharp, and fiery spirit in him, which Christ will have removed before He comes to dwell there. Before that, He will have this harshness and bitterness laid down, that they shall be smooth and level before Him—the frame of the heart shall be as meek as a lamb. The Lamb of God will not lie in a den of lions, and if we break out into harsh and unsavory distempers afterward, we shall damp the life of God in us. The life of Christ will be dead in us. And therefore, if you desire to entertain Christ into your hearts, then lay aside all harshness, and bitterness, and roughness, and all guile of crookedness (1 Pet. 2:12). Then you shall have life in the Word, and find Christ to be yours. This is the first thing whereby we receive Christ.

The Second Way of Receiving Christ

Secondly, suppose He be come, there is thus much more required to have Him and to keep Him there. We must look there be no unholy thing remaining there. All vain and common things must be removed. No profane matter must stay there. "Touch no unclean thing" (2 Cor. 6:16). And if Christ come unto you, you must not only remove all sinful and unclean matter, but also all common matter. And now everything must be dedicated to God, and you must go about your callings as becomes Christians, and you and all yours must be dedicated to God. Your silver and your gold must be dedicated. And only spent upon such uses as God calls for, and therefore look at everything so as God may have glory by it. And let Him not be dishonored in anything by you. All that you are and have must be dedicated to God: mind, and judgment, and conscience, and heart, and affection, love and hatred; your whole man. And all your labors, and all you can reach lies as a consecrated thing, else God will not dwell livelily in you. Unless you have a care to keep everything clean, you shall find this to be true. Christ loves to lie clean, and religion loves to lie clean. And if He see nasty sluttishness in us, He will be gone and will not tarry there. He would not have natural uncleanness to appear among you, but let all such be covered, and let no such defilement be seen among you, He would have all kept in a holy reverent frame, such as might become the presence of God.

The Third Way of Receiving Christ

Thirdly, the receiving of Christ into our hearts as into a temple implies to keep the charge of His Ordinances and holy things, to offer to Him all our sacrifices, and to look that all be performed in such a manner as Himself requires. God charges it as a sin upon His people, "You have not kept the charge of My holy things" (Ez. 44:8), but "you have set keepers of My Ordinances in My sanctuary for yourselves." God will not dwell among them when they set up the uncircumcised to offer up their sacrifices. God will have every man to take charge over his own temple.

Have a care of yourselves, put not off your care to others, you may not put off the charge of God's holy things. Every man has a charge to look to the things of

God; not only to see that all unclean things be removed, and all common things dedicated, but to see that every morning and evening, sacrifice be duly performed, and all things done in a right manner. Else you will find little life in Christ. And if He see this care in you, then Christ will come into His Temple and dwell there, and you shall have life in Christ, and that in abundance. You cannot have God for your God, but you must have a place readily prepared for Him, and keep it in fitness, and comeliness for Him, trim it up for a habitation for Him. This God requires of every soul that will have God for his God.

In a word, therefore, do but consider whether your hearts have embraced Christ or not. Are your base hearts exalted to look after heavenly things? Are your proud hearts brought low to the obedience of Christ? Do you find your ways of hypocrisy made plain before God? Are your rough passions made smooth before God? Then you have Christ, whether you see Him, or feel Him or not. And do you find that when you have Christ, you dedicate yourselves to Him, and suffer no unclean thing in yourselves or yours? Do you keep the Ordinances pure, and offer up your morning and evening sacrifice yourselves? Then you have received Christ, and it is your faith by which you do thus receive Him. But if it be not thus with you, then say you have not received Christ. Or if you have, you are to be humbled for your great neglect, and want of keeping Him.

PART II

THE ACTUAL HAVING OF CHRIST

Having Christ Himself, Not Just For His Benefits

He that has the Son has life, and he that has not the Son has not life.
(1 John 5:12)

There yet remains two things for signs of having Christ. For in all this point of our Christian faith, there is no word but of more than ordinary and common use. And therefore when he says, "he that has the Son has life," some signs may be gathered from the word—*having Him*, and some from having Him as a *Son*. And some from this word *life*, by which we may know, whether we have the Son and life in Him.

We now come to speak of the second sort of signs, "He that has the Son has life," then if we would have life in Christ, we must have Him as a *Son*.

The thing then to be opened is: What it is to have Christ as the Son of the Most High God? And that will give further light to the text, and to the consciences of them that would see the ground of their hopes settled upon a foundation, "He that has the Son has life."

There be three things implied in having Christ as a Son.

HAVING CHRIST HIMSELF

First, it implies that such as have Christ in truth, and so having Him, have life by Him. They do not rest in having any of the benefits of Christ, though they be spiritual, but they chiefly affect to have Himself, not so much his benefits as Himself. He does not say, "He that has such and such spiritual gifts has the Son." No, though you have never so many gifts, and they such as do accompany salvation, but that which He principally commends to us is Himself.

You shall read of a company of professors that had Christ, and affected to have Him so far as they might have loaves from Him. But our blessed Savior bids them in seeking Christ, "seek not for loaves that perish, but labor for the meat which endures to eternal life" (John 6:26-27). And that is only the Lord Jesus Christ Himself: Labor not for any loaves, whatsoever you might find in your pursuit after Christ. It was this by which Peter did discover the hypocrisy of Simon Magus. He desired the gift of the Holy Ghost, but for Christ Himself, his heart was not set upon Him, but he only desired that in which lay most profit. For had it been in his power that upon the laying on of his hands upon any, tongues might have been given, and sicknesses healed, he might have grown mighty in the world by that trade (Acts 8:18-19).

And Balaam was somewhat more upright in his desire than Simon Magus was. One would think that he had sought after Christ, for he wished not for any temporal thing in this world, only that he might have a comfortable end. He would feather his nest with immortality, and invest himself with the robes of incorruption. And such kind of other glory as the saints in light do partake of. But it was no more his desire than the other—to desire Christ for himself, but only a blessed end that he might be translated into immortality and glory, and so might be kept from fellowship with those devils and evil spirits he had been acquainted with all his life long, that he might not have fellowship with them when he departed hence. But did not desire Christ for himself, and therefore whatever gift he had, as he had a notable spirit of prophecy, as the Spirit then came upon him, speaking of the marvelous blessings reserved for God's people. Yet notwithstanding, he never sought Christ in any of them. And therefore, though he might have some glimpse of the vision of God, yet of Christ he had none. Whereas there is no true Christian that does most esteem the having of Christ, but does not only seek Christ without respect of loaves, or money, or of a quiet conscience in time of death. But even in the very time of this life, when he seeks after the Ordinances of God in this life, there to live according to God, and to find pardon of sin, and peace of conscience, and subduing of his lusts, and strength of grace, and power of godliness, yet even in seeking the very Ordinances of God (out of which these are not to be found). Yet in seeking of these, he does not so much seek these, or any blessing they do afford, as the finding Christ in them.

The story is notable and famous in 2 Samuel 15:25-27. When David fled from Jerusalem, the priests and Levites carried the Ark after him, and when David saw them overtake him with the Ark of God's presence, in the enjoyment whereof stood the life of his life, the assurance of the pardon of his sin, the assurance and presence of God's favor, strengthening of his spirit in grace, and subduing his lusts, yet says he:

> "Carry it back again to Jerusalem, if I shall find favor in the eyes of the Lord, He will bring me back again, and show me both it and His habitation; but if He thus say, I have no delight in you, behold, here am I, let Him do to me as seems good to Him."

He would not wrong himself, nor do the Church of God so much prejudice as to wrong God. And his sacrifice, they were not to offer sacrifice elsewhere. Nor could they find any solemn presence of God anywhere but there. There were they all to meet, and it was the place where God had put His Name. And he considering that he could not have the Ark with him, but God's Name should be dishonored, and the Church of God would find much prejudice with the loss of God's Ark. Therefore, rather than God should be dishonored, and the people discouraged and prejudiced by the want of it, he would send it back again, and is content to loose outward blessings. His care was not so much about outward things. His chiefest care was, if he might have had his wish, that he might all his time "dwell in the house of the Lord" (Ps. 23:4). And oh, that he might be but "a door-keeper in this house, rather than to rest in the tabernacle of wickedness." But yet, when he could not have this great blessing, but with dishonor to God, and prejudice to the Church of God, he rather lays down the comfort that he might have from God's Ordinances, and the help he might have from them, and those helps were very great—as pardon of sin, and peace of conscience, growth in grace, subduing of lusts, and establishment of his heart in assurance of his election, and vocation. Yet he is content to let them all go that he might have what he has without sin to himself, and dishonor to God, or wrong to the Church.

This is a notable sign of a man's integrity and uprightness of heart. He would not have anything whereby God might have dishonor. He would not have the Ordinances with the Church's loss, but rather sit out, and shift for himself as well as he could, and would adventure the loss of them all rather than he will stand to contend for them with the loss of Christ Himself.

And this kind of frame of spirit was in Moses. He entreats God that He would not destroy the Israelites in the wilderness lest His name should be dishonored, but rather blot his name out of the Book of Life then cut them all off (Ex. 32:32). Such is the uprightness of the frame of the heart of a child of God that he desires not spiritual blessings singly for himself, not for the peace of his own conscience, nor for the subduing of his lusts, nor for the strengthening of his grace, further than may stand with the glory of God. And above all things else, he seeks the honor of God, the coming of His Kingdom, and the doing of His will. And if these concur not in his way, he would rather lose them than dishonor Christ by having of them. He has a singleness of heart in seeking spiritual blessings, he seeks them not for his own ends.

As you see in David's desire: "My soul thirsts for You, my flesh longs for You, to see Your power, and Your glory, as I have seen You in the Sanctuary; because Your loving kindness is better than life, therefore my lips shall praise You" (Ps. 63:1-3). He desires not there the enjoyment of the presence of God, or the subduing of his lusts, that he might live at more ease, and have more comfort (though that be a lawful end). But he would see the power of Christ more magnified in him. He would see a mighty increase of the grace of God in him, not that he might be more excellent than his neighbors, more eminent in gifts, and so be better than others, or so esteemed.

But he desires that all his lusts may be swallowed up, and that the life of Christ might more mightily over-rule, and over-sway him, and dwell mightily in him—that he might not live after his own will, nor to himself, nor would he live by the graces of the Spirit in him. But the life that he would live is "by the faith of the Son of God" (Gal. 2:20), that Christ and His life in him might work all His works in him and for him. And in that at any time he desires death, it is not that he might be freed from evil and misery, but that he might be "dissolved, and be with Christ" (Phil. 1:23). Though the other be a lawful desire, but chiefly his desire is that he might see Christ, whom from his first conversion he has most loved, and in whom he has lived all his life, and now to be wholly possessed of Him, and wholly acted and swayed by Him, not that he might have his heart filled with joy, but that he might be with Christ—not only as chiefest of ten thousand persons, but as the chiefest of ten thousands benefits of God. That should God give us pardon of sin, His Word and Sacrament, and victory over all our lusts, strength of every grace of God, and everlasting life, and therewith fellowship with all the blessed saints and angels, yet to us Christ is the chiefest of them all, none greater than the gift of Christ. This is the sincerity of a Christian's soul. He desires more any benefit for Christ's sake than Christ for any of His benefits' sake. For he whose heart is set upon Christ more than upon the pardon of sin or salvation, that soul has Christ, and life in Him. He that has Christ in his eye and heart above all blessings, he indeed is a true Christian, and has Christ.

Reason: Christ must so be had, and we must so receive Him as God gives Him. Now God gives us first Christ in all His Ordinances, and then in Christ all other things, all benefits in and through Christ: "We preach to you Jesus" (Acts 8:35); we offer you Him, all lusts laid aside, all sinful corruptions put away, whatever separates between God and us, that being done away—we now offer you Christ, and in Christ, plenteous redemption. But if we be without Christ, we are without true life.

CHRIST OR HIS SACRAMENTS?

As in the Sacrament, first you have the body and blood of Christ set before you (Matt. 26:26). And then sealed up and confirmed to you in the Sacrament, and together with that—justification. And further degrees of the sanctifying Spirit, and further pledges of everlasting life and glory. No benefit, but it's conveyed through Him. Christ first, and then the benefit. It is true, Herod received joy, but Felix trembling, and Jehu zeal, but none of these received Christ. They received the husk, but wanted Christ. They had the shell, but not the marrow and kernel within. They received the benefit, but Christ they did not receive, and for want of Him they had no life at all. Simon Magus believed (Acts 8:13), but he had no lively faith because he would receive the benefit, but Christ he minded not to receive. Unless the heart be knit to Christ, and the soul more seek Christ then pardon of sin, or subduing of lusts, he has no life in truth; "he that has the Son, he has life." Not so, he that has the gifts and benefits of the Son: But Christ first, and in having Christ we have all.

Christ must be received as God gives Him. We must acknowledge there is no life in any grace, but in Christ (cf. Hos. 14:8). "On Me is your fruit found, and without Me can you do nothing" (John 15:5). Now then, carry this truth home with you and gather from hence a true estimate of your own estates, whether you may judge of yourselves as living or dead Christians. Upon our having or not having of Christ depends our having or not having of life. How will you know, whether you have life or not? You say you have Christ; how know you that? Is your heart more set upon Christ than the gifts of Christ? Do you labor more for gifts, or for Christ Himself?

And if you find this, that in the truth of your hearts, you come not to the Ordinances, but to find your Beloved there, not out of unclean and wanton spirits, but to seek Him whom your soul most desires. Whose favor and countenance you would rather behold, than to hear the voice of a pleasant singer, and you are not satisfied with anything unless you find Him? Then shall you find life in so coming to the Ordinances? "By night in my bed

I sought him whom my soul loved, *etc.*" (Songs 3:1-3). The bed was the Temple wherein God did reveal Himself in His Ordinances, and disperse Himself to His people in the bed of His love. She came to the Temple, not to seek any of the priests and Levites there. She goes indeed to the watchmen and makes her moan and complaint to them that she could not find Christ in His Ordinances. And she durst not rest upon their opinions. But faith, have you not seen Him whom my soul loves? Can you tell me any news, or give me any intelligence of my beloved Savior? Thus she inquires of the watchmen. And from them she goes to the daughters of Jerusalem, to her Christian friends and charges them to tell Him, that she is sick of love.

Now, if this to desire Him is to find Christ, then there is no more to be doubted of in such a case as this. But the heart thus seeking Him in His Ordinances, and the affections gone after Him there, more than after any of His benefits, then in truth we have the Son. He could not have our hearts if we first had not Him. And therefore, it is a strong evidence we have Him because our hearts are set upon Him. We search for nothing so much as for Him. This is part of the meaning of that place in Psalm 73:25, "Whom have I in heaven but You, or in earth in comparison of You?" He desires nothing more than Him, neither peace of conscience nor joy in the Holy Ghost, nor anything so chiefly and principally as God. But if we have a longing affection after pardon of sin, and peace of conscience, and assurance of salvation, after subduing of lusts and growth in grace. These be blessed desires, and usually upright and sincere, but there may be hypocrisy even in these very desires, and in using the means to attain these.

SPIRITUAL HARLOTRY

For sometimes by this means we seek Christ, and Him in His Ordinances, not so much for Himself, as for the benefits we have by Him, which is a spirit of harlotry. As in a woman that it may be has a strong affection to match with such a man; but it is, but that he might pay her debts, and that she might be well provided for. For the world, and that he might be a veil, and a protector to her, these be lawful ends to aim at. But if it be only and chiefly for these ends, it is not true conjugal affection. For if another man could do this for her as well as he, she could make choice of another as well as of him. And she desires him, not for his, but for her own ends.

And just so it is alike in this case: If a man desire the Lord Jesus Christ to this end that he may have his sin pardoned, and be furnished with grace, though these be spiritual ends, yet so much as we prize the benefit above Christ, so much are we halting in the truth of our affection to Him. If a woman in true conjugal affection look at no more but at the very bare man, if there be true love in her towards him, she is content to have him, though she have nothing else but his person. So if our hearts be truly set upon Christ, we are content to have Him, though we should never see good day with Him. Though we should never see peace of conscience with Him, though no comfort of grace in Him. Yet would the soul that is truly affected to Christ say, "Give me Christ, and I have enough"? Who or what is there besides Christ? What is there? Why, there is variety of excellent graces: But "whom have I in earth but You?" As if you should put all other things in comparison against, or with Christ; they are nothing to Him, then surely you have Christ.

ALL OR NOTHING

But how much will this discord from the fellowship of Christ, the sons and daughters of men, who when they see the costliness of the ways of Christ. They will neither seek after Christ nor His benefits but as for pardon of sin, as it passes all understanding, so it passes their desires? And for peace of conscience, they hope they have a good conscience. Or if not, they do not search to know it; and as for the graces of the Spirit, and subduing of lusts, they have a good hope, and believe as well as the best. And for the Kingdom of glory they hope if God grant them mercy they shall come to heaven at the last. These men are far from having the Lord Jesus and life in Him. They are so far off from seeking the Son as that they do not so much as seek those mercies and benefits which in Christ are conveyed to their souls. They neither have Him nor none of His.

They say to the Almighty, "Depart from us, for we desire not the knowledge of Your law" (Job 21:14). Of such God says, "They would have none of Me" (Ps. 81:11). Not only have Him, but none of Him; that is, nothing that was His, not any saving benefit of His. The world we would have, but none of those choice and heavenly blessings of Christ—no pardon of sin, no peace of conscience, no care of Christianity, or faithful ministry, no fear of God, nor keeping of His Commandments. Dear hearts for us, how shall we ever conceive that ever we should have life in Christ, when we do not so much as desire the very benefits of Christ? Yet a man may desire and lose all too, and when a man has not so much as an affection to the things of Christ it is very dangerous.

HAVE CHRIST, AND THEN THE BENEFITS

But secondly, when a man is in this case, that there is a desire in a man after the benefits of Christ, more than after Christ Himself; all this while you want that sincerity upon which Christ will give us a comfortable meeting, and speak peace to our souls; we are not yet come to that condition, as in which he will say, "My well-beloved, You are all fair, and there is no spot in You." He yet sees not a true conjugal affection in us towards Him, so as that though we should never find grace nor glory by Him, yet He is the chief desire of our souls. Suppose a woman should see a man that has a desire after her, but he chiefly aims at her estate to provide for himself, and looks no further, wonder not if she should say to him, "You seek not me, but mine," she may well rid her hands of him in such a case. And truly so is the case here between us and the Lord Jesus, so long as He finds that we come to Him, and seek, and pray, and wrestle, and what would we have?

Oh, pardon of sin, and peace of conscience, and power of grace, to be but as other Christians are; that we could pray, and believe as they do, and find such comfort as they have, and this is the thing that the soul is chiefly set upon. Now, all this while that we come thus to Christ, we must not think that Christ is to blame if He tarry a little longer than we expect. For we may seek Him and not find Him because we seek not so much Him as His benefits. And the rich treasures of grace, and mercy, and peace that are laid up in Him without measure; the greatest part of the world do not love their souls, nor the Lord Jesus so well as to love Him for His grace and goodness sake. But yet among better men, there is a world of self-love. Many a man would have his sin pardoned because he would have his conscience at quiet. We may thank ourselves for such affections as these, not but that such affections may spring from the grace of God. For men by nature never dream of such things as these be, but yet though such affections may spring from the grace of God. Yet you shall ever find such souls to detain the grace of God in unrighteousness, and out of self-love, use them all to their own ends, and look not that God may be glorified in and by them, nor that His will be done.

But oh, that the soul might have peace, and that sin might be pardoned! And there it rests when our desires is chiefly set upon spiritual gifts. If we lose much comfort and fellowship with Christ that else we might have had, we must not marvel at it. For our desires are set not chiefly upon Christ, but upon the things of Christ. Our desire is not after the person, but after the goods and benefits of Christ.

Observe the Apostle's expression in Romans 8:32: "He has given us His own Son." He does not say, "He that has given us peace and pardon of sin, will not he give all other things also?" Or, will not He give us Christ? He reasons not from Christ's benefits, but to Christ. Thus he reasons: "He that has given us His own Son, will *with* His Son," and *after* His Son, "give us all other things." At the second hand comes in all these benefits of pardon of sin, and strength of grace, and power against our lusts, *etc.* These things come in as attendants upon the former. And therefore, if God give us first to look at Christ, that in Him, we have life of justification. And sanctification, and consolation, eternal glory, peace, and grace, and all.

Then we have Him, and life in Him, else we may have the outward comforts, but stand long enough at Christ's bed-chamber door, before He let us in.

SEEK CHRIST!

Let it therefore be a word of direction and exhortation to every soul that desires to have that truth of life, and peace, and grace wrought in his heart that will never die. Have you respect chiefly to the Lord Jesus Christ, and long and seek more after Him than after all spiritual blessings and much more above all worldly blessings? If you shall therefore refuse Christ because you think He is but a melancholy person, you will never have Him. If you stand upon such terms, if you will not have Him unless He be thus and thus qualified. Then let Him alone, never talk of Him. Rest not in looking after any of His benefits. It is a good thing to look for such benefits as accompany Christ. But rest not there. Content not yourselves in such wrestlings. Never think you are of a right spirit, and that you have a lively life, and such as by which you shall maintain constant fellowship with God, unless you find your hearts longing after Christ. "My soul is athirst for the living God" (Ps. 42:1-2).

Let your hearts be chiefly set upon Him for His own sake. You can tell what it is to set your affections more upon a person than upon their estate. And you must know that your affections are more set upon Christ than upon any benefit He has. Unless you find Christ more than His gifts, you shall find little peace in your way. You must see that all, even the worst of His things are beautiful and comely, and is more to be desired than gold; it is sweeter than the honey or the honeycomb. He that thus has the Son he has life, the Son of God; God and Man, as He is our Son, and our Savior.

Let the desire of your soul be unto Him, and your affections run out after Him. Be you for Him, and then He will be for you. Stand not so much upon this, what Christ will be for you, but be sure that you be for Him. Let friends and all go, and be sure you be only for Him. Though Christ love us first, yet He will make us no assurance of His love to us until He see us love Him. And if we choose Him first before and above all His benefits, then we shall have Him. Make Him then your assurance, and your kingdom shall not be shaken. Think not that He will make you a feoffement[2] before you be married to Him.

But we must be content to come to Him, and take Him as He is, and stand upon no conditions with Him. You must not look for assurance of Christ's benefits until you have Himself. And if you choose Him, then you shall have assurance to your souls that He has chosen you first. You cannot ask more than He will give, but first

---

[2] A *feoffment* was a transfer of land or property that gave the new owner the right to give it to his heirs as an inheritance.

you must have Himself. He will give you a kingdom, but you must first be a little flock. "All is yours, and you are Christ's, and Christ is God's" (1 Cor. 3:23). Thus choose Him above all His benefits, and you shall have Him, and life in Him.

HAVING THE SPIRIT OF CHRIST

He that has the Son has life, and he that has not the Son has not life.
(1 John 5:12)

From the second part of the words, "He that has the Son," there are three sorts of heads of notes drawn. One is already hand-led; to wit, that such as have the Son, they have not so much, nor do so much stand upon, nor so much desire the *benefits* of the Son as *the Son Himself*. This is the spiritual life of a Christian. While some men labor more for spiritual gifts than for Christ Himself, the true Christian is only for Him, and let His gifts go. We now come to the second head of notes from the word *Son*. A man is said to have the Son when he has the Spirit of the Son.

A man is said to have Christ when he has the Spirit, and therefore you may read 2 Corinthians 3:17: "Where the Spirit of the Lord is, there is liberty, and the Lord is that Spirit, *viz*." He had spoken before of a Spirit of righteousness and of the Spirit of grace dispensed in the ministry of the gospel. Now, the Lord is that Spirit, not only so called because He is the giver of that Spirit and grace, but also as there is a secret fellowship between Christ and the Spirit.

So that, have one and you have both, have not the Spirit of Christ, and you have none of Christ. "If a man have not the Spirit of Christ he is none of His" (Rom. 8:9). And notable to this purpose is that in Galatians 4:6, "Because you are sons, God has sent forth the Spirit of His Son into your hearts." And verse 5, "He redeemed them which were under the Law, that we might receive the adoption of sons." Implying that, to whomsoever Christ came for into the world to save and redeem, all those have fellowship with the Son, and into all their hearts He has shed abroad the Spirit of the Son. So that, look how Christ is and was in this world, so are we in the world, he that has the Son, has the Spirit of the Son.

Now that I may the better open this point unto you (because it is of special use for our direction in a Christian course). There is a threefold spirit of a Son, dispensing Himself three ways, and bestowing a threefold gift upon us, which gives us the Lord Jesus Christ to be ours, and us to him, to be His.

THREEFOLD SPIRIT OF THE SON OF GOD

First, a spirit that does knit us to the Lord Jesus Christ, and Him to us,

Secondly, a spirit of liberty.

Thirdly, a spirit of prayer.[3]

---

[3] The discussion of prayer is continued beginning in Sermon 12.

These three the Holy Ghost takes special notice of in this case.

THE FIRST DISPENSATION OF THE SON TO US: BY UNION

First, the Spirit of God, wheresoever it is shed abroad in any member of Christ, it does make us one with the Lord Jesus. It unites us into one fellowship of nature—a likeness in affection and disposition, and a likeness in all the graces of God. As in John 17:21, our Savior prays the Father "that all those whom He had given Him might be one with Him, as You and I are one."—'You in Me by Your Spirit, and I in You by the same Spirit; and this Spirit is such, as makes not only Me one with You, but them also, one with Me; and they also in like sort, one with another.' It makes us and Christ as it were one. Hence it is, that as soon as we receive Him, we "of His fullness receive grace for grace" (John 1:16). There is a conformity between Christ and us; one and the same image stamped upon us both (cf. Rom. 8:29); a like in grace, a like in affection, and in continuance of affection, a like in everything.

For a little further clearing of the point: The same Spirit of Christ, being shed abroad into the heart of every one that has Christ, does work a threefold conformity or likeness between Christ and us.

First, a likeness in *Nature*.

Secondly, a likeness in *Offices*.

Thirdly, in *Estate*, both of humiliation and exaltation. And all this is done by the mighty power of the Spirit of Christ.

Unity through Threefold Conformity: A Likeness in Nature

First, for the *Nature* of Christ, by the precious promises of God which are made unto us, and which the Holy Ghost does apply to us: "We are made partakers of the divine nature" (2 Pet. 1:4). There is a likeness and a participation of the divine nature, and we are made partakers of the like grace in Christ Jesus. And that "grace for grace"—Look what grace anywhere you see in Christ, the resemblance of it is stamped upon every child of God by the Spirit of Christ. Hence it comes to pass that (which is worth your observation) those who have Christ, they do reason from the nature of Christ to justify the temper of their own spirits, and the course of their own lives.

As is the Apostle Paul's own argument in 2 Corinthians 1:17-19, some of the false apostles took up an argument against the Apostle Paul to prove his levity, and inconstancy, and forgetfulness. And how does he free himself, "did I use lightness?" No says he, "our words toward you were not yes and no." And thus he reasons from Christ's nature, "The Son of God who was preached among you was not yes and no, but yes and amen: Now He which establishes us with you is Christ, *etc.*" So that look as Christ is "yes and amen, the faithful and true witness of God," what He speaks He confirms, and fulfils in due season.

Now says he, when Christ was preached among you, it was not an uncertain Christ, carried about with lightness and unsettledness. But what is once gone out of his lips, it is "yes and amen." Therefore make account that God that has poured the same Spirit upon us has "established us together with you." To show you that, by reason of the participation of the Spirit of grace, there is such a spirit in us, as that you may argue all these. The nature of Christ, the nature of the gospel, and the nature of the frame of grace in the hearts of God's people, to be all alike. They do mutually show the face one of another in the frame and carriage one of another. That as Christ is "yes and amen," so is the gospel, and such are they that believe the gospel, and established by the gospel in Christ Jesus (vv. 21, 22). "And He has sealed us, and given us the Spirit in our hearts"— the same Spirit of Christ that breathed in the gospel, and in the preachers of the gospel, and the believers of it, is "yes and amen" in them all. A Spirit of truth, and innocency, and gravity, and purity, whatsoever is the Spirit of the one is the Spirit of them all.

So that this is an evident sign that we have Christ. When we have the Spirit of Christ; when you may reason alike the one from the other, though in us it be the weaker, by reason of a spirit of corruption found in us, and not in Christ. Yet this is an evident argument of the stability and gravity of our hearts, which though in regard of weakness, we might think the Apostle might have been excepted against. Yet because there is no weakness in a child of God, but if he have Christ, his heart is in the same condition with Christ, and with the gospel also. Therefore he may comfortably argue a likeness between them; what he speaks, that he thinks in his heart, and it is the desire of his soul that it may be effected. And though he may be hindered, yet his heart is still the same, and he was by no means to be taxed of any lightness because he did not perform his word, the fault was not his levity. His spirit was the same, but some occasion fell out otherwise by the providence of God. And so it is with every child of God. If he have Christ, the spirit of a Christian is ever the same. If there should be any inclination to lying and inconstancy, the frame of the spirit is altered, but the true bent and frame of a Christian is to be one with Christ, as Christ is one with Him.

Unity through Threefold Conformity: A Likeness in Offices

Now, as there is a likeness and conformity and unity in nature between Christ and a child of God, so there is also in us a conformity to Christ in His *Offices*. The meaning is, whosoever has the Son, he has the offices which the Son has. As He was both King, Priest and Prophet to God His Father, so are we (cf. Rev. 1:6). As kings, to rule over all our lusts, and to rule all those whom God commends to our government according unto God. As kings, to get victory and to conquer over the world, and to over-wrestle any difficulty as we meet with. As kings, anointed with the spirit of a king of a royal spirit, though not invested with fullness of glory till the last day. Yet of a heroic noble spirit can easily overlook all earthly drudgery, and resist any enemy we meet with.

And priests also we are, so as we are able to offer up sacrifices of prayer and thanksgiving to God, "A broken and a humble heart is a sacrifice," much set by of God (Ps. 51:17), and Philippians 2:17, "offered upon the sacrifice and service of your faith." We are now enabled to go to God and to offer up praises to Him, which are as incense before Him. And in offering up any other sacrifice of a holy life, we are priests unto God the Father.

And so are we also prophets. He pours out His Spirit in a rich and plentiful measure. He pours out His Spirit "upon all flesh" (Acts 2:17). Whence it comes to pass that the servants of God understand many secrets of God's counsel (Ps. 25:14), and whence also it comes to pass, that many a godly man by the same spirit discerns many secret hidden mysteries, and meanings of the Holy Ghost in Scripture, more than ever he could by any reading or instruction. And many times discerns some special work of the Spirit of God which enables them to foresee some special blessings, most useful for their spiritual estate, and so leads them on to many good things which they did little think of. And so makes them of prophetical spirits, and bows them to teach others also, to lead on others of their neighbors in the ways of God.

And now I say that as these be the Offices of the Lord Jesus Christ, so there is no child of God that has the Son, but he has all these in Him. He is now a man of a royal, and priestly, and prophetical spirit.

And you are hereby (I mean by the Spirit) not only called to these Offices, but enabled to discharge them. For that is the difference between a Christian in heart and a Christian in appearance, fall short of ability to perform these Offices.

Unity through Threefold Conformity: A Likeness in Estate (Humiliation & Exaltation)

And as there is this conformity to the Nature and Offices of Christ in them that have the Son, so thirdly, there is a conformity in their *Estates*. You know Christ waded through an estate of humiliation and exaltation. These be the main principles of religion that look as it was with Christ's estate. It was sometime, the time wherein He was humbled in this world, all the course of His life was a time of humiliation, and that unto the very death, or else His state of exaltation in heaven. That then when He was most mortified, then was He most glorified, triumphing openly and mightily, showing forth Himself to be the Son of God, even then when in man's sight, He was separated from God, and banished from the Church. So as that all men cried, "Away with Him, crucify Him!" and all Hs own disciples forsook Him, and not a soul acknowledged Him, but one poor thief upon the cross with Him. Yet even then was He so gloriously magnified, as that well might the Apostle say, "He triumphed openly upon the cross, having therein made a spoil of principalities and powers" (Col. 2:15).

Now this very estate is the estate of every child of God, and so far as he has the Son, so far does he express this estate in his whole conversation (for an estate of humiliation), "great and many be the afflictions of the righteous" (Ps. 34:18, 19). There is their debasement in the world, but the Lord delivers them out of all. There is their exaltation mixed together; many ways humbled, and exalted by deliverances, "The Lord will beautify the meek with salvation" (Ps. 149:4, 5); that is, He will beautify them by their manifold deliverances.

Nay, besides deliverances, you shall find this to be the beautiful frame of the spirits of God's people in their estates. Take it in their outward condition in the world, an estate of means and affliction. If he be a man of a fair outward estate, and of good means in the world, yet you shall see a marvelous spirit of self-denial in him, so as that in the midst of many worldly comforts, he sits loose from them, and lives besides them. These are not the things that he has set his heart upon. As our Savior said to His disciples concerning the stones of the Temple, so as that though God had done much for them, and given them many comforts, yet there is a more hidden matter in their hearts. Better than these things can reach unto, they are not a Christian's crown and glory, but "He is crucified to them, and they unto Him" (Gal. 6:14).

And if so be that God give him any great or eminent gifts of spiritual grace, it is strange to see how they are clad in Him with a garment of Christ crucified, over shadowed in self-denial. As they said of Paul, mean in outward view, and speech of little or no value (2 Cor. 13:3), and yet even in this very meanness which any of them labor under in regard of want of outward things. And all their meanness and lowness of carriage, and self-denial of all the outward blessings and contentments they have received, yet you shall see a mighty power of Christ, triumphing in the baseness and mortifiedness of a Christian soul, so as that the Apostle fitly and suitably expresses their estate: "Though He was crucified through weakness, yet He lives by the power of God; for we also are weak in Him, but we shall also live with Him by the power of God." So that as it was with Christ in His estate, so it is with us in our estate, weak in Him; meaning, that as Christ in His outward man seemed to be weak and contemptible, so we (as it is in the original) are weak with Him, but we "shall live with Him by the power of God."

So that suppose Christ be indeed weak in outward view, so as he that looks once would not look twice at Him. Yet when He seems to be most weak and base, then is He most powerful and glorious. And so the very death of Christ, wherein He is most exposed to such infirmities as follow man's nature, yet then He performs the greatest work of our redemption—satisfies the Father's wrath for us, procures us pardon of sin, and redeems us from the bondage of hell, and purchases for us a Spirit of grace and power. And truly there is a certain kind of conformity even in this very point between the Lord Jesus and every servant of Christ. As He is weak, so are we; as He dies, so do we; as He is in His great debasements and advancements, so it is with us. And hence it is that you read these phrases in Scripture: "we are dead with Christ" (Col. 2:20), and "risen with Christ" (Col. 3:l), and "crucified with Christ" (Rom. 6:6).

Now these be strange phrases, that Christ who is dead one thousand six hundred years ago, and risen again so long since; what is this which the Apostle says, we are thus *dead*, and *crucified*, and *risen* with Christ? What is the intendment of his discourse? The true meaning is, that by the same Spirit of Christ, which was shed abroad into His heart above measure, we are so knit unto Christ, as that we are not only of the like nature with Him, but of like estate with Christ. That as He was in this world, so are we while we are in the world, weak as He, yea glorious as He. And as He rose again out of all contempt and reproach and persecution, so do we rise again (out of all our many and great afflictions) mightily by the same power of the same Spirit of the Lord Jesus. So that this is a point that inwardly flows from this having of Christ;

"he that has the Son has the Spirit of the Son," whereby he is made one with Christ in Nature, in Offices, and in His estate. And this is evident in the experience of God's servants, and by testimony of the Holy Ghost in Scripture. And therefore examine we ourselves in this particular, if we have the Son, we have the Spirit of the Son.

THE SECOND DISPENSATION OF THE SON TO US: BY LIBERTY

The second work of the Spirit is that it is not only a spirit of union, but it is also a spirit of liberty. For of all the kinds of temper in a Son, there is nothing more expresses the frame of a Son (next to His likeness and union with the Father) than liberty does: "Where the Spirit of the Lord is, there is liberty" (2 Cor. 3:17). "And if the Son has made you free, then are you free indeed" (John 8:36). It is a real liberty if the Son shall give you liberty, and He speaks of such a liberty as appertains to Sons, and not to servants that may be turned out of doors; but the "Son abides in the house forever." And it is a strange kind of liberty which the children of God are advanced to by the Spirit of the Son. It is a phrase of much importance, a spirit of liberty.

Liberty from the Fear of Sin & Death

First, liberty from the fear of sin, and the fear of hell; from fear of the grave, and of all the enemies of our salvation; a freedom from fear of any of them. A servant, if he offend, is afraid of extremity from his master, but the son walks with more liberty. "We have received the Spirit of adoption whereby we cry, 'Abba Father'" (Rom. 8:15). We look at God as a Father, and we walk before Him not in fear, but in liberty. And therefore we are free from the fear of death, to which, "some are all their life time subject to bondage" (Heb. 2:14, 15).

Now this is a spirit of liberty, to have the heart set free from all fears. It is the sum of all security, He has redeemed us, "that we might serve Him without fear all the days of our lives" (Luke 1:74, 75, 78). We are free from fear of death, and hell, and of the world. And we do not "fear what flesh can do unto us" (Ps. 3:5, 6). His meaning is that the fears of men should not break his sleep, but he would walk in a childlike confidence before God and man. And he would lie him down quietly and sleep securely, "though ten thousand had compassed him round about." And the like you read in Psalm 56:3, "What time I am afraid I will trust in You." And verse 11, "In God will I put my trust, I will not be afraid what man can do unto me." It is a usual phrase with David, and the usual frame of the spirits of God's people, and this kind of holy tranquility of heart, and liberty to walk with evenness and comfort of soul, against all the fears of this and another world. This kind of inward liberty from all fear is the natural property of a Son.

A son never greatly fears ill measures from his father. All his care is to approve himself to his father's will, and then he knows his father's care is more for his own provision and protection than his own can be. And if at any time he fall short of doing his father's will, he makes his peace with his father upon as good terms as he can, and there he rests. But this is his father's will, and you need not possess him of that; and if he be a son, he will look for protection from his father. A child of God knows his heavenly Father will support him, and he fears not what sin, and hell, and the grave, and death can do unto him. He fears not persecution, nor sword, nor famine, the Lord is with him, and he fears none of them; "I am persuaded" (says Paul) "that in all these, we are more than conquerors" (Rom. 8:37, 38). This is the liberty of the spirit of a son.

Liberty from the Power & Dominion of Sin

Now, as there is by the Spirit in the heart of the child of God, liberty from all fear of sins, so he has liberty from all the power and dominion of sin. He is not subject to the dominion and bondage of sin. Sin has not that power over him as to carry him captive to it, but he walks at liberty (Psalm 119). And therefore at liberty, because "he is not under the law, but under grace" (Rom. 6:14). And notable is that speech in Romans 8:2; "the law of the Spirit of life which is in Christ Jesus has freed me from the law of sin and of death: The Spirit of life, *viz.*"—that Spirit of life which has a legal power in it, a power like a law, and has a ruling power over me as the law has. And in both these respects called, a law of God; a kind of spiritual life, because there is a lively spirit in Him. And this law of the spiritual life of grace "has freed me," set me at liberty from the law and trade of sin and of death. Sin and death set him a course and trade, which this law of the Spirit of life has set him free from, so as that he is but a bungler in sin now; not now learned in the law of sin, as sometimes he has been.

But the law of the Spirit of life has freed him from the skill of sin, and from the command of sin. The law of sin has had a sovereign power over him, but now he is freed from the act and trade of sin. And now he walks at liberty even from the dominion and usurpation of sin. Time has been when nothing would withhold him, and he could have followed evil company and unlawful games. They were as lawful to him as to any and he had no power to resist them. But now the law of the Spirit of life has helped him against them all. This is another part of the Spirit of liberty; a liberty from the bondage and dominion of sin, and it is a marvelous comfortable liberty indeed. Many a valorous-spirited man has so little fear of death, that he rushes upon the pikes as the horse into the battle, as if it were their meat and drink; but yet wants this liberty, he is not at liberty from fear of danger by the redemption of the Lord Jesus Christ, but as Aristotle faith, valiant, because ignorant of the danger.

And besides, such a natural man, though he be of a magnanimous spirit in respect of fear of danger, yet such a man is often captivated of many base lusts, and sinful courses, and is not able to resist ill counsel, nor ill company. Whereas a godly man is free from all these—free from the bondage, and dominion of sin, and all the law of sin he looks at it as a cobweb-law, which he may easily break through, and accordingly does so, and overcomes all his former sinful lusts.

Liberty from the Service of Men

Thirdly, there is another frame of this spirit of liberty as it is the Spirit of the Son; it frees us from the service of men (1 Cor. 7:23). Not that it forbids civil subjection: not so to make men free, but if God have called you a servant, live as a servant (1 Cor. 7:12-20), but use your liberty the rather if you can. But if you must needs be a servant, then know, "that he that is a servant is the Lord's free man, but be not you the servants of men," that is, though you owe and do your bodily service to men, yet towards God walk at liberty. And if your labor be great, and your reward little, yet do your service, and look for more wages at the hand of Christ (Col. 3:23), than from men. In serving men, serve Christ; and therefore, go about your Master's service, "not with eye service, but in singleness of heart serving the Lord, and not men." In serving of men, they do faithful and diligent service to the Lord, and therefore they do it willingly and not grudgingly, but in much quietness of spirit, and are more free for Christian duties, and have more quiet time for seeking God than ever after. "He that is married cares for the things of the world" (1 Cor. 7:22). And it is true, he that is most free is but a servant to Christ, but a free servant though. But he that is a servant is "the Lord's freeman." The meaning is, not only to do the work of his own service with a free spirit, but he is not only a free man when he is most bound, but then he goes about the service of God with much more liberty of spirit than when he is his own man.

It is oft times wonder to see servants being called, what care they will have of Christian duties, what time they will steal to call upon God and to examine themselves, and what a grief it is to them to see this and that duty neglected in the family. And they are very free to God. But afterwards, when they come to be free men, and are for themselves, that they may now have as much liberty as they will, pray when they will, and take what time they will, to instruct those that are about them, which time they wanted when they were servants, and which they then mourned under. And yet whereas then they would serve God with much freedom and liberty of spirit, were then free from the law of sin, and free for any duty. There is now a secret kind of bondage come upon them. Their hearts are more embondaged, and ensnared, and encumbered, and entangled. And so duties come not to be performed, either with that constancy and care, or not with that enlargement of heart, as they were when they were servants. And therefore that is the reason why the Apostle bids them, not be over-ready to challenge freedom.

But this shows you that there is a marvelous liberty even in those that are servants. They are free from the service of men in their hearts and consciences; and then most at liberty to serve God, when they are most bound to serve men. Yet in their hearts and consciences they are free from their service. They are not bound in conscience to do anything but what is the will of God. And this is a marvelous great freedom that a man is not bound to become a slave to other men's will, and to do as other men do. He is not bound to do anything that is unlawful, and this is a spirit of liberty that makes even a servant to have a spirit of freedom. He is a free-man, his heart is free to God's service, and this is from nothing else but from this spirit of a son, a spirit of liberty.

The Christian's Duty

Now, on the contrary side, as by this spirit of liberty, a child of God is free from the fear of sin, so he has a certain kind of privilege of peace in his soul, and of freeness and readiness to every Christian duty. And also he has a certain privilege of dominion over all the creatures. It is the nature and proper definition of liberty: freedom from evil and liberty unto the enjoyment of some good things.

It sets me free from sin, and gives me liberty and peace of conscience from the same Spirit of the Lord Jesus. It sets me at liberty to "run the way of God's commandments" (Ps. 119:32). And God's people are a willing people (Ps. 110:3). This is indeed a spirit of liberty. It enlarges me to dominion over men; no creature in heaven or in earth, but a Christian is able to rule him to his own advantage. A Christian servant will turn his Master's government to his advantage, and so all his enemies' tyranny; he will be sure to be better by them all, and he will grow and thrive in his spirit by all the dangers and evils that can befall him in this world.

I know not in what better to instance than in that of Genesis 25:23. The Oracle of God said to Rebecca, "the elder shall serve the younger." And this is a thing in much dispute among Divines, wherein this was ever made good, and say that Esau was never a servant to Jacob. For you shall find in the 32nd and 33rd chapters of Genesis that Jacob uses this word, "My lord Esau," and beseeches his lordship "to go before," and "his servant would follow after;" and so it stood in their outward condition. And Divines say, though the promise be true of the persons both separate from the womb, yet the service was not so. But we need not straighten ourselves for the explication of it, for Esau lording and domineering over Jacob was as serviceable to Jacob's spirit as if he had laid aside his state, and come and served Jacob, and kept his sheep. The bitterness of Esau against him did him more real service than all the service of all Jacob's servants could reach him. Whence was it that Jacob went a pilgrimage from his father's house? And that in a strange country God so prospered him, that whereas he went out but with his staff in his hand, he returned back again with two bands or two droves? And whence was it that Jacob made such a solemn vow to God, and kept it in so much faithfulness, that if God would keep him in that journey, God should be his God forever.

Did not all this come from the rage and wrath of Esau towards him? Esau did him that good service, and when he came back again and heard news, that Esau came out with four hundred men against him, and thought to come to spoil them all. What a marvelous service was this to Jacob, as you may read in chapter 32, from verse 9 to the end. Esau, by this means set him on wrestling with God by prayer, and therefore wrestles with God all that night, and so wrestles, that God changes his name upon it. "You shall not be called Jacob, a wrestler, but Israel a prevailer; though have prevailed with God, and you shall prevail with men." And now he is past the worst with his brother. And when he meets him, expresses much natural affection, and is marvelous glad to see him, and offers to help him to drive his flocks, to show you that the very emulation, and envy, and cruelty, and ragings of the enemies of God's servants; even when they are most incensed against them, and most tread them down, and insult over them, then they do them the greatest service that is possible to be done through the mighty power of the Spirit of the Lord Jesus Christ that turns all into contraries; that even when men do most domineer over them, then they do them the best service.

Look as it was with the tyrants of Syria and Egypt that made waste of God's people. It is a notable speech that in Daniel 11:35-36, it is "to purge them, and to cleanse them, and make them white." A scullion in the kitchen, when he scours his pewter, when he first takes it in hand, you would think he would quite spoil it. But he but scours and clears it up, and makes it more bright than it was before. The end of all is, but to take away the filth, and to make it clear and bright. And so a housewife that takes her linen, she soaps it, and bedaubs it, and it may be defiles it with dung, so as it neither looks nor smells well. And when she has done, she rubs it, and bucks it, and wrings it, and in the end all this is but to make it clean and white. And truly so it is here, when as tyrants most of all insult over God's people, and scour them and lay them in lee, or dung, so as the very name of them stinks, yet what is this but to purge them, and to make them white, and it is a great service they do to the people of God in so doing. And this is a great measure of liberty that a child of God can tell how to make an advantage of all the afflictions he meets with in this world. These things do but serve his turn, and afterward he will say, he could have missed none of them; so that this is a second work of the Spirit of the Son, it is a spirit of liberty.

CONCLUSION

Only take this word for a conclusion, and that is thus much: examine now, and try whether you have the Son or not, which you may know by your having or not having the Spirit of the Son. Say then, have you the Spirit of the Son? Have you that Spirit of the Lord Jesus Christ that makes you to be of one and the same nature with Him, of the same Offices, and same Estate with Him? Can you find this in truth, and that with comfort and honesty you may reason? This is the frame of my Spirit, such is the Spirit of Christ. And such is the spirit of the godly, and if in anything you fail, your spirit is against it. Do you find that you are in some measure invested with a royal spirit that you can overcome yourselves and the temptations of this world? And are you able to offer up spiritual sacrifice to God of prayer and praises? And do you find a spirit of prophecy shed abroad into you that makes you sensible of and privy to the secret paths of God? Do you find that Christ was most glorious when He was most humbled, and so are you? And when you enjoy outward blessings, your hearts are not puffed up with them.

These are not the goodly stones that your hearts and eyes are set upon, but you have greater matters than these to mind; then I say, it is the very Spirit of Christ that makes you to die with Christ, as well as Christ to die for you. He may die for many men, but He only dies with those that are brought on to the fellowship of His grace. If a Spirit of Christ so knit you together, that He is yours, and you are His, then you have the Son, because you have the Spirit of the Son, because you are sons. God has sent forth the Spirit of His Son into your hearts, but now if there be no proportion, no conformity to Christ in holiness and righteousness, not patient and meek as He is.

And though we be not such, yet we allow ourselves in not being such, and are ever and anon starting aside from Him. And if we have not His Offices, nor rule over our lusts, nor over the world; and we can neither pray nor prophesy, and show forth no spiritual life in our lives, cannot deny ourselves that we may show forth the hidden man of the heart, then consider that for the present we have not yet Christ, because we have not the Spirit of Christ. And also, if we be not yet free from the fear of death, and take no care to be free from the dominion, and power of sin, but sin has still a power over us like a law, and are not yet free from the service of men, but as our masters and governors say, so it must be. If we yet know not how to rule men for our own advantage, we have not yet received the Spirit of Christ. We cannot tell how to serve our masters with liberty of spirit, we know not how to make advantage of them.

~ Sermon 6 ~
HAVING THE SON AS LORD & PRINCE

He that has the Son has life, and he that has not the Son has not life.
(1 John 5:12)

It now remains that we come to show what it is to have the Son by a spirit of prayer, but of this we shall have further occasion to speak in verses 14, 15, and 16, and therefore we shall leave it now, and speak to it then.

You may remember we said there were three notes to discern whether we had the Son or not. The first was: If we desired not Christ for His benefits, but chiefly for Himself. The second was: If we have received the spirit of the Son. We come now to speak of a third sign, a point more easy to be gathered than the former, but though most common, yet not to be neglected; but being well applied, will be of special use to the edification, and salvation of the hearers, for every truth in his place is divine and precious.

And therefore the next note is this: He that has the Son, he has Him not only for a Savior, but for his Lord and Prince. A point which upon sundry occasions has been touched, but now to speak of it more fully.

There is no man that has the Son, but as he has Him for his Savior so he has Him for his Prince. "Him has God exalted with His right hand, whom they slew, a Prince and a Savior" (Acts 5:31). So that he that has Christ has Him not only as a Savior, but as a Prince. To whomsoever He is a Savior, to them He is also become a Prince. It were a wonderful dishonor to Him to save them whom He does not rule; to save them from the power of the grave, and to leave them still in their sins, and unbroken off from their evil ways, it were much dishonor to Him. It is a dishonor to parents to have children, and to have them untaught and unmannerly. And God has given the life blood of His own Son to purchase us unto Himself, and therefore He would not only save us, but rule us, or else we shall never have Him for our Savior. So that here is two points to be opened.

First, he that has the Son has Him for his Savior.

Secondly, he that has the Son has Him also for his Lord.

HAVING CHRIST AS SAVIOR

It is an usual saying, every man would have Christ for a Savior, but rare are those that will have Him for their Ruler and Governor. But though the saying be true in respect of the common conceit of men, yet in truth I say, they are but rare Christians that will have Him for a Savior, so far off are they from desiring Him as their Lord.

For two things there be that go to the having of Christ for a Savior.

Looking to Christ Alone for Salvation from Sins

First, He that will have Christ for a Savior must look up to Him for salvation in all his ways, and distresses that we have other saviors, but not Him, if we look for salvation elsewhere. "Look unto Me all the ends of the earth, and be saved, there is no God nor Savior besides Me, and therefore look to Me, and be saved" (Isa. 45:22). So that if a man will have God for his Savior, he must look to Him from one end of the earth to the other. We are at the utmost corner of the earth, and if we will be saved, we must look up to the Lord Jesus Christ for salvation. As David looked towards the Temple at Jerusalem for salvation, so they who look towards the Lord Jesus for salvation, may be saved in what place soever they are. Wait for salvation from Him, and long for salvation by Him. And look not to any means, but so far as they are guided and ordered by Him, and in whatsoever distresses you are, whether in conscience or in distress, through bodily sickness, or penury, or imprisonment, yet "look to Me, and be saved."

You may read the like in Isaiah 8:17: "I will wait upon the Lord that hides His face from the house of Israel, and will look for Him." The prophet at that time saw the Church and Commonwealth of Israel much distempered, and in much distress, both in regard of sin and misery. Now for him to look for, or expect such princes as might reform it in the Commonwealth; or such priests as might reform things amiss in the Church, it had been a vain thing. For they were all bent to backsliding till the wrath of God burnt out, and took hold upon them. But though there was no hope in any of the princes, nor priests, yet "I will wait upon the Lord that hides His face from the house of Jacob, and will look for Him." Though God suffer all things to go to wrack and ruin, yet I will wait for Him, and look for salvation from Him, and by Him.

So that, suppose God should hide His face from any soul of us, that we lie in darkness and in the shadow of death, or if that we should see ourselves in distress of the outward man, or see Church or Commonwealth in many sinful distempers. It is not now for a man to look about him, hither and thither for help and succor, but to the Holy One of Israel. And this is indeed to have Him for a Savior. He that has Him for a Savior waits for Him in all distress.

So in Isaiah 17:6-7, the time will come when God will gather His people unto Him, "as the gleanings of berries, when they shall be left like the shaking of an olive tree, two or three berries in the top of the uppermost bough; four or five in the outmost fruitful branches says the Lord. Now, at that time shall a man look to his Maker, and his eyes shall have respect to the Holy One of Israel." Which shows you that those who are God's gleaned ones from the world, that are brought on to fellowship with Christ in the election and salvation; these are they who look to their Maker, and their eyes are unto Him, the Holy One of Israel.

And so God is said to be, not because He is so in Himself, but because He makes Israel His holy one, and therefore his eyes has respect unto Him. You know in the cast of an eye, we show respect. When the creature looks after this and that in the world, and fastens and sets his eye upon anything there, he has no respect to the Holy One of Israel, but to the creature only. But when the creature being conscious of his own insufficiency to help itself, by any means itself can use, but has respect to the Holy God that makes Israel holy, and is acknowledged of Israel to be holy. This is indeed to have God for our Savior, and so He is to all such as are gathered together unto Him.

This is livelily expressed in the example of good Jehoshaphat in 2 Chronicles 20:3. He sought the Lord, and in the audience of the people he made a solemn prayer to God, and concludes with this in the latter end of the twelfth verse: "We know not what to say or to do, but our eyes are unto You." Now, this having our eyes upon Him in time of distress. Whether of war, or pestilence, or famine, or anguish of conscience, or poverty, and yet we have our eyes towards the Holy One of Israel. We know not what to do, and our power will not reach us any help without God's blessing. No, not in outward things, but our eyes are unto Him. This argues that surely Jehoshaphat had the Lord for his Savior because he had such respect unto Him.

Notable is that expression, "I will lift up my eyes unto the hills from whence comes my help; it comes even from the Lord" (Ps. 121:1). The Lord dwelt upon Mount Zion and Mount Moriah. There He manifested Himself in His Ordinances, and therefore He put not His confidence in the valleys and pits of the city. But in Him that dwells in the hills, and looks for salvation from thence. As He expounds Himself in the next words: "My help comes even from the Lord." So then, if so be that we do indeed look up unto the Lord for salvation, and for help and preservation, and deliverance, and restoring of any comfort we have been deprived of; sometimes justly, and sometimes unjustly; whatsoever our condition be, if in all our distresses we can look up unto Him, and our hearts wait for salvation wholly from Him. This argues that we have Him for our Savior because we have such respect unto Him, and elsewhere we look not, though we may use lawful means, yet our eyes are not upon the means, but we look a great deal further, and no further expect deliverance from any means than we see the Holy One of Israel, the God of our salvation, expressing and revealing Himself in the means.

And to add this one instance more of Jonah chapter 2: One that went away from God, and was unwilling to be directed by God, and therefore he was overwhelmed in the sea, because he would not be ruled, and bowed to the will of the Lord Jesus. And therefore God sent forth the most unruly creature that God has made, set aside the devils in hell. And it may be they have a hand in it too, in raising the horrible tempest that raged against them. And when Jonah was cast out, the most unruly creature—a whale—meets with this unruly prophet of God, and swallowed him up, that he thought himself in the belly of hell. Now when God had in some measure broken his heart, and in the whale's belly begins to consider how unruly he had dealt with God, and said in chapter 2, verse 4, "I am cast out of Your sight, yet will I look again towards Your holy temple"—implying, that though he had been most unruly, and of a good man, the most of all you read of; yet when he saw God for his unruliness meet him with such afflictions, yet when he said, he was "cast out of his sight," yet, "I will look again towards Your holy temple." How could he tell which way the Temple stood when he was in the whale's belly? Yet his heart was towards the Temple, which was a type of Christ. He in his heart had respect to the place where the Temple stood, and therein he showed his respect to Christ. And so having respect unto Him, he had Him as his Savior, most unruly Jonah. Yet he having respect to Christ as his

Savior, he is delivered and saved. So that you see, he that has Christ as a Son, he has Him as a Savior; and those that have Him for a Savior, they wait on Him, and only look for salvation from Him.

Looking to Christ for Salvation from Distress

There is a second duty for every man to perform that has Christ for his Savior, and that is, he does not only look for salvation from Him when he stands in need of it, as we daily do; for salvation is deliverance out of danger, and preservation in a good estate, and he looks for all salvation from Him (Psalm 3). Salvation belongs to God, and though many means may be used, yet it is the Lord and His mercy and blessing that saves and delivers, and nothing else, and God's servants they know it.

But there is a second duty in having Christ for a Savior; and that is, in looking up to Christ, and cleaving to Him, and not only desiring salvation from Him, from all our distresses, but salvation also from all our sins. And he that has Christ for a Savior, he would be saved from all his sins, as well as from all his miseries. "God has appointed Him a Prince and a Savior, to give repentance to Israel, and forgiveness of sins" (Acts 5:31). There is therefore this salvation to be had in Christ, not only deliverance out of the hands of dangers, but from the hands of all our sins and rebellions, and to be saved from them by turning from them and repenting of them. And we desire not only forgiveness of them, but salvation from them, to be saved from our stubborn spirits, and saved out of our covetousness, and wantonness, and worldliness, and carnal vanity of heart and life that we are subject to; to be saved from the vain fashions, and in all these we look for salvation from Christ. We desire to be saved not only from all our distresses, but especially from the sinful distempers of our souls.

It is notable in Psalm 130:3-8, "If You, O Lord, should mark iniquity, who should stand? But there is forgiveness with You that You may be feared. I wait for the Lord, my soul does wait, and in His Word do I hope; My soul waits for the Lord, more than they that watch for the morning. Let Israel wait for the Lord, for with Him is mercy and plenteous redemption, and He shall redeem Israel from all his iniquities." And He is therefore called Jesus in Matthew 1:21. And notable is that expression in Hosea 14:2, "Take away all our iniquities, and receive us graciously, so will we give You thanks." Thus they desire salvation from all their iniquities, and not so much salvation in the pardon of all their iniquities, for there is more in it than forgiveness of sin, but a turning them from them. They desire both *pardoning* and *healing*, and God so understood them, as appears by verse 4. God answers them, that He would pardon them, and heal them. He will remove them all away from them, not a hoof be left behind, but all taken away. There is a generation of men that are marvelous unwilling to yield to this, so that you see it is an ordinary thing for men to say they have Christ for a Savior, but it is a rare thing to be so indeed.

You know how affectionate our Savior's speech is in Matthew 23:37, "O Jerusalem, Jerusalem, how often would I have gathered you under my wing of salvation, but you would not be gathered?" The body of the Church of God, though some was gathered, yet others of them would not be gathered. And if it was thus with Jerusalem, it is no wonder if you read the like of Babylon—"We would have healed Babel, but she would not be healed" (Jer. 51:9). God sent His Church, and kept it there seventy years among them, that some of them at least might embrace the salvation of God, but she would not be healed. We have used the best means we could to heal her, but it will not be, she will not be healed of us, and therefore let us be going home again. God would not send His Church among them for nothing, but He looks for some fruits among them. But since either none were gathered, or so few, as that they were not a considerable number, therefore God will send His people home again, when they say, "Let us break their bonds asunder, and cast their cords from us; then God will take no further pains" (Ps. 2:3).

It is a notable place that in Jeremiah 2:25, God calls upon His people most affectionately that they would be healed, but they snuff up their iniquities as the wind, and like unto wild ass colts would be at liberty, and take plea-sure in their running at random. And God said, "With-hold your foot from being unshod, and your throat from thirsting after such vanities, but you say desperately, 'There is no hope, I have loved strangers, and after them will I go.'" What a marvelous speech is this in God's own servants, when God would withhold them from running for salvation elsewhere, and from such other sins as they thirsted after. No, there is no hope but the course they had taken they would take, and no means should save or draw them from their haunts. So that you see it is no easy matter for a man to be willing to be saved by Christ, and though many would be saved by Him, yet few there be that would look for all salvation from Christ, and are not willing to be saved from all their sins, but are willing to keep some sins still alive in their souls.

Are they not ready in their hearts to say as they said in Matthew 8:29, "Have You come to torment us before the time?" It was when Christ came to save two men from the possession of a Legion of devils, the men spoke it, though the devils acted it in them. So when Christ comes to bring salvation, it is a torment to our souls. The two witnesses vexed men, and they came but to save men.

It is a torment to men to have sin pulled out of their souls, as you read in Acts 16:19, when the apostles had cast out of the maid the spirit of divination. When their masters saw that the hope of their gain was gone, they were in a rage, and caused them to be stoned and left them for dead. Now when men take it ill that they should be saved, or are loath that their children, or servants should be saved, take it ill that they dare no more lie and swear and couzen, and buy and sell on the Sabbath day. And such and such a gain is thereby lost, and this they cannot endure. It is a dangerous sign of an ill heart, and therefore however it is a usual saying, that every man will have Christ for a Savior; and yet if in truth we consider it, I assure you in plain English, we will not be saved. That is our resolution when it comes to the point.

HAVING CHRIST AS PRINCE (LORD)

It is a use of trial that we are upon in this discourse, and therefore to proceed to the next part of the point; those that have Christ for a Savior, they have Him also for a Prince. "God has appointed Him for a Prince and a Savior" (Acts 5:31). If you will have Him for a Savior, you must have Him for a Prince. Resign up yourselves, you and yours, to be guided and governed by the Lord Jesus, though you have never so many strong oppositions, yet it must be so. "Unto us a Child is given, unto us a Son is born" (Isa. 9:6). How shall I know that Christ is born for me, and this Son is given to me? Why by this: "The government shall be upon His shoulders"—If the Son be given you, then you are wholly governed by Him. And if you are so, then He is born and given to you, and you shall call His name "*Wonderful*."

If you can behold a wonderful glorious majesty in Christ, and he to whom He is given, they shall acknowledge Him their Counselor, the Prince of their peace. And to whomsoever He is given, the government of Him is upon their shoulders; know therefore whether He be your Governor or not. And two things there be in having Christ for our Prince, to open them plainly to you.

Resign Yourself to Be Ruled By Him in All Your Ways

First, when you resign up yourselves to be wholly ruled by Him in all your paths, so as that you lean not to yourselves not so much as in one thought, but all your thoughts stand in subjection to His will. "The weapons of our warfare are not carnal, but mighty through God to cast down every high imagination, and to bring into captivity every thought to the obedience of Christ" (2 Cor. 10:4-5). God leaves us not one thought free, nor are we willing to have our thoughts free. "The thoughts of the righteous are right" (Prov. 12:5); that is, they come from a right rule, the Word of God, and aim at a right end, the glory of God; not a man that has his part in the Lord Jesus, but his thoughts are right.

Objection: *You say, "But who has his thoughts so rectified and set upon the Lord Jesus; but he has many vain, and covetous, and proud, and stubborn thoughts? Who can say, I have kept my* *heart clean? Who can say that every thought in him is subdued to the obedience of Christ?"*

Answer: It is true that you object, for in Jeremiah 4:14, it is a complaint and an earnest speech: "O Jerusalem, wash your heart from your wickedness that you may be saved, how long shall your vain thoughts lodge within you?" So that you see a man that would have salvation by Christ, he must be content to subject all his thoughts to Christ, and not leave one vain thought to lodge within him. It is true, Satan may cause them to flutter in his mind, but he must give them no entertainment. It is one thing to have a sturdy beggar that comes to the door to rush into my house before I be aware and enforce; and another thing to bid him welcome, and to bid him stay and lodge there all night, and to make provision for him. So it may be there is many a proud rebellious thought rushes in, and calls for this and that, and will be served in this and that, and every faculty, and part, and member must bestire itself to satisfy such a thought, and all must be as this thought will, and sometimes scars all the house, puts the whole man to agitation to consider what to do, to give it content. Yet they who have Christ for their Savior, they will look to Him for salvation from such sturdy thoughts as these be. They will not suffer them to lodge there, but get them out again, and are not at quiet, but the whole man is disturbed till they be dislodged, and cast out again. So they who have the Lord

Jesus for their Savior, they must not give lodging to a vain thought, much less to a malicious, and proud, and desolate thought, or any other wicked thought whatsoever. It is true indeed, there is no Christian man but he will have vain thoughts come in upon him, but you shall observe this difference.

Christians Differenced by Their Thoughts

First, a man that has not Christ for his Prince, he has not one good thought comes in his mind, or if it do, he does not give it lodging there. All, or every imagination of his heart is evil, and that continually; the original is (*omne figmentum*) the whole frame of a man's heart; the bent and scope of his thoughts, the whole suggestion of them first and last, not a good thought comes in him. Many a man will say, "It is very fitting and meet it should be so, that one day we should turn home to God, but not to give entertainment to him at this time, but let him come another time, and them he shall have lodging." And so we deal with all good thoughts that God suggests into our hearts. We like good thoughts well, and sometimes we are loath to give them offense, but yet are not willing to give them entertainment, but are more willing to be shut of them, and to turn them out of doors. But a godly man, if a good motion come into him, it is most welcome to his soul, and he entertains it with the gladness of his spirit. He sees it is of God his heavenly Father, and he lodges it in his heart, and conscience, and affection, and rejoices in it, and desires after it, and cherishes it, and is loath to part with such thoughts when he is gotten into such a good frame.

Now I say therefore, this is a difference: a carnal man never gives entertainment to a good thought, nor do his thoughts ever aim at good ends. They never go higher than himself, and therefore never could good thought find lodging in him. Out again it is thrust, sometimes somewhat courteously, sometimes discourteously, but however there it must not lodge. There is a world of matter to quench and damp it, and to use means to be shut of it. But it is not so with a true Christian. He entertains Christ as his Prince, and he will have every thought in him to be set upon Him. If a wicked thought come into a carnal man's heart, it is natural to him. It takes place, and is suffered to lodge there, anger rests with him all night, and "he suffers the sun to go down upon his wrath" (Eph. 4:26, 27). The devil lodges there, and there he may rest, and he never takes pains to be cleansed of those evil thoughts, and he cares not how long they are there.

But if a godly man have a wicked thought come upon him, he stirs up all the faculties of his soul, and the graces of the Spirit against it, and does what he can to expel and banish it. And if he cannot prevail, then he will call for aid from his Prince from heaven, and will acquaint his dear Christian friends with it, and say, "I am troubled with such thoughts of malice, and pride, and vanity, that I know not in the world what to do, they lie down with me, and they rise up with me," and therefore entreat their help. And as they look to Christian friends, so will they especially call to the Prince of their salvation to save them from their vain thoughts, and much more from these wicked speeches, from these things they are most careful to be delivered. And therefore they stand not devising plots against their Prince, but He will tell him that such wicked rebellious thoughts devise mischief against Him, and therefore he craves help against them.

So did David in the like case, "Search me, and know my heart, and see if there be any way of wickedness in me" (Ps. 139:23). As if he had sent to heaven for a privy search, he would not have any one thought within him, but he would that God should know it, and therefore desires that God would try and search and know his thoughts. He was not like them of whom you read in Isaiah 29:15, "that dig deep to hide their counsels from the Lord." But a child of God would have God to be well acquainted with his thoughts: "see if there be any way of wickedness in me," any wicked thought or vain affection in my heart, I have labored to find, and to cast them out what I can, but there may be many more that I know not, "but search and try me, and lead me in the way that I shall go."

Good thoughts are of everlasting use, and of everlasting durance, and they will continue to everlasting life.

God's ways are everlasting ways—"lead me in the way everlasting." Thus a man has every thought brought into subjection, though evil thoughts may come rushing in. Yet he will not give them entertainment but complains of them to Christ, and such a man has the Lord Jesus for his Prince. For He is not a Prince that only governs the outward man as earthly princes do, who can take no hold of what we think, but God takes notice of our thoughts. And you may apply what I say of thoughts to words and actions, and so make use of it to all.

There be many men that never think good thought, but let wicked thoughts rest in them, can be wanton and unclean, *etc.* Whatever it be that makes a thoroughfare in the heart, let it there lodge, let it come and go as it will, and that is part of the meaning of the highwayside ground. It keeps, and is a thoroughfare to all beasts to all sorts of travailers, to thieves and robbers, takes no notice of them, lets them come and go and stay as they list. Then we have not Christ as our Governor. We do not put the government of our thoughts and actions upon His shoulders, and are not in subjection to Him, "but casts His cords from us" (Ps. 2:3). And say, "we will not have this man to reign over us" (Luke 19:14). What, are not our thoughts free? And are not our tongues our own (Ps. 12:4)?

David takes them for atheists that say, "their tongues are their own." He prays that God would "keep his lips" (Psalm 119). Only God's people would have all that is in them bowed to the obedience of God's will. Some men there be that will not have God to rule over them, so marvelous is the profaneness of our hearts while we are carnal that we that should be servants to God. We are not ashamed to make Him a servant to us. We were never subject to any man, nor do we mean so to be Pharaoh-like. Who is the Lord? I know not who he is.

Notable is that you read in Isaiah 43:24, besides that, I had no service from you, "you have made me to serve, with, or under your sins." See the desperate spirits of the hearts of the sinful sons of men. They draw in God to serve them, and He complains that He is pressed under their sins "as a cart is pressed under sheaves"—men load the patience of God, and lay upon Him one bundle of wickedness after another. They lay so much wickedness upon Him till the patience of God will bear no longer, as long as ever He will bear, and suffer us to live in this world. We will load Him with sheaves upon sheaves, load the very majesty of God, and His long sufferance, and make use of His providence many times to serve our own lusts. We will do that which is wicked in God's sight because we can do it, and because God has given us means to do it. We can maintain our pride and covetousness, and God gives us these gifts, and these liberties, and we will make God to serve with them, and here is a double service put upon God.

We load His patience and forbearance by our continuance in sin. But besides that, we abuse the very gifts of

God, as our wealth, and good parts of nature, and our common graces. And (by your leave) the very saving graces of God's Spirit, we will not stick to abuse them against God. And is not this much rebellion that we should make God to serve such a wearisome service. He is provoked every day, and weary to suffer us in a sinful course one day to an end. But when day after day, and year after year we lay load upon God's patience; and if He will suffer us long so He may; and if we do set God at liberty from His drudgery, it must be at the last gasp, and He shall be our Ruler then, if He will. Wonder not therefore if sometime God say, "Rebellion is as the sin of witchcraft" (1 Sam. 15:23). And that is in a double respect.

First, as you see a witch gives her soul to the devil that she may have her mind fulfilled for her lifetime, so a rebel deals with the devil to have his own lusts fulfilled. He makes a covenant with hell and with the devil. He is at an agreement. He knows he does wickedly, but to serve his own turn, he is content to do it.

But secondly, as a witch will have the devil to wait upon her, so at last she will wait upon the devil. So it is in this case: The devil must serve a witch all her lifetime, and she will serve the devil at her death. Far more monstrous is this wickedness in this kind. We will have God to serve us all our lifetime, and when death comes, we will do God this favor: we will serve Him then. As a witch deals with the devil, so do we with God. He shall supply our occasions, and we will make use of His bounty to serve ourselves. But at last gasp God shall rule us, to do Him all the service we can, and give Him all good words. There is great and plenteous mercy to be found in Him, and now we will do Him all the honor we can. And will God be thus served, do you think? Do you think to put Him off, as witches put off the devil? Will He (think you) take your service then? Consider of it: This is to make God our Prince, when we give up ourselves to serve Him.

Do All Your Service unto Him

There is a second thing, wherein the having of Christ for a Prince does stand. And it requires that you do all your service to Him as to a Prince. It should all be Princely service, such as becomes a Prince. "When you bring that which is torn or lame, offer it to your prince, and see if he will accept it" (Mal. 1:8). Implying that God is a Prince, and if a Prince, then where is His princely service? If you will serve Him, serve Him of the best of that you have. God looks for no more but what you have; but when you come and offer Him a lame and peremptory sacrifice, and be loath to come off with the fat and strength of your affections, and are loath to crucify your dearest lusts. Then you deal not with God as with a Prince, you offer Him such a sacrifice as is loathsome to Him. God curses such deceivers who have in their flock a male, and sacrifice unto the Lord a corrupt thing. "For I am a great King," says the Lord of Hosts. To pretend Him to be a Prince, and yet to serve Him like a peasant, this God curses. God accepts Abel's sacrifice because he brought the fattest and best of the flock to sacrifice (Gen. 4). When we bring the strength of our hearts, the fat of our strength, this God accepts, and then we offer to Him as to a Prince.

Notable was that speech of David in 2 Samuel 24:24, "I will not offer to God a sacrifice of that which will cost me nothing." A man offered royally to the King; "I give them all freely to you; as a king, he gave to the King." If a man give to a king, he must give of the best he has, "behold all are yours." And as if David should say, "If you will be so bountiful to me, shall not I much more that am a king, give like a king, to the King of kings?"—We must give our best strength, the best we have of anything to God. "I and my household will serve the Lord" (Josh. 24:15). All is little enough so give to God. Make it a point of our service in our best duties, this God looks for, we should do it the best we can. If we would have Him for a Prince, and as to a Prince, we should freely part with all.

CONCLUSION: IS CHRIST YOUR LORD AND SAVIOR?

And therefore to conclude this point, know that this point is the principal sum of the gospel, and this duty is of great necessity. And let us therefore sum it up together, and lay it to our own hearts. You would know whether you have life or not; if you have life, you have

Christ. How will you know that? Ask then your hearts this question: Has God exalted Christ to be a Prince and a Savior to you? Consider, if you have Christ for a Savior and a Prince, and if you so have Him, then you have the Son. And if you have the Son, you have life.

And therefore meditate upon this seriously. Do you find your hearts looking to Christ for salvation in whatsoever distresses you are in? Some will say, "I am in distress, and anguish of soul, comfortless in my spirit and troubled with fear of God's wrath, and sense of the torment of hell." Another man says, "I am in distress through bodily weakness and sickness." Another says, "I am in distress through great poverty." Another in debts; another is in distress through the great untowardness of wife, and children, and servants. These be deep and great distresses. Yet consider: Christ is a Savior from all distresses. God has not limited His salvation to this and that, but it reaches all the evils we are subject to. Then whether does your heart look, and upon whom do you wait for salvation? If your heart tells you that in the midst of all these desertions you look for salvation from the Lord Jesus, and your eyes are unto Him, and you do find your spirit willing to wait for salvation from Him—then you have Him for your Savior. And He will save and redeem you from them all, and it is an evident argument we have Him for a Savior.

But if in our dangers and distresses we look to this and that means, and to this and that friend, and sometimes put ourselves to flight from pestilence and famine (though in some cases we lawfully may). If you only consider lawful means, and use them according to God's will, and for God's honor, then you wait upon God for salvation. Else not, if you look to Him which "hides His face from the house of Israel." If God hide His face from Church and Commonwealth, and yet "our eyes are towards Him," and we know not what to do for our consciences, and liberty, and estates, and health, and peace, *etc.* But our eyes are unto Christ, such a look at Christ is a saving and healing look. And as they were saved and healed by looking at the brazen serpent (Num. 21:9), so truly the Son of Man is exalted that whosoever looks for salvation from Him should receive it, though they be not yet come to the full persuasion that the Lord is their God, as they shall in time come to. But if they look with a wist sad look at Him, and rest not satisfied till salvation come, this makes Him their Savior; "Look unto Me, and be saved." But if we look to friends, and means, and our own hands, and doings, then no hope of salvation from Him.

There is this difference between the cony and the hare. The cony is a thing not strong, yet reckoned among the wise people. When they hear the noise of a dog, they run to their rock and shroud themselves, and so are safe. Whereas the wild hare has no help but her heels. She runs through fields and pastures, runs every way, but has no protection, but her heels, and is of all creatures most destitute. So if we run to the Lord Jesus for deliverance from all our evils. He will spread a wing of preservation over us. But if we run to any creature we can have no rest, nor peace, and then it argues we have no Christ, because no Savior; and no Savior, because we look not to Him. And if you look to Him to save you from your miseries, and not from your sins, you have Him not as a Savior. You would be excused in this and that, spare me but here only; Felix would be spared in his Delilah, but if you would be spared in any sin excused for, nor parting with any iniquity, then you have not Christ for your Savior.

Remember what our Savior said to the man in John 5:6, "Would you be made whole?" He said, "Yes Lord," and he was healed. So this is the point, will you be made whole? If God so far turn the stream of our hearts, that unfeignedly we would be made whole, not a member in our bodies but we would have it healed. We would not have an unclean lust in our souls, but we would be perfectly made whole. Would we be saved from all our sins? Then we have Him for our Savior. And there is not a sin in us but we shall be healed of it, and this is life, to look to Christ for universal salvation.

And so consider, have you Christ for a Prince? Are your hearts willing to subject every thought unto Him? You say you are somewhat unwilling to it. But does not the Apostle say: "Every thought must be brought into subjection to the gospel of Christ, into captivity"? And were it not better to be free and voluntary? It is true, God's people know that when they were first brought on to God, they were carried captive and drawn (John 6:44), but afterwards they find the service of Christ to be perfect freedom. And therefore how do look you at your thoughts? For I principally take notice of them.

Are you not willing that a vain thought should lodge within you—thoughts of pride, and of revenge come into your heart, but what entertainment do you give them? Does Satan, when he comes, find your house fit for his purpose? If you give these guests such entertainment, then you have not Christ for your Prince. But if they come like stubborn rebels into you house, and they disturb you, and you call to your friends to help you, and you cry out to your Prince in heaven for a privy search to be made to find them out, and would not have any one wicked thought to rest in your heart, then you have Christ for your Prince.

But if you give them willing entertainment, and lodge them next your heart, and fatted and fed yourself in such thoughts of wrath and lust, and hug them in your bosom, then your heart stands in rebellion against God. If these rebellious lusts be your friendly companions, then God is not at peace with you. But if you are burdened with them, as soldiers come into the houses of men that live in the Palatinate, and they are forced to entertain them. But if you would cast them out, then you have Christ for your Prince.

But if you refuse His government, and your thoughts are your own, and you will have God to serve your turn, and you burden His patience with one wicked course after another, and you make use of God's patience to the sinful provocation of His wrath; and you deal with God as witches do with the devil, He shall serve you now, and you will serve Him when you die.

Consider what sacrifice you offer to God. Anything is good enough for God, and the ways of His grace are a burden to you, then you have Him not for your Prince. Now in the name and fear of God, consider what has been said. Everyone take his portion, and the Lord give you a good understanding in all things.

PART III

THE SIGNS OF LIFE

Discerning the Life by its Causes & its Effects

He that has the Son has life, and he that has not the Son has not life.
(1 John 5:12)

We now come to a third head of signs by which it may appear whether we have Christ or not. And that is from the third word in the text (which is "Life"), for it is an argument of like strength and value to argue the one from the other. "He that has the Son has life, and he that has life, he has the Son." And therefore now at this time to open to you some signs, or marks by which it may appear to us whether we have life, or not; that spiritual life here spoken of: to wit, the life of righteousness in our justification, and of sanctification, of comfort and consolation, and of eternal glory.

And the signs of life are of three sorts; either you may discern the life of God's grace by the *causes* of it, or by the *effects* of it; or by the *qualities and properties* of it, as we call them.

DISCERNING THE LIFE BY ITS CAUSES

First, for the causes. The Holy Ghost usually sets forth the causes of our spiritual life, and if we find these causes to have been the work of that life which we conceive our souls to be endued with, we may from thence argue the truth of our spiritual life, and from thence the truth of our fellowship with Christ.

CAUSE 1: THE WILL OF GOD

The first cause of our spiritual life is the holy and gracious will of God. "Of His own will He begat us" (Jas. 1:18). It is that therefore to this life by which we are begotten, for all generation is unto life. It is of His own will that we are begotten to this life.

And the Apostle John sets it forth by the removal and denial of all other causes. "We are born not of flesh nor of blood, nor of the will of man, but of God" (John 1:13). Not of godly parents; for men may have godly parents, and yet themselves degenerate, and therefore it is not to be ascribed to parentage. It is not from the parentage but from the covenant, and from God's will in the covenant, that begets a child of God. Nor is it of the will of the flesh; that is, of corrupt nature. Nor of the will of man, nor of the best pains that they can take, though they take much pains for us. Yet all may be in vain, so as that unless God set in with Christian friends, and with the blood and covenant of our ancestors, we shall not be brought on to live a spiritual life in God's sight.

It is that which God Himself speaks of in Ezekiel 16:6, "When we were yet in our blood, yet God said to us live." When we were in our blood like an infant, gasping for natural life and ready to perish, even then when none could help us, then God said to us, "Live!" and then we lived in His sight. And therefore, in a word, you may take this for an evident sign of the true life of grace. Wherever you find the work of grace wrought in any soul, you shall find the heart speaking of it as the work of God's own hand.

Take you a man in the estate of nature, and he will say, "God be thanked he had always a good mind," and his parents would never say no less of him. But he was always a toward and hopeful child he thanks God. And thus a man will speak that is only well nurtured, he will say it is a work that was ever in him, and he ever thought so of himself. But now take another man that is indeed born to a new life, and has this life in him that springs from Christ, he will tell you as Paul was wont to say, "When it pleased God to separate me from my mother's womb, and called me by His grace" (Gal. 1:15, 16). There you shall as in a pattern discern what the manner of the expression of a living soul is. He does not say it was wrought when he had a good mind to hear such a man, or to take such a course, so it may be will flesh and blood say. But when you come to a heart that indeed lives in God sight, he expresses himself thus. But when it pleased God it was done.

I, for my part, ran clean another way. I never had a desire after God. I had indeed a kind of form and show, and could comply myself to my governors and neighbors, that I might be flattered and encouraged by them, and I should never have taken better course of myself. But when it pleased God to call me by His grace, there is the life of a Christian. He fetches his life from the highest heavens. It pleased God to call me by His grace and to reveal His Son in me. When it pleased Him to show me the estate of my soul, and the sinful rebellion of my heart, and when He revealed Christ, not so much *to me*, as *in me*. He was revealed to him in Acts 9, in the first vision and work upon him. But when He revealed Christ in me, then he went that way the Holy Ghost led him. Thus you shall easily discern it plainly; though it be hidden in the pleasure of God, yet it will show itself evidently in the expression of a Christian man. When he comes to speak of the life of his spiritual estate, they never attribute it to good inclination, nor to the good instructions of others. But they say, when it pleased God, thus and thus to reveal Himself in me, when He showed me myself, when God laid about to find which way to hem me in, then it pleased God to do it, and since then I have lived.

CAUSE 2: THE WORD OF PROMISE

A second cause of my spiritual life is: The Word of God; the word of Promise. For so the Apostle tells you: "Not all that are of Abraham are the seed and children of Abraham; but the children of the promise are counted for the spiritual seed"—that seed which is elected of God, and chosen to everlasting life. That is the seed of promise, that is, such as are begotten of some promise of God or other. Every Isaac is a son of the promise. And least you should think it peculiar to Isaac alone, the Apostle opens it sweetly in Galatians 4:28 as a thing common with Isaac to all the people of God. It is a like privilege given to the Galatians, and to all others that were born of God. "We brethren are children of the promise." It was not peculiar to Isaac alone to be born of the promise, and yet of the promise he was born in a kind of peculiar manner. For before he was born, God gave Isaac to Sarah by promise, and by virtue of that promise was he born, even a natural life.

Now so far indeed it was a special peculiar prerogative to Isaac and Jacob, but the Apostle would from thence gather that the spiritual birth of us all is by a word of promise. All of us, one and other is born, by a word of providence. But if we speak of our spiritual birth, then we brethren are children of the promise. So that you shall observe this to be a holy truth of God; that every child of God is born of the promise of God. So that then have you a new birth, and you do live a new life. Tell me then, what promise was it that did beget you to God, that begat you to this new life? What word of God was it by which you were begotten? It is a general speech that, in Romans 10:17, "Faith comes by hearing," and by the doctrine of faith preached (Gal. 3:5), that is, the gospel of faith.

So that this is the point: There is some promise, which being reported to the soul in the ministry of the Word, is laid hold upon by the hearts of God's people. The same word of promise, working that faith in the heart, by which the soul cleaves to such a promise. Then do but consider if you be born of God, what cause was there of your birth? Were you born of the Word of God, or of your own conceit? Or of the good opinion of Christians? Or is there some Word of God, which you have placed your confidence in, and upon which you have been reformed? And since that day to this, God has turned your heart and way to another course, and given you to live in His sight?

It is true, it may be many a good soul cannot readily tell you what promise did first bring them on to God. But though you cannot always tell, yet a word of promise it was; and ordinarily, a word of promise which the word preached did apply to your soul, and caused your heart to reach forth and to lay hold upon it. But though you be not always able to reckon up the first promises, yet this I say (and mark it): There is no Christian soul but has some promises of God on which his heart is stayed upon, and by which his life is nourished, which argues it was bred of those promises, of which it is now fed, though a man be not always able to tell what promise it was. Sometimes a word of reproof or of counsel may sink deep into a man, when God sets it well on, and may make a deep impression in the heart of a man. And may so turn about the course of their lives, as that thereby they may reform all common and outward, and known soul sins, which before was ever cause and matter of reproof. But that is not so safe a work of Christ, not such a strong evidence of our spiritual life, when such a word of reproof or counsel has set us in such a course, and we have thereupon refrained gaming and breaking of the Sabbath, and vain fashions; this is well, but it is not so safe a sign of our new birth. For this may befall even a hypocrite. He may be so convinced by a word of grace, and wise counsel, as may strongly turn the stream of his course another way, and yet be without any life and power of godliness. Only the Word of Promise is able to work grace and life in the heart of a man.

For the ground of the point is this: we cannot have a spirit of life wrought in us by the works of the Law, nor by the words of the Law. "He that ministers to you in the Spirit, and works miracles, does He it by the works of the Law" (Gal. 3:5)? As if he should say, did you ever receive the grace of Christ by the works of the Law? Or by the counsel of the Law, or by the commandments of the

Law? Or by the reproofs reached forth from the Law? He excludes it as impossible, and as no ways able to do it (v. 21). And therefore he does ever lead us unto some word of the gospel, to some promise of grace for the ground of all our spiritual life. As if ever we would be able to say we are begotten to a new inheritance, we must be able, and are able to say, we have some word of promise which has wrought this in our souls, which has bowed us to look to Christ, and to cleave to Him for strength, and increase, and growth in grace.

For it is true indeed, the works of the Law may indeed cut us off from some bad ways. But when it has done so, it leaves us there; leaves us in an estate wherein we would not give offense, and would not displease men that are grave and wise. And this we may reach unto without respect to the glory of God, or any inward regard of His holy fear. But when as we are quickened to live by virtue of some promise, then the love of God constrains us to live to obedience and good ends, then our respects can reach heavenly and spiritual ends.

And therefore observe this as of necessary use for any man; that as he would be loath to be deceived in a counterfeit piece of money; so much more let him be careful in the main points of his everlasting estate. On this depends our having or not having of life. And therefore it behooves us to be sure that we be not disappointed in this great mystery of godliness, and consider seriously upon what your hopes and confidence was bred, and whence it was grounded.

Question: *You will say: "But is it not ordinary that the word of the Law does humble and cast down the heart and spirit before God, and cut them off from all confidence in the flesh, before they come to lay hold of the promise of grace in Christ?"*

Answer: True, it is so indeed that ordinarily some word of the Law, some word of conviction prevails with the heart, and makes him in sense of sin; say to his Christian friends, "What shall I do to be saved?" This is true, but yet this is not it that makes him a new man in God's sight. It may reach to the reformation of his outward man, and to the alteration of sundry of his former courses, which no means else could have reclaimed. But yet this makes him not live a spiritual life until he be not only humbled by the Law, but in some measure, brought on to look after the promise of grace in Christ, and to long after them, and to say, and desire, "Oh, that I had but my part in this or that promise, what a mercy of God would that be to me, could I but lay hold upon them." But thereupon the soul of a Christian does stand poring and plodding, and wistly gazing upon them till in the end the very sight of a promise has so seasoned us with a spirit of faith, that we begin not only to long after that promise, but to cleave to it, and in time come to receive it into our hearts, and come to embrace it, to rejoice in it, to acknowledge it, and find our happiness and life and comfort to be wrapped up in it.

CAUSE 3: THE SPIRIT OF GRACE

A third cause of our spiritual life is the Spirit of grace. "That which is born of the Spirit is spirit, whatever is born of the flesh and no more is but carnal, but that which is born of the Spirit is spirit" (John 3:6). There is a shedding abroad, the Spirit of God's grace in the heart of man that makes him of another spirit. He is not the same man that he was before his spirit was changed; his inclination and disposition is changed.

For spirit is nothing else but the *inclination* and *disposition*; the habit of it. The spirit of wisdom is a habit or inclination to wisdom. The spirit of grace is a habit of grace; the spirit of prayer is an inclination or a habit of prayer. They are several words, but all mean the same thing: "Be renewed in the spirit of your minds," that is, be renewed in the inclination and disposition of your mind (Eph. 4:23). And not only be renewed in the mind, or judgement, or understanding of a man, but there must be a renewal of the whole soul of a man, the disposition and inclination of the whole must be changed and altered.

Caleb and Joshua were of another spirit. They could judge of things otherwise than other men could do. Other men not renewed in the spirit of their mind have no alteration. But the truly regenerate they see a great change. They never saw the danger of their sins before, nor ever before judged themselves for their sins, but now their spirit, and soul, and affection is changed. And now a spirit of fear, and love, and care, and every affection is altered. Now a man is turned quite off from earthly things, so far as they hinder him in the enjoyment of his spiritual life. And now we are set upon the things of God, so as that he that is born of God to a spiritual life, is become "a new creature, and old things are passed away" (2 Cor. 5:17).

He has a new mind, and a new heart, new affections, new language, and new employments that he was never wont to do before. Now he can read God's Word, and confer with God's people about the things of God, and can instruct others, and fashion himself to a new mold, and all upon the renewal of the spirit of his mind. So that if you see that God has put another spirit into you than ever you had before, so as not only this or that part, but the whole man is changed, and put into another frame, that though there be still a taste of the old man, yet the frame both of the body and soul is of another mold, and "all things are become new" in some measure. Then you live a new life indeed, else it is not a perfect change, though this and that alteration be wrought in you.

By these causes you may clearly discern whether God has given you a new life or not. Consider it, therefore, I beseech you, how do you now find your hearts apt to speak, when you speak of that estate you are in? Are you in your closets wont to say that time was when you have been thus and thus led in the vanity of your mind, and the hardness of your heart, and custom of sin. But when it pleased God, who called you by His grace, when it pleased God, then it took place; you had been in good company before and had used many means, but never anything would work. But when it pleased God, then it wrought, and from that day to this it has been so and so with me?

It is a good sign to you, if withal you can recall that such or such a word of promise it pleased God to pitch your souls upon. You have long looked and waited for salvation, but in the end, it pleased God to wrap up your souls in life by such a promise. And if you can call to mind that such a promise your souls did cleave unto, then are you indeed born to a spiritual life, because you are right bred, bred of a promise and of the holy will and pleasure of God. But if you find yourselves to be of another frame, and you are bowed to walk with God, and to reform your course of life by outward bounds, this is not so safe. But if your whole man universally be bowed to a godly holy frame, and all things are become new—new friends, new affections, new desires—if you find such a universal change, then you are right bred Christians.

And indeed no Christians are right bred but such Christians. But if you make a great stir about the great reformation that is wrought in you, and it is from the good inclination and disposition you have always had; you ever had a good mind, and in the end (you thank

God) you have reformed such and such evils as you have been blamed for. Time was when you could have freely played at cards and dice, but since then you see the vanity of it, and you take better courses. And do now comfort yourselves with well-ordered and stayed company? You had always a good mind to be better, but you could not do it suddenly, and so in the conclusion your reformation is but a good inclination or disposition of your mind.

And if you see that much good has been wrought upon you by the counsel of such and such friends, and by the good example of such and such wise and discreet friends; and if you find that there is some strange change in your carriage, your course of life is much altered, you are not so light and wanton as you were. But you take a far more grave, and wise, and stayed course, and to much better purpose both for Church and Commonwealth wherein you live.

Now I say, if you shall go on and look for that spiritual life, which only springs from Christ Jesus, and will lead on to eternal glory, and therefore rests not in any reformation of yourselves till you find there be such an inward and whole change wrought in you, which the heart is wont to speak of to the praise of God's grace, it was God's will, else it could never have been wrought, and you could not speak of it till now; and you never rest satisfied in such a change, as word of reproof or counsel that has wrought such a change or reformation in you, that stayed in the outward man, or in some affections, till you found your hearts to sanctify the name of God's grace in the acknowledgement of the Word of Promise and of the Spirit of grace, making you new, that you may be able to say, that in very deed you have Christ, and with Christ life, and that life which will never decay, but will hold to all eternity.

And therefore now to speak something of the signs of the life of our justification.

DISCERNING THE LIFE BY ITS EFFECTS

Therefore a second sort of signs is taken from the effects of spiritual life. You see what are the causes of it as the good pleasure of God: the word of promise, and the Spirit of grace. These be the first sort of signs.

Now a second sort of signs is from the effects and fruits of life, and herein take notice of some fruits of your life of justification. It is a principal part of our spiritual life to have our sins forgiven—"Blessed is the man whose iniquity is pardoned, and to whom the Lord imputes no sin" (Ps. 32:1, 2). And therefore it is that forgiveness of sin is called justification; then God accounts us righteous, and this is called "justification of life" (Rom. 5:18), because in the pardon of our sins is our life. As when a malefactor by the law is condemned, he is by the law a dead man. And if his pardon come, his pardon is his life, and it is so indeed. So is it in this case, the pardon of our sins is the very life of our souls. And if God give us to find that life, there is no fear of the life of our sanctification, or consolation, *etc.*

EFFECT 1: INWARD PEACE OF CONSCIENCE

The first effect then that flows from the pardon of our sins is some inward peace of conscience; some inward refreshment and satisfaction yielded to the heart that it could never attain to before. For sin may be pardoned in the sight of God, and yet that pardon is not manifested and declared to my soul until God vouchsafe me some measure of peace. And a manifestation of the free pardon of my sins, I can have little rest. It is a notable saying, "Being justified by faith we have peace with God through Jesus Christ" (Rom. 5:1). A man justified is one that has his sins pardoned, for what was it that all our life time before made us afraid of God's displeasure, and we had much disquietness about our estates. Oh, the sin of our souls that we had committed all our life long, the sin committed many a day ago that now lay heavy upon our souls, and the want of pardon lay as heavy as our sins! But now if God come and say, "Your sins are pardoned," then follows a sweet tranquility of peace in the soul.

A matter that philosophers have talked of—to quiet the mind, to lull men asleep—and with applying remedies did stupefy for a while, and take off the heavy burden, or the sense of the burden, rather than the burden itself. But so soon as ever God pardons sin, there is shed abroad a spirit of peace in our souls. And sometimes in that unspeakable measure, as that it passes the understanding of a man to conceive (Phil. 4:7). But I do not so conceive that every Christian as soon as ever his sin is first pardoned has such an unconceivable peace in his soul. But he finds a great deal of ease sometimes, as if you had thrown a millstone from off his body.

Notable is that expression in Isaiah 32:17, "The work of righteousness shall be peace, and the effect of righteousness quietness and assurance forever." He speaks of that righteousness, whereby we stand righteous before God, and the imputation of Christ's righteousness to our souls. The work of righteousness shall be peace; from this work and effect you may gather what the causes of it is. Blessed are such, it is quietness and assurance forever. Not that there is an everlasting sense of that peace, for the sense of it is sometimes obscured for want of watchfulness, and want of experience in the ways of godliness. And sometimes through the buffetings of Satan, or desertions from the hand of God, and so many times our peace may be over-clouded, and the sense of it taken away. But the work of righteousness is peace. If sin be pardoned, peace will follow upon it, and the fruit of this righteousness is quietness and assurance forever. The heart is now peaceable, quiet, and assured that God has wrought this and that grace in me, which will abide in me forever.

EFFECT 2: QUIETNESS

That you may be further instructed in this point, see a second effect of this life of justification of the life of righteousness, which is of special use for the right discerning of our spiritual life. And that is this: Look as in all natural life, no man has received life, but is careful to preserve it—"Skin for skin, and all that a man has he will give to save his life" (Job 2:4). And if his life be struck at, he will have his hand cut off rather than have his head wounded. He will expose himself or any member to any danger rather than lose his life. And so if God vouchsafe pardon of sin and peace of conscience, you will find this an evident sign of pardon and peace together, and an evident effect of them both. A serious care, and a constant endeavor to maintain and keep that peace, that as you see God has been very gracious in speaking peace to you. So you would preserve that peace above all the blessings in the world, that whatsoever you lose else, though you lose friends, and goods, and lands, and trades, health, and liberty, you would not lose your peace, though you hazard the loss of them all to preserve and maintain your peace. That peace when it was given you was so unspeakable and glorious that life itself was not to be compared to this mercy which God has vouchsafed us when He gave us peace, "Your loving kindness is better than life" (Ps. 63:3).

A man that has found something that is better than his life, he will lose his life rather than it, and much more anything else. And therefore it you see God incline your hearts to be tender and chary of your peace. Then God has bestowed peace and pardon upon you. And it is evident, because you are so loath to break it. A man that never received this peace, he makes no conscience of sin unless it blemish him in the eye of the world. He makes no great matter of conscience to run into any sin because the old score is yet undischarged. Christ is not wont to discharge that score which we make no conscience to run into again.

And if they do, he can tell how to make them feel the smart of playing such prodigals. But when God has blotted all our sins out of His sight, that there is no more mention of sin between God and our souls, that the heart of a Christian will be marvelous chary and solicitous, that it sin no more against God. He that has his sin pardoned and knows what it has cost—both on God's part and on his own—he is very careful of running into sin anymore, and is very careful to walk more holily forever hereafter. Notable is that example in Genesis 39:9, when Joseph was tempted to a pleasing sin; Oh (says he) "How shall I commit this great wickedness, and so sin against God?" How should he now break his peace with God and run upon a new score with God? It is certain, he had sinned before, and he had found pardon of it. And how should he now sin any more against God? This is the constant care of every Christian man; he is fearful of every sin.

I grant you, it is true that sometimes, even those that have their sins pardoned, and the writing of transgression by which they had engaged themselves to everlasting torments has been cancelled, yet even they have afterwards turned the grace of God into wantonness through sinful lusts—as David and Peter, *etc.* through some corruption or other. But you shall also find this to be true, that as they have been overtaken and overwhelmed with such corruptions as those be, so they have held forth as much repentance, and affliction in this case; that if you had taken many lives from them, you could not have grieved them so much as in this case they are put to.

The blotting out of the sense of this pardon has been more bitter to them than death itself. And if it be not so, that Christian men in such a case do not more shame themselves before God, and loath themselves for all the evils they have done in God's sight; they will either lie down seared and benumbed, and their spiritual life will evaporate away. And then it will argue, it was never true and sincere. And if it were true, it will lie so close and hidden, that you may plainly see what a slaughter Satan has made, and what heavy load he has put upon such as are careless to maintain that peace with God, which he has vouchsafed them. And therefore, if God give us hearts to keep our peace, it is an evident sign God is at peace with us.

If we fly from sin, as from the grave or hell, then surely those sins are pardoned which we do abhor, and that peace and reconciliation is procured which we desire; that is the nature of spiritual life. It desires to maintain itself, and to expel all that is contrary to it. If the body have taken any noisome and hurtful thing, it will vomit and cast it out, and will not let it rest there in quiet. If it be an enemy to our life it will strive against it, if there be any spiritual life in us, it cannot let sin rest in us. It will strive against it, and never rest till it be shut of it, anyway, some way or other, out it must, though he shame himself for it by an open confession. And though it many ways trouble him, yet out it must, it is an enemy to his life, and out he must cast it. And therefore if God give us hearts to be fearful of sin and careful to maintain our peace; it is an evident sign of the truth of our spiritual life. And this is a sign of life, for he feels not his peace because it is clouded in him. He discerns no life in him, and he fears what he had was but a delusion. Why, how stands your care to preserve your peace, and to avoid the danger of the loss of it? If God gives you a heart desirous and careful to maintain your peace, though it be not so lively as sometimes it was, yet it is certainly true and good.

EFFECT 3: ASSURANCE

A third sign and effect of the life of righteousness is that which our Savior gives. "Her sins are forgiven her, which are many, for she loved much" (Luke 7:47). So then, this is a third sign that our sins are pardoned and of the life of our justification—our love of God. Love of God, proportionable and suitable, according to the greatness of the sins that have been forgiven and pardoned to us; this is a good evidence of the life of our justification. This is not a dead and lifeless pardon. A prince may pardon a malefactor of his former offence, but he can put no new principle into him. But God's pardons do convey life into the soul, and it has this work in it; when the soul sees that all its sins are done away, and those sins many and great, as many and great sins are forgiven him.

So is His love great and manifold, and this is of the same nature of the love there spoken of. She was a wicked woman, and very notorious for uncleanness, for so said the people, "Surely if this man were a Prophet, he would know what manner of woman this was, for she is a sinner" (Luke 7:38, 39). And when they say, "A sinner," they mean not such a sinner as other men and women ordinarily be, but such a sinner as was a notorious wicked woman, and therefore a shame for Him that professed Himself to be a Prophet to come so near her. She begins "to wash, and to kiss His feet, and to wipe them with the hair of her head, and to anoint Him with precious ointment." Now says Christ to Simon the Pharisee (and he was none of the worst of them neither) for Christ seems to imply that he had some sins forgiven him:

> "I have something to say unto you, Simon. There
> was a creditor had two debtors. The one owed five

hundred pence, the other fifty, and when they had nothing to pay, he frankly forgave them both. Tell me therefore, which of them will love him most? Why, says he, I suppose him to whom he forgave most. And Jesus said, you have rightly judged, since I entered into your house you gave Me no water for my feet, *etc*. Wherefore I say unto you, her sins which are many are forgiven her, for she loved much" (vv. 40-47).

She showed wonderful much love, she sat behind him weeping, when she though she had not been so much seen, not presuming to come into His presence. Now therefore her sins, which are many, are forgiven her. You may see it plainly because she loves so much; and you that have showed less love, you have less forgiven you. But they that have many sins forgiven them, they have much. And therefore if a man's sins be forgiven him, and God give him peace in the pardon of them according to the measure and multitude of his sins. Such is the measure and variety of his love, the greatness of his love to God. And as God has forgiven him many sins, so he gives God manifold measures of love. He loves God greatly, the very feet of God; the lowest and poorest members of the Body of Christ. He is content to stoop to the meanest office of love to Christ, or to any of His servants; anything wherein love may be showed to Christ, or His members, he is content to stoop to it. According to what is your forgiveness, such is you love.

And because no man has so little forgiven him, but if anything be forgiven him at all, he knows that little is so much, and so great, as would indeed have plunged him into the nethermost hell. And therefore no true Christian is conceited of the smallness of his sins, but he thinks it a very great matter to have any one sin forgiven him. But he knows if God had cast him out of his sight for any one of them, just had his judgements been, and if at any time his love decay, he renews it by repentance of that sin, for which before God had vouchsafed him pardon. And thus you see a six-fold sign of our spiritual life—three from the *causes*, and three from the *effects*; and the latter, the three effects chiefly concern the life of our justification.

And therefore do but apply it home to your souls because the whole discourse is but an application and a use of the point. But I pray you consider what you have heard, and lay it to heart, and draw near now into the closet of your spirits, that you may discern what God has done for you. Did you yet ever see any peace of conscience? You say, "I never had a troubled unquiet conscience all my days." But to you I only say thus much: your peace has neither a good root, nor will it bring forth any good fruit, not well rooted. For I pray you, whence came it? Did it come from any word of God's promise? Or any work of the Spirit of grace? Or from your self-love? Or is it not a benumbed peace? And if so, then it is not well rooted.

And truly it has and will have as bad fruits. For if you say your sins are pardoned, then what care have you to keep that peace and to preserve it? Does not a sin befall you? But it is an annoyance to your spiritual life, and you cannot rest till you be shut of it. And cannot be satisfied till you be wholly discharged of it. It is well, but if you find that you can live quietly in known sins, and your soul is never troubled about them. This is then but a barren and false-hearted peace, and will deceive you. And in the midst of this peace you may sink into hell unless God heal this distempered peace in you; and if God have given you such a peace, what love do you then return to God? Where is that great and manifold love you give to God? If this love be wanting, and your care to preserve it be wanting; if your peace be groundless and fruitless, then spiritual life is wanting.

But if God has been pleased, and your own heart can find it so, and bear witness to your soul that God has pardoned your sins, then that peace which is in your soul will refresh you. Have you ever found such a peace in your soul as has been unspeakable and full of glory, and you have been sweetly quieted when many troubles have been about you, and have you found comfort from hence in any of the Ordinances of God? And do you find that though that peace then gotten be in a great measure lost and decayed, yet you have as great a care as may be to preserve it, and to maintain it, and to renew, and to recover it again by repentance, and art careful to preserve yourself spotless before the world? And do you find that according as God has been merciful to you, so your love is great and manifold? Can you never love God so much as He has done you? Can you never answer the thousand part of His love and mercy showed to you? And then no service of God, or office so mean that He calls you to, but to the utmost of your endeavor are willing to spend and be spent for God. Then it is an evident argument that justification is conveyed to your soul; for God has given you peace, and has given you a heart to love Him back again.

~ Sermon 8 ~
The Effects of Life of Our Sanctification

He that has the Son has life, and he that has not the Son has not life.
(1 John 5:12)

The causes of this life you have heard, and some of the effects of it also. The life of justification you heard has these three effects or fruits in the heart; *peace*, *quietness*, and *assurance* forever. Care to keep our conscience pacified in some measure, careful to maintain that peace we have had so much ado to get. And also love of God according to the abundance of sin that has been pardoned to us.

We are now speaking of the effects of life, and now to speak of the effects of the life of our sanctification. "He that has the Son has life," not only in the pardon of his sin, but he has likewise the graces of God's Spirit, which are the life of sanctification—a frame of grace wrought in the soul, which is the life of holiness.

Now because sanctification is found, partly in the heart and partly in the life, let me now show you some such effects of spiritual life as are found in the heart of a Christian. And breathe forth themselves in his life by those habits and gifts which are principally within.

And the sum of what I shall now say is thus much. There are certain variety of the graces of God in themselves so different and opposite. As that in nature they are seldom compatible to one person at one and the same time, or least of all to be found in one and the same business. And yet are found wherever the heart of a man is sanctified by the Spirit of grace. Where you have the life of sanctification in a Christian, you shall find variety of graces in them. Some of them of such diversity and opposition one to another, that in nature the like temper is not to be found in one person at the same time, and in the same business. They are certain kind of conjugations, or companions of grace so fitted, and joined together in the heart of a man, as that nature is not able to compact such sanctified affections unto such uses upon any occasion; much less able to bring them forth upon any occasion, they are so different in themselves; to name some of them in particular.

THE FIRST EFFECT: JOY & GRIEF

First, if you look at the grace of God as it works in the heart, and exercises itself in the conversion of a sinner, you shall find that when the soul discerns any life of grace in its heart, that sin is now pardoned, and God is pleased to frame it anew, and to give it a new life. At that time the heart is taken up with these two contrary effects. It is both enlarged with no small measure of *joy*, that ever God should redeem him from such a desperate condition as his soul lay in, and yet withal full of *grief* of heart, that ever he should have so much displeased that God, that has done so much for him. And so plain, as that you shall evidently discern the voice of your own joy from the voice of your own grief.

I know not better how to instance in it than to fetch a resemblance from the return of the children of Israel from captivity to Jerusalem. Read Psalm 126:1-4, "When God turned the captivity of His people, this was their affection; then was their mouth filled with laughter, and their tongue with singing, *etc.*" Now the same people that so rejoice to see themselves redeemed by the arm of the Lord, when they do rejoice to see themselves set at liberty from the captivity, they do at the same time as sadly grieve and weep. To consider the unkindness they have put upon God and their unworthiness of such a mercy from Him, as you may read in Jeremiah 50:4-5, speaking of the same people, and of the same time, their return from the captivity. And he tells you, "They shall come, going and weeping shall they go, and seek the Lord God, and ask the way to Zion, with their faces thitherward." If the psalmist speaks of it, he says, they were out of, and beyond themselves for joy, as in a comfortable dream. The news seemed to be too good to be true, and they rejoiced with exceeding great joy. And if the prophet Jeremiah speak of the very same people, and the same time, and the very same action; he tells you, "They go to Jerusalem, weeping, they go to seek the Lord, and ask the way to Zion." They rejoice at the greatness of the mercy, and weep in sense of their unworthiness of it.

And truly this kind of combination shall you find stirring in every soul that is converted to God, when the pardon of its sin is sealed to its heart. It breeds a certain kind of inward joy, and comfort in the Lord that has thus graciously pardoned their iniquity. And yet more abundantly mourning for the evils, it has so displeased God with. Nor is there any mourning so deeply wounds the soul as that which arises from the sight of Christ crucified. Then the soul mourns full bitterly (Zech. 12:10). He will mourn exceedingly to think that he should deal so unworthily against that God that has all this while had such wonderful thoughts of peace towards him. This is the first combination of graces that is found in the soul after sin is pardoned, and the heart restored to a new life. For we spoke before of prizing Christ in our judgements by certain preparative graces, but now we speak of that kind of life of sanctification, which puts forth itself after some sense of our justification. This life of the mixture of joy and mourning, bears witness to our life of sanctification.

THE SECOND EFFECT: JOY & FEAR

Secondly, in the worshipping of God in those duties of the life of sanctification, you shall find another combination of mixed affections, the like of which are not, and cannot be found in nature. And that is joy and fear, according to Psalm 2:11, "Serve the Lord with fear, and rejoice with trembling." A Christian man, when he is in a good frame, and the life of grace most stirs in his spirit, he never comes to a holy duty but with some holy fear and trembling before God, before whom he then stands, and yet there is no duties he goes about with more comfort and joy than those, when his heart is not dead. It is true, a dead-hearted Christian comes to good duties like a bear to a stake while they are in such a temper. If they can shun duties they will, but take the heart of a Christian when it is alive, and then they are a willing people (Ps. 110:3), they come with some inward gladness of heart. It is the joy of their spirits to hear of an opportunity when they may hear the Word, and pray, or perform any duty acceptable to God. But how? When their hearts are most joyful, and they go about duties most willingly. Yet then most awfully, for take you a Christian when he comes unwillingly, his heart is not much affected with fear and trembling. But then he is most awful when his heart is in the best frame towards holy duties.

These two affections never meet in other things, when a man goes about any business gladly, he is not afraid of it. Or if he be in fear, he goes not about it joyfully. The sun trembles not at his course, but rejoices to run his race. The horse rejoices at the battle, he never trembles at the matter. Or when any man goes about any work with joy, he never trembles at it. But a Christian man, when he goes about any spiritual duty, though he have much joy and comfort in it, and is glad of the occasion, yet he is most fearful. As with Psalm 130:4, the very consideration of the greatness of God's mercies makes a soul fearful of the presence of God. So the more rich God in grace and mercy is to us, either pardoning sin, or sanctifying the heart, or quickening us to any duty, the most fearful is the soul in such a condition. And hence is that you read, the Lord is said to "be fearful in praises" (Ex. 15:11); when the heart is most enlarged to praise God with comfort, then does it most fear God, so that here is another combination of graces that are not commonly found together in other businesses of ordinary affairs. But where the heart is spiritual, they meet together in the same thing.

THE THIRD EFFECT: JOY & SADNESS

Thirdly, take you a godly man in affliction, and when he is most able to bear them, and yet when afflictions are most heavy, if he find his heart able to grapple under them, yet then you shall find much joy and sadness of heart mixed together. It was a sign of the election of the Thessalonians because they "received the word in much affliction, and with joy of the Holy Ghost" (1:6). When they found much affliction either by the word, or in the outward man, though much affliction, yet inwardly joyous; "No affliction is joyous for the present, yet it brings forth the quiet fruits of righteousness" (Heb. 12:11). By how much the more affliction makes their spirits sad, yet so much the more is the heart enlarged with joy and comfort in the Holy Ghost—"We rejoice in tribulations" (Rom. 5:3). Tribulation is such a kind of affliction, as is a threshing us like corn out of the chaff drives us out of all the comforts of this life, and that is not in nature, to rejoice in any measure, when the heart is in grief and discouragement, it ever wants something to raise it up.

THE FOURTH EFFECT: PATIENCE WITHOUT ALL FORBEARANCE

Fourthly, there is this mixture of affection in our carriage towards men which argues the life of holiness in us. In our conversing with men, you shall have the same heart full of much patience, but without all forbearance. And those are such as are not found in nature, nor in a hypocrite, yet in a Christian heart you shall find them together the more patient a man is towards others, yet the less able is he to bear with evil. Read Revelation 2:2, "I know your works, and your labor, and your patience, and how you cannot bear them which are evil." A man would think it were a very strange expression.

A man of known and proved patience, and yet cannot bear—for what is patience, but bearing and forbearing?

Yet says God, "I know your patience, and that you cannot bear them that are evil," implying that such a soul, if it were a matter to be put upon himself, and affliction or trial put upon himself, then I know your patience in bearing of it. But if it come to a matter of evil, not of punishment, but of sin, then I know you cannot bear it.

Take you any patient man that only has a moral virtue of patience. And if he have so much patience as that he can bear with crosses and afflictions, he can as well also bear with evils committed against God. But this is the nature of spiritual patience. It is mixed with zeal, so as that the more patient a man is, in regard of injuries done to himself, the less patient he is in respect of injuries done to God.

THE FIFTH EFFECT: GENTLENESS & MEEKNESS

Fifthly, you shall have gentleness and meekness sometimes mixed in a man, with much austerity and strictness, which is very much they should meet in one man at one and the same time. The wisdom that is from above is gentle and meek, and easy to be entreated.

It was said of Moses, "he was the meekest man upon earth" (Num. 12:3). Take Moses in his own case, and his carriage towards men, as they had respect to himself. And then he was a meek man, soon persuaded, yet same Moses, when he saw the matter concerned the cause of God, he is so stiff and immoveable, as that he will not yield one jot, he will not "leave a hoof behind of all that appertained to the children of Israel" (Ex. 10:26). He would not only have men, and women, and children go forth to serve the Lord, but their cattle and their stuff. He will not yield a little here; no, not for the king's pleasure sake. A man would much wonder that such a man, so meek and gentle, and so easy to be persuaded in his own cause that yet when it comes to a matter of importance and concerns God, he will not there yield. He is now inflexible, nothing can persuade him to give way to it. This is a combination of graces that are not wont to be found in men thus mixed together. But it is found in the people of God that live a sanctified and holy life.

I know not better what to instance in than in the liquid air. Of all other things the most easiest to be pierced through. Of itself it gives way to every creature, not the lest fly, or least stone cast into it, but it gives way to it of itself. Yet if God say it shall be as a firmament between the waters above and the waters below, it then stands like a wall of brass and yields not. It will not suffer the water in the clouds to fall down, but if it do fall to water the earth. It shall strain through the air as through a sieve, the clouds sometimes are so full that one would think they would burst through the air and fall upon the earth. But God having set the air to be a firmament, or expulsion between the waters above and the waters below, though of itself a very liquid thing, yet it stands like to a wall of brass. And truly so is it with a Christian spirit, though of himself he is as liquid as the air, you may easily pass through him, and go an end with him easily. He is easy to be entreated, very gentle, but take him now in anything wherein God has bid him keep his stand in his course, and there he stands like a wall of brass that were never such high and great matters put upon him, ready to bear him down. He will not shrink, nor give any way at all. This is another mixture of affections which are found in Christian men that do enjoy this life of holiness.

THE SIXTH EFFECT: MODESTY

In the sixth place you shall have modesty mixed with such magnanimity, which is rarely found in men, endued only with moral or civil gifts, but in nature the more modest, the less magnanimous. But a Christian, the more modest he is, the more magnanimous. Look at Paul, and touching the "righteousness which is of the Law," he is endued with many carnal privileges according to the Law. But now all these are but loss and dross, "and dung, that he might win Christ" (Phil. 3:8). All his good parts of nature and all his common gifts of grace, yet all of them but dross and dung. This was the modest spirit of Paul, a man who sometimes said of himself, he was not inferior to the very chief apostles (2 Cor. 12:11), yet again says he, "I am nothing," there is his magnanimity.

When he is opposed and vilified by the false apostles, has Paul forgot his modesty, now that he knows not how to submit himself, nor to compare himself with his equals? No, but though chief of the apostles, yet "am I nothing." He looks at everything he had as nothing: "This I am," but yet "I am nothing." He sometimes calls himself, "the least of all the apostles" (1 Cor. 15:9, 10) and yet other whiles, not inferior to the very chief of them. Sometimes he calls himself, "the least of all saints" (Eph. 3:8), and yet sometimes, "not inferior so the very chief apostles." And this "he had learned," he had been instructed thus to deny himself. He desired that he might know nothing but Christ, and Him crucified.

See the noble spirit of this self-denial servant of God. Sometimes when the magistrates had done him wrong, see then how he stands upon his privileges, he complains, "they had beaten him, a Roman, being uncondemned" (Acts 16:37). And when they heard this, they would have sent him away privately; nay, "let them come and fetch him out." See now, a man of a great and magnanimous spirit, though a man as fit to put up wrongs as any man. Yet when he sees the glory of God is interested in his person, and his calling, or his cause is called in question, then he knows how to stand upon his worth. And if in such a case he sustain open wrong, then he will plead the liberty of a subject. Whereas at another time, he would have done more to a far less man than a magistrate—"He is become all things to all men, that he might save some every way." So gentle that you may turn him about your hand anyway, but else he will stand upon his worth. And not inferior to the very chief apostles; those that are greatest and chiefest, such "who seemed to be pillars," he is not inferior to any of them, the greatest of them all. Equal to the best of them, if not before them all, and yet "labored more than they all" (1 Cor. 15:10). To show you the marvelous modesty of the spirit of grace, a work incompatible to nature, but is found only in a spirit of holiness, and there only they are combined together in the same person, at the same time, and in the same business, with the same breath he can tell you; "He is not inferior to the very chief apostles," and yet, "I am nothing."

Notable is that expression of David to this purpose, "My eyes are not lofty, nor my heart haughty, but I have behaved myself as a weaned child" (Ps. 131:1, 2). Now you would think if a man were such a weaned humble creature, he could not tell how to speak, nor to take any great things in hand. But when he comes to speak to that, you shall mark the frame of his spirit. "Stand open you everlasting doors, and be lift up you everlasting gates that the King of glory may come in" (Ps. 24:7, 9). When he looks at earthly things—yes, the best of them—his heart is so weaned from them that he knows not how to have a high thought. Weaned even from a kingdom as a child from the breast, and yet the same soul that is thus weaned, and thus mean in his own eyes, when he comes to spiritual matters. It is wonder to see the height of his spirit; these things are too low, and too shallow for him. He knows not how to close with, nor to content himself with such poor things as these be: crowns, and scepters, and dignities—his heart was weaned from them all. All of them things too low, and too mean for him to be exercised about.

Now, "be lifted up you gates," and he means the heart and conscience of a man, the affection of his soul, lift up there to the ways of God, he would now be of an higher strain, so that a man would wonder at this, though the matter be great and high, every way far above all earthly things. Yet notwithstanding he looks at them all as matters fit for his heart to be raised up unto. He looks at the favor of God, and the blood of Christ, and pardon of sin, the kingdom of glory. He looks at all these high matters as fit objects for his heart to be set upon. "His eyes were not haughty," and he "did not exercise himself in great matters" concerning earthly things, and yet, was it not a great matter to be King of Israel? Yet is it not a greater matter to be the Son of God than to be the son-in-law to a king? But "his eyes are not haughty." He does not exercise himself in such things as these be, but yet he exercises himself in greater matters than these things are.

And therefore, when as Christian men are thought to be of shallow weak spirits, and know not how to carry on end matters in this world, yet when they come to spiritual matters, there they can tell how to set their hearts a work about such matters about the inheritance of the Kingdom of Heaven, about the favor of God, and the light of God's countenance. These be great matters, when they come to have the eye of God upon them, they can look for the glory of His presence, and the fellowship of the angels. And they can discourse, and tell you of great blessings that God has laid up for them in Christ. Then they can exercise their hearts in such great matters, "Let the high praises of God be in their mouths" (Ps. 149:6).

What a strange speech is there for a man that sometimes said, "Great matters are too high for him," yet now, as it is in the original, "High things, the high glorious things of God, the great things of God, the magnanimous things of God, the high praises of God," the high Majesty of God, the high praises, and thanksgiving of God, "let them be in their mouths." The mighty power of God, let that be in their lips, and a "two-edged sword in their hands." He speaks of a word of prophecy and instruction to the people; the word is called, "the sword of the Spirit," whereby kings are bound in chains, and lords in iron bonds, and such honor have all the saints. He would have all the saints of God to invest themselves with this honor that they might speak of such glorious excellent things, as their words might be like to a two-edged sword, to cut asunder the hearts of great princes, to bring kings and great lords in chains of horror, and anguish of soul and conscience. Such chains as out of which there is no redemption, but by the high words of the saints, by the high promises of God to speak peace to the souls of princes. But let the high threatenings of God be in their mouths, the high commandments of God in their mouths, and those will bind kings in chains, and lords in fetters of iron. And then let the high promises of God, the spiritual promises of grace be in their mouths, to set princes at liberty, and to teach their senators wisdom.

A strange kind of combination in the Spirit of grace wrought in such hearts. They can call upon their hearts to be lifted up to the high things of God. Nothing then too great for them to exercise themselves in; no mercies, nor judgements too great, no not the unsearchable counsel of God, the depths of the mysteries of God, nothing is too high for them. It will be prying, and looking into the secret counsels of God, and yet both together with most modesty, when the soul is most lifted up in the ways of God. Yet at the same time he looks at himself as nothing, and get notwithstanding so far forth as God will be pleased to reveal it to him. He will be searching into the deep things of God, and yet all this will he do with a very modest spirit.

Thus you have seen six combinations severally of the gracious affections that are not to be found in nature; no, not set upon civil objects, much less upon spiritual, but upon civil objects, they cannot be so combined together.

The Seventh Effect: Diligence in Worldly Businesses

Seventhly, there is another combination of virtues strangely mixed in every lively holy Christian. And that is diligence in worldly businesses, and yet deadness to the world. Such a mystery as none can read, but they that know it. For a man to "rise early, and go to bed late, and eat the bread of carefulness," not a sinful, but a provident care. And to avoid idleness, cannot endure to spend any idle time, takes all opportunities to be doing something, early and late, and loses no opportunity, go any way and bestir himself for profit. This will he do most diligently in his calling. And yet be a man dead-hearted to the world, "the diligent hand makes rich" (Prov. 10:4). And you read of the godly woman that she "rises while it is yet night" (Prov. 31:27), and of this you read (Prov. 15:13; 18:19, 27).

Now if this be a thing which is so common in the mouth of the Holy Ghost, and you see was the practice of the greatest women then upon the earth; the greatest princes in those times, the more gracious, the more diligent, and laborious in their callings: you see it will well stand with the life of grace, very diligent in worldly business. And yet notwithstanding, the very same souls that are most full of the world's businesses, the more diligent they be in their callings, yet the same persons are directed "to be dead with Christ" (Col. 3:1–3). "Set not your affections upon things below, but on things that are above, for we are dead with Christ." Meaning, dead to all these earthly things, and all the comforts here below, they are not our life, but "our life is hid with Christ in God." And therefore to this world are we dead.

And Paul therefore so speaks of it, "The world is crucified to me, and I unto the world" (Gal. 6:14). The very same men that are so crucified to the world, yet the spirits of those men, though their affections be in heaven, yet their labors are in the earth. "Our conversation is in heaven" (Phil. 3:20), but our employments is here upon the earth, diligently taking pains in our callings, ever very busy in outward employments.

"Observe the ant, learn her ways, and be wise" (Prov. 6). Be busy like ants, morning and evening, early and late, and labor diligently with their hands, and with their wits, and which way soever as may be the best improvement of a man's talent. It must be employed to the best advantage. And yet when a man has labored thus busily, yet his heart, and mind, and affections are above. He goes about all his business in obedience to God's commandment, and he intends the glory of God. And he thereby sets himself and his household at more liberty for the service of God in their places, and so, though he labor most diligently in his calling, yet his heart is not set upon these things. He can tell what to do with his estate when he has got it.

Say not therefore when you see two men laboring very diligently and busily in the world, say not, "here is a couple of worldlings." For two men may do the same business, and have the same success, and yet a marvelous difference between them. The heart of the one may be dead to these things, he looks at them as they be. Indeed, but "crumbs that fall from the children's table," he looks not at them as his chiefest good, but "the bread of life," the spiritual food of his soul, that is the thing which he chiefly labors after. Another man places his happiness and felicity in them, and makes them his chiefest good, and so there is a manifest difference between them.

So then you see seven combinations of graces that are in the life of holiness, and all of singular use in this kind.

THE EIGHTH EFFECT: LOVE OF ENEMIES

Eighthly, the last virtue is a single one, and that is love of enemies. "I say unto you, love your enemies, that you may be the children of your heavenly Father" (Matt. 5:44-45). Love your enemies. This very grace whereby we do love our enemies. It has a contrary work to nature, for naturally, this we shall find to be the frame of our hearts towards our enemies. We are cold and undisposed to do any good office unto them, very hard and cold, and frozen towards them. Those who are our enemies, we take no pleasure in them, but now in such a case as this, the love of a Christian will come and warm the heart, and thaw this cold frostiness that is in our souls. Whereas before a man was cold toward his enemies, his heart now begins to reflect upon him in pity and compassion. And instead of hardness, his heart now melts and is made soft within him, to see what ill measures it could have put upon its enemies.

But on the contrary side, the same hatred in a man that is towards his enemies, it makes a man of a hot distemper with boiling in heat of wrath against his enemies. He is all upon it to do him any harm. His heart is full of hot and bitter wrath. So as that love which was as heat and fire to thaw and warm, cold and hard hearts, when it comes to the fire of wrath, it is as it were cold water, and allays that heat and bitterness and harshness, which else our hearts are subject to.

This is the nature of love, as it is the nature of water to cool hot distempers. And as it is the nature of fire to thaw and soften hard frozen spirits, and so though it be but as one entire grace. Yet in the act it puts forth a kind of variety of work, whereby one would think it did cross itself, but it does not, but does all by the life of Christ. Thus you see what the effects of the life of sanctification is in the heart of a man, after that God has begun to root the life of justification in us. And he discerns that God has wrought a change in him, and then these several graces, though in themselves, and work one apposite to another; yet in a Christian heart they can meet and join together.

THE EFFECTS REHEARSED

And therefore now do but lay this to heart, "he that has the Son has life." Will a Christian say, how shall I know that I have that life, in having of which, I may know I have Christ? Why, do but consider with your own soul, not now of the life of your justification. But have you found that ever God did fill your heart with joy, so as your soul has said, "The Lord has done great things for my soul, whereof He has made me to rejoice"? And have you found that when you have most rejoiced in the wonderful mercy of God, then have your heart most melted before the Lord your God? And you have been ashamed and confounded within yourself, and never open your mouth against God anymore—Do you see that the more God reveals Christ to you, who was crucified for your sake, the more bitterly you moan for your wickedness? Then it is a strong evidence of life and peace in your soul.

Were it not the mighty power of the life of Christ in you, you could have had neither of both these graces, much less combined together to work the same thing, at one and the same time. If therefore God had helped you to look at the great mercy of God with joy, and yet with shame and bitter mourning that ever you should dishonor such a God; certainly God has vouchsafed your life. And such a life as in which you shall live. You shall have many a soul that is marvelously comforted in hearing the word, rejoice exceedingly in what they hear, and go home and say such a word was good and very comfortable. And never man spoke like that man, and he never thought before that there was so much to be found in the word, as now he conceives there is.

But now, if this were the joy of God's elect; if it were such a joy as would not vanish away like lightning in the air—a flash of joy—it would sink down into the heart, and leave so much the more deeper impression mourning by how much the more it has had joy. I grant that sometimes the joy of God's own servants may soon vanish away, but it was never known that the joy of a living Christian did so soon vanish and depart away, but that when it did most abound in the heart, it did cause inward mourning. And if not weeping, yet an affection of grief and sorrow of soul, that ever we have so displeased God, the more God has been merciful to us, the more are we ashamed of ourselves, and inwardly grieve for our shameless carriages.

If therefore you only find joy in hearing that may deceive you, it is not the shortness of the continuance that argues the unsoundness of the joy, but the want of this combination that will argue the falsehood of it. If God yoke not spiritual joy with spiritual mourning, then suspect your joy, for it does not accompany salvation unto life. And in very deed, this you shall find to be true, the joy of living souls in Christ, though that oftentimes be soon gone, yet it leaves this spirit of mourning, which keeps possession for it, and that many times for a long time. And you may read your comfort in the sorrow that it has left behind. For there is as much cause of comfort in this sorrow, as in the joy when you had it. When you see your souls can mourn unfeignedly, for that you see so good a God to such a wretch—this very comfortable sorrow that is left in your heart is an undoubted pledge that it is not a vanishing joy, the power and work of it lasts long, and will abide in the soul forever. A man will in such a case mourn for his sin while he lives. If you have therefore found your joy mixed with sorrow it is right, else it is but a fading, hypocritical, and false joy.

Again further, how do you find your heart affected with the duties of God's worship? Do you come to duties marvelous unwillingly, that if you could avoid it you would not keep such duties in your house, and if it must needs be, you put it upon anybody rather than upon yourself? You may be a living Christian but your heart is in a dead frame at that time. And if it be always so with you, you never did truly live. But if you find your spirits, at least your hearts coming on most willingly to Christian duties that you perform them like free-will offerings, not free, so as without warrant from God's Word, but free in respect of grace. Do but observe thus much, it may be you may come off freely before God, because He has given you spiritual gifts, and you can quit yourselves well in the performance of them, and that makes you come the more boldly.

But consider, if the more willingly you come to Christian duties, the more trembling your heart goes about them. The more the soul is prepared, the more it fears before the Lord. And the more lowly the spirit is, and awful in the sight of God; if a man can serve the Lord with joy, and trembling together, then the service you perform to God is heavenly, and spiritual, and lively. And such as in which you live, they come from a living heart, and the sacrifice is lively and acceptable, and argues you have life, and therein you have Christ the God of peace. But if a man have only fear in a duty, but no joy—or joy, but no fear—his heart is not in a good frame, we must bring a better frame of heart before God then so, before we can say that we have the life of sanctification.

Again, for another sign: How do you find yourselves in your tribulations? Are they altogether matter of burden and weariness to your hearts? Have you no joy in them? Have you many afflictions in inward, or in outward man, and no comfort in them? It is an uncomfortable sign to you; the life of sanctification is not so shed abroad in your hearts that you may gather you have life. But if you find that in the "multitude of your thoughts within you, God's comforts delight your soul" (Ps. 94:19, 20). In the midst of sorrow you find some comfort, if your life in Christ makes your saddest times joyful and comfortable to you. And so in outward afflictions, though afflictions may seem to be grievous, yet wait a while, and you shall see the more weight and burden that lies upon you. And the "more your afflictions for Christ have abounded, so has your consolation abounded much more" (2 Cor. 1:6).

Again, observe your carriage with men. It is good to be patient when you meet with evildoers (2 Tim. 2). Yet notwithstanding not so patiently as to bear with them in everything that is evil, to allow them in any sin; no, if God give you place and opportunity show some kind of zeal to cleanse them from their evils, and this may well stand with your patience. Be patient in things that concern yourself, but bear not with them that are evil in their evil deeds.

Again, do but observe the frame of your Spirit in the things that you suffer. Are you meek and gentle and flexible? That is a good virtue; but how are you in the things of God? Are you stiff and immoveable there? (1 Cor. 15:58); that though they may persuade you very far in any reasonable thing concerning man, but in things concerning God, you will not bait anything of the peace of your conscience for any man's pleasure. Are you immoveable in such a case? Both these together do very well, steadfast and yet soon persuaded; such a heart as is thus mixed, and knows how to temper and frame his spirit according to God. He is a living soul, and has life, and Christ the Prince of life.

Again, you are a modest creature, and thinking mainly of yourself, and art weaned from this world. It is a virtue, but how is it coupled. For God couples every grace with another grace, that they may poise one another. As Christ sent out His disciples, by two and two together; so all the graces of the Spirit join one with another. They balance one another that he may not be too high on the one side, nor too low on the other, but that all things may be carried according to God. And therefore you are modest.

It is well, but have you withal a high and a lofty spirit, that if it be heavenly matters you are to be exercised in, they cannot be too high for you. Let a man tell you of state matters, coming before princes. And tell you of nobility, you are ashamed, and know not how to set about such things as those be. But tell you of an inheritance in the Kingdom of glory, and the making it sure to you in a way of God's grace. Tell you of pardon of sin, and of the Spirit of grace, and the riches of the precious promises of God, and your heart can look at these highly. Then you are of a magnanimous spirit. Then is your modesty in outward things well-coupled. But he whose spirit is most lofty should be most humble. Couple them together and they well suit one another. When they go hand in hand, righteousness and peace go together, modesty and magnanimity, humility and courage go together. They make an amiable set of grace where ever they are so coupled. If it be of things concerning yourself, you have not a heart to stand out against any man of place, but he may bow you round about. But if they wrong you so far as God's honor is interested in the thing, you can then stand upon your lawful rights. And if therein you be impeached, you can come off with this, "you are not inferior to the chief apostles," and yet "are nothing," nor are able to do anything.

Again, look at your worldly business, are you diligent in your calling? It is well; and you say, "Cursed is he that does the work of the Lord negligently," and the work of his calling is the work of the Lord. But how stands your heart affected in the midst of your business? Is your heart dead to the world, go not about it with a worldly heart, go not about it for profit sake, but because God sets you about it? And you are more free to the service of God, and to do more good. This is the life of sanctification.

And lastly, if God give us hearts so abundant in love that it both thaws our cold and stiff hearts towards our poor brethren, and also puts a watery temper to cool the wildfire of our wrath towards our enemies; it is a mighty power of the Spirit of grace to turn itself so many ways. For the right ordering and framing of a Christian in the course of his sanctification. These be comfortable signs of our life of sanctification.

~ *Sermon 9* ~
THE EFFECTS OF SANCTIFICATION IN THE NATURAL LIFE

He that has the Son has life, and he that has not the Son has not life.
(1 John 5:12)

Now we come to speak of such effects of the life of sanctification as show themselves in the lives of Christians by observing of which in ourselves we may know we have Christ, and life in Him. Now these effects are suitable to the effects of *natural life*, and they are principally five.

THE FIRST EFFECT OF NATURAL LIFE: MOTION

The first is *motion*. When a creature is able to move itself unto the duties of its place. It is an effect of natural life. When it is able to move itself in its place, then it is said to live such or such a life. If you see a creature stirs and moves not further than by the help of another, then you say it lives not. But if it stir of itself, then you say it lives. Nor is it strait way alive if it move unless it be in its place. For you see earthly things will move downward, if they be upward, and light things will move upward. But these are out of their places, they are rather moved then themselves do move, when they are out of their place; and it is not so much from a power of moving, but rather an affection to rest than a power to move themselves.

And further, suppose they should move themselves, meet it as they should move themselves to such actions as argues as argue this, and that life which they express. Suppose a tree moves itself, and nourish itself, and grow, and that in its place, yet it does not move itself to see, nor hear. And beasts that do move themselves to see, and hear, yet they cannot move themselves to acts of reason. And men that can move to acts of reason, yet cannot move themselves to any spiritual duty and work of grace. So that, that motion which argues the life of the soul is a power to move itself, and in its place unto spiritual duties, that is the true nature of the life of sanctification. Do you therefore see a creature no further moving itself than according to its lightness?

You shall sometimes have men to move themselves out of their levity, come to an eminent duty in the pride of their natures, and will lift themselves up to some duties. But this is not out of an inward principle, but out of the lightness of their spirit's desire to be above, will move them to this and that duty, and rather move from hence than from any inward principle of grace. And so sometimes creatures, out of their heaviness and baseness of mind will be doing spiritual duties, but as the one does them to be seen of men, and perform the mere letter of the duty, and in the pride of his heart, not out of any inward affection to such duties. So there be others that for profit sake will move themselves basely unto spiritual duties. As Christ said of His hearers, they followed Him "for loaves" (John 6:26).

So that it is one thing to move to such or such a business, or to be stirring about such duties out of an inward affection to the duty and inclination of heart. And love of such a work, and another thing to be carried to such works out of an inward levity of nature, or because by such duties a man may excel others and go beyond his neighbors. And it is one thing to be acting and stirring in spiritual duties out of an inward love to them, and another to perform them out of a base respect to the profit, and pleasure that may be found in them in outward peace and rest. As sometimes the case so stands that if a man do betake himself to spiritual duties, he shall perhaps find the more favor in the eyes of men and to please authority, if it take the better side. And so from a heavy baseness of their hearts to such regards, they will have respect unto spiritual duties. But these do not move but as heavy things move, downward, and light things upward; a stone will move downward, and fire upward.

Absalom had a marvelous strong affection to be doing. He tells them every man should have justice, "if he was but made king in the land, so all Israel desired after him"

(2 Sam. 15:4). But Absalom was now out of his place, but as soon as ever he got into the place he desired, the first thing he intended was to cut off his father's life—an act of the greatest rebellion that ever could be done. So that men out of their places are apt to be stirring and moving, but it is but either from the baseness or lightness of their hearts. "O that I were but in my master's place," says a servant, "I would have duties performed in such time and place." And when they come to be in place, and might order and command their families, then they grow as bad as their masters. And it may be worse, but this are we apt to do when we are out of our places, apt to be moving, but it's not true life. Because only that which moves in its place that only lives. And yet further, a thing may move in its place, and yet move from some kind of outward respects; as a watch, or a clock, it moves, but it is from the weight that lies and hangs upon it, and so it is rather a violent motion than a natural.

So is it many times with men, the weight of the law, or the weight of the authority of governors does so carry them an end in those ways they walk in that they go through with it, and yet it is but from an outward principle from some outward weights that hangs upon them. But yet, suppose men should be doing in their places as Jehu was. He was mighty in his place, and was very much against Baal, and destroyed the house of Ahab, and his children, and his friends. But yet notwithstanding though this was all in his calling, he had a special calling given him of God to that end. But though you should perform duties in your places as a tree though it move in its place upward, yet it puts not forth. So many a man may do good duties in his place, and yet be wanting in the graciousness and spirituality of them.

Requirements of Our Spiritual Duty

Now to make a duty spiritual requires not only that it should be for the better a good work, but that it should be wrought.

First, in sense of our own insufficiency without Christ, and yet so, as that by and from Christ we are able to do it.

Secondly, that we have some respect to the Word of God for our warrant.

Thirdly, that in all we do, we have respect to the glory of God in all our performances, "I live by the faith of the Son of God" (Gal. 2:20). "The just shall live by his own faith" (Hab. 2:4; Rom. 1:17; Gal. 3:11). As if he should say he no further puts forth a work of spiritual life, further than he denies his own ability, so far he lives by his faith and depends upon Christ for supply in every duty he goes about. Whether he pray, preach, or receive Sacraments, or be diligent in his calling, or in his carriage towards any that stand in relation to him. So far as we are sensible of our own failings, and therefore do depend upon him for strength; there are not such as come from common graces, but do accompany sanctification to life.

Common Gifts

It is true, if men be invested with common gifts, they may be acted and moved to many duties in their places, and put out very sweet affections to the duty. And yet do it rather out of the power of their own strength, and rather for their own glory and applause than from any dependence upon Christ. So that spiritual life has the Lord Jesus for its root, and the Word for its warrant, and for its rule to walk by: "Then shall I never be ashamed, when I have respect unto all Your commandments" (Ps. 119:6). All such actions will be acceptable to God, and serviceable to men, and also aim at the glory of God for the end, that is, their last end. And all such other ends as are subordinate unto that, the building up of God's Kingdom. "When you did eat, did you it unto Me, says the Lord? Nay, did you not do it to yourselves?" (Zech. 7:5-7). "They have not cried unto Me with their heart when they howled upon their beds" (Hos. 7:14). Did you desire in your prayers to bring in any service to God, to tend to His honor and glory? And did you debase your own souls before Him, that you might find help from Him? Or, did you not this to yourselves, or for your own deliverance, and redemption, and freedom from such bondage and other miseries that lay upon you, so that if God see men go about such duties merely for themselves, they are wanting of this spiritual life?

So then, do but lay these things together. Do you find a man that is desirous to be doing good duties, but is it to please others, or is it out of the bonds of authority that lies upon him? Do you see them have affection to duties, but out of their place and calling, or in their calling? They do such duties but rather out of their own strength than from the strength of Christ, and not out of a conscionable respect to all the commandments of God. Or if it be from outward principles, and to wrong ends, the glory of God not sought after, nor tending to the building up themselves, nor others in grace. All these are such as men may be carried to do from outward respects. They may do something that one would think would argue life, but all the duties they do by their own strength is like a spider that weaves a web out of her own bowels. We follow not the rule of the Word exactly, but are ever wheeling about to our own ends, and to those respects that concern ourselves rather than to the glory of God and the Church's good.

It is true, no man has common graces. Men that have gifts of preaching, and gifts of praying may love to act, and move them, or any other zealous gift; but yet notwithstanding you shall find this to be true that till the heart be sanctified by the life of Christ, we ever detain all the graces of God in unrighteousness. As the Romans and Gentiles did detain the truth of God in unrighteousness (Rom. 1:18). So we by a spirit of hypocrisy detain all the graces of God in unrighteousness and in hypocrisy. Whereas God has given us every grace, and the manifestation thereof to edify Himself and to glorify God withal. We wonderfully magnify ourselves withal, and make ourselves goodly in the eyes of men. We are full of ourselves and think we have this and that in us that will serve our turn, and reach our own ends. This is not a life of grace, but is indeed a dead work all that we do, and therefore rest not in any such kind of life and motion.

But if you find an inward inclination of soul to spiritual duties, and to those duties in special that are pertinent to your place, and if they be not within the compass of your calling, you dare not reach unto them; and in your calling, you do them not out of desire to be seen of men, but you are doing good duties out of a sense of your own inability to reach any duty in your calling, much less of God's service, and in them all you observe every commandment of God, and the ends you aim at are singly that God may be glorified, and that God may see you, and not man; that good may be done by you in your places, in church, and family, and commonwealth, and that thereby others might be brought on to God and His Kingdom increased. This very motion and inclination of your hearts is an argument that you have a stirring spirit to spiritual duties, and this is spiritual life in Christ. And therefore, by how much the more God shall give you a heart to be doing your works and duties in this order, so much the more comfort you shall gather to your souls that undoubtedly Christ has shed abroad His Spirit in you by which you are able to do that which else you could not have reached unto.

THE ISSUE OF DEADNESS OF HEART

There is the question: You say unto me, may not a good Christian man have his heart so dead that he is unfit to pray, or preach, or to instruct his family, or for the duties of his calling; fit, and good for nothing: And is a soul in such a case as this altogether void of spiritual life, and sanctification? Is there not sometimes a kind of a coath[4] come upon a Christian that so benumbs his spirit that he performs no duties at all, but if he might have his own mind, he would not pray at all, nor receive Sacraments? Is not this sometimes the case of a Christian? And will you say that such a one is a dead soul, because he is altogether listless, and dead-hearted to move to any spiritual duty?

CAUSES OF DEADNESS OF HEART

It is true, there may fall such a deadness upon the heart of Christian men, that they are both unable and unwilling to any spiritual duty. Which commonly God leaves His servants unto when He has found them acting and moving in their own strength, and upon their detaining of the graces of God in unrighteousness, and diverting

---

[4] sickness, disease

them rather to their own praise in the world than the edifying of the people of God, or the glorifying of His own name. When God sees we are much of ourselves and think we can do much by the strength of grace we have received, then God is wont to leave us cold and dead. So as we know not in the world what to do, nor are we willing to do anything. The very presence of a duty, and the thoughts of it, is a horror to such souls in such cases. We have been too busy in our own strength, and too mighty in the grace we have received. And rather aimed at ourselves than at Him, and then no marvel if God leave us to a world of deadness.

Remedies Against Deadness

But when God has thus by this means let us see that all our life is in Him, and that we are dead-hearted further than we have life from Him, then God is wont not to fail, but to help us thus far at the least, to look with a wist, and a sad eye upon the forlornness of our estates, and to cry out of ourselves, "O what dead hearted creatures, and dull-spirited things are we!" And bemoan ourselves as Paul did in Romans 7:18, "I see that in me, that is, in my flesh, dwells no good thing." Sometimes I have a mind to do good duties, but I find that I have no strength to perform. Paul comes to Macedonia, and he had an open door, a fair calling to preach, but he had no heart to it, because he found not Titus his brother there. Now when this is the case of a Christian man, that he is straight and dead-hearted, he groans under the burden of it. And he looks at it with a sad countenance, and sees he is not well, but is ready to complain of it. Now this sense and complaint of deadness, and using the best means to raise himself up out of this deadness, this is an action of spiritual life.

It is an act of spiritual life for a man to be sensible of his own deadness, which in time works the soul of a Christian to a more constant dependence upon Christ for life, and makes him more observable of the Word, and more ingenuous and sincere in looking at the glory of God, and the Church's good more than his own. And by how much the more we come to this pass, and the more we have respect to the Word as our daily rule, so much the more all our stirrings in our callings is a motion of spiritual life, and argues the life of sanctification, shed abroad in our hearts.

THE SECOND EFFECT OF NATURAL LIFE: FEEDING

Secondly, another action of life is feeding, the creature that feeds itself is able to live; "Except you eat My flesh, and drink My blood, you have no life in you" (John 6:53). He does not speak of the Sacrament of the Lord's Supper there, for it was not then instituted. But yet it is true of that as well as of any other Ordinance of God—the body and blood of Christ, fed upon in Word and Sacrament, and Christian communion, in hearing and reading the Word. And if Christ had ordained more Ordinances than He had, yet when He has ordained any spiritual ordinance, the feeding upon Christ in that Ordinance had been an argument of spiritual life. "Except you eat His flesh and drink His blood, you have no life in you."

This is an argument of spiritual life. When a man in every duty that he takes in hand, and is sensible in them all in some measure, though not always easy to be discerned at first. But if in every duty of Christianity that you perform, and in every Ordinance of God you feed upon Christ, then you have life in Christ. So that, let a man observe it: you hear the Word, and you receive Sacraments, and you partake in Christian company—Do you eat the flesh of Christ there? And drink His blood there? If so, then it is well. When you hear the Word is the blood of Christ, or is the flesh of Christ there? Or is either of both there to feed upon? Or in prayer, or in any other duty that you take in hand, do you feed upon Christ in it? If you feed upon Him there, you have life, and he that feeds not, lives not. If a man forbear his meat he cannot long subsist. It is true, a man may live for a while and find no relish in anything, but in time he must find relish in them, else he cannot be preserved.

Question: *But how shall I know that I do feed upon Christ in every Ordinance?*

Answer: First, whether do you find an inward longing desire in your souls after the Lord Jesus Christ in the duties you go about? Do you come with a desire to find

Christ in His Ordinance, hungering and thirsting, and not satisfied unless you find Christ? That is the nature of hungering and thirsting, and so is the case here. This desire and thirst is such an unquenchable desire as that without Christ it is by no means satisfied. Do you therefore find an inward longing to find and meet with the Lord Jesus in the Word that you read or hear, or in the Sacraments that you receive? And such a longing desire as that, if you find not Christ there, you go away poor and dead, and finding your hearts unsatisfied is an evident sign of life, for you came to an Ordinance, and desired to find Christ there, and there He was not? What then in Songs 3:1-3, to the bed of the Ordinances? The Church goes to seek and to find Christ, "by night I sought Him," that was in a time of calamity, that she could plainly discern she found Him not, and she sought Him in every other Ordinance, but found Him not. Or sign of life; she hungers, and sought out after Him, but could not find Him, and when she missed Him was not satisfied.

If a man come to an Ordinance and find nothing there, and yet when he is gone, he is satisfied, he is well enough. That soul has either no life at all, or life in a swound,[5] or cold without stirring and motion; there is not an hungering desire after Him, when you can come and go away unsatisfied, and yet be well contented too.

---

[5] the act of fainting

Secondly, feeding has another work. The former is but a preparation, or supposition of feeding. But a man also then feeds when he finds some sweetness and relish in the meat that he eats that does ever accompany feeding. And is a sign that a man does feed, the stomach does well affect the meat it feeds on. Have you then found some sweet relish in the Ordinances? "The gospel is a sweet savor to them that are saved" (2 Cor. 2:15, 16), and as for savor to smell, so as a sweet savor to the taste. Do you therefore find some kind of sweetness, a spiritual sweetness in the Word you hear, or read, or Sacraments you receive, or prayers that you make? Are they such a comfort or sweetness to you that you find in this or that promise, or commandment, or doctrine, any word of life? Do you find strength and sweetness in it? It is an evident sign of life because you find sweetness in it. It's a sign of health to relish a sweetness in our meat. For a sick man, it may be he eats and drinks, but he finds no sweetness in it. And that is a part of his complaint that he cannot relish his meat. And it is true, it may be a man that has some life in him feels no relish, no favor in any Ordinance. But then he sees he is sick, and he complains of it to God, but yet notwithstanding if a man do find sweetness and relish there. It is an evident argument not of life only, but of health, and such as will maintain spiritual life. But if a man find no sweetness in it he cannot live, for were there life, it would find sweetness.

Thirdly, in all feeding there is a taking of the meat down, and not spitting it out. But we receive it down, and there it lies in our stomachs, and we chew upon it, and there it rests. But if we cast it up again, then we feed not. It is an ill sign when we cast it away as soon as we receive it. If God's Word abide with us, and in us, that we do not reject it, but "hide it in our hearts, that so we might not sin against God" (Ps. 119:11). And receive it by a wise applying of it to our own souls, receive it into the inward man. And apply ourselves to every duty commanded us, so far as concerns our callings, and our estates, and takes notice of every threatening, that we had need look to it, so far as we might sin against God. If we thus take the Word of God down into our hearts, and make it our own case, and therefore keep it within ourselves, and give up ourselves in some measure to be bowed by it, and hide it in our hearts, and lets it sit next our hearts, then truly we do feed upon it, and it secretly conveys strength into us, though sometimes we less discern it.

Fourthly, all feeding contains in it a conversion of the meat into the thing nourished, so as that which we feed upon, it becomes ourselves. It is all one with ourselves; in time it is so digested, and turned into our nature that every part has sucked in its own nourishment. Every part has received something of that which was inwardly received. This has been anciently observed. This is somewhat more than receiving Christ by faith, for when we apply every word to ourselves and make Christ ours, that is receiving Him to be ours. Yet it is a further work to be conformable to the Lord Jesus Christ in everything to be confirmed and established in the promises. And to be quickened by them, to be terrified by threatenings, and to stand in awe of every word of God, and to be bowed to an inward subjection to Christ, day by day, by the word we receive; this is a further mighty work of grace.

If therefore he be a Christian that by the Word and Ordinances he receives, he is fashioned and made conformable to Christ; meek, and righteous, and lowly, and holy as He is. And willing to do any good office for the Church of God, and go up and down doing good, and needs no further motion this way. But as Christ moves him, it is a sign that he feeds upon Christ. Christ is turned into his nature, or which is more, his nature is rather turned into the nature of Christ; the nourishment being so strong makes us become "such as He is in this world."

Now, when we are conformable to the Lord Jesus Christ by the Ordinances that we partake in, it is an evident sign that we there feed upon Him. And therefore try yourselves by this sign of sanctification: if you live, you live, you feed on Christ, and except you so do, you have no life in you. So then consider, do I "feed upon the flesh of Christ, and drink His blood," and do I find a spiritual appetite to the Lord Jesus raised up in my soul? And do I find any spiritual refreshment and strength by that which I do partake in? And that which I so find sweetness in, I apply it to my own estate, and convey it into the inward part of my heart, that I may be able to drink it up as my lot and portion. And do I by this strength of grace grow like to Christ? And do I more "adorn the gospel of Christ" (Titus 2:10)? This is an evident sign you live. For you feed upon spiritual food, which is an argument of spiritual life. So man can feed upon spiritual food, but he that lives, and such a life as he lives in Christ. Let a man come to the Word without an appetite to it, and when he comes find no nourishment nor refreshment in it, and applies nothing as is said to him; but let such and such look to it, he never hears profitably that does not particularly apply that which he hears. And if he apply it, he rather storms at it. It is an evident argument that such a man has no life in him at all.

Not that you should here look at the natural body and blood of Christ, for that were a cannibal eating and drinking. That which the Church of Rome puts upon the Church of God at this day. But our Savior tells you the meaning of this place, "It is the Spirit that quickens, the flesh profits nothing" (John 6:63). Had a company of Roman Soldiers fallen upon Christ, and either out of wrath against Him or love to themselves had pulled Him in pieces and eaten Him, goblet by goblet, it had profited them nothing. Had men eaten the real body of Christ and drunk up His blood, and joined with others in so doing, and left none of Him, all this had profited them nothing. No, it profits nothing.

For the Capernites ask the question, "How can this man give us His flesh to eat? It is a hard saying," they thought it incredible (John 6:52). They would think it a savage brutishness to fall upon Him in that manner. And therefore our Savior so confesses that it is no part of His meaning that they should eat and drink His real body and blood. But He means the breathing of the Spirit in the Ordinances. If you can relish, and feed upon that, and grow to be such as Christ was in this world that was the meat and drink of his soul. If you grow humble and meek, and be transformed into the spirit of Christ, if you see your spirits conformable to the will of Christ, it is a sign of the life of holiness in your souls, which God has given you through Christ.

THE THIRD EFFECT OF NATURAL LIFE: GROWTH

A third effect of the life of sanctification is *growth*. For that which lives, grows till it come to its full perfection. So in all natural, vegetative, or sensitive life; if it live, it grows, till it come to its full maturity. When it comes to its full vigor and strength, it may decay and stand at a stay. But a Christian's life never comes to that till it come to the life of glory to the full measure of the stature of Christ. In this life we cannot come to that, but therefore it is that we grow to the end of our days, and then are forthwith translated to immortality, "you desire the sincere milk of the word, that you may grow thereby" (1 Pet. 2:2) and "grow in grace" (2 Pet. 3:18). And God has given us ministers to teach and instruct us, "will we all grow to be perfect in Christ Jesus" (Eph. 4:11-13); "Increase with the increasings of God" (Col. 2:19), with divine and enlarged and spiritual increasing, so does the body of Christ grow, and all the members of it. They grow in grace, and in the knowledge of the Lord Jesus Christ.

So that this is a third effect of life, if a man can find his heart to grow.

Question: *But does not many a Christian stand at a stay, and sometimes grow backward, and fall from their first love, fall from the fruitfulness and goodness and rootedness in Christ, though not wholly cut off, yet falling from the firmness in grace, and the power of grace, and from fruitfulness, and the abundance of the work of righteousness.*

Answer: It is true, many a soul does so for a while. But if so be that God do give a Christian man not to grow, we must not say therefore he does not live. Not but that a man for a time may be weak; as a living man in sickness may be very weak, his spirit fail, and his strength fail, and his work and employment fails him. And he can do nothing, neither eat, nor drink, no not so much as lean upon a staff, but may lie bedridden. But yet such a man feels a sensible distemper of his body, and he ceases not to use the best means he can, and so in the end he comes to grow and recovers his first love again in some measure. Some also there are that by sinful lusts waste, instead of growing, as a thief in a candle wastes it, but if there be a thief in the heart, a lurking lust in the soul. A living soul is not well till it be removed, by some good means or other, that so it may recover itself.

It is sometimes the case of a Christian, as David speaks in Psalm 39: "Oh, spare a little that I may recover my strength." So a Christian man, if he find himself in a decay, that he is dead and heartless in every spiritual performance. Oh, then spare a little, that I may recover my strength. Now he is afraid to die in such a case, but he would now have some time that he may recover his first love and his first fruits, and that his faith might not vanish away in ashes and smoke. If he see that his spirit decays, he considers then "whence he is fallen…and repents, and does his first works" (Rev. 2:4, 5). This is the nature of repentance—it purges out. It purges out the noisome humors that brought the body into languish and decay. Repentance is the chiefest purge. And so then we do our first works, and attain to our first love, and grow more at the last than at the first (Rev. 2:19). And therefore this is to be considered of—A Christian man is a growing man, if not always in the bulk, which is easy to be discerned, as to grow in strength and rootedness, *etc.* yet surely he grows to more sweetness of spirit.

An apple is sometimes grown to full growth upon a tree yet grows not sweet till a good time after, but in time it will. So a Christian, though it may be he shall never get more knowledge than he has, or more ability, but though the case so stand, that you are like to grow no further; yet you may grow to more sweetness, and mellowness, to more love to your brethren, and be more ready to deny yourselves of that arrogance of spirit, and pride he is now addicted to.

And so a Christian grows in sweetness, and grows in rootedness of spirit, and sees his more want of Christ, and gets faster hold on Christ. And though he cannot grow more tall in his outward expression, nor more painful, yet in these two no Christian that grows. But if he be living and healthful, he grows in firmness and rootedness in Christ, and in great dependence upon Him from day to day in his ways. And he grows in more sweetness, aims more at God's glory, and is more in love to his brethren, and more denies himself in his own matters.

And if he grow not here, he is either no living Christian in truth, or no healthful Christian. And if a man see this, and not bewail his not growing in these, he has no life at all in him. A man that grows harsh and unsavory, and does not take a course to repent of it, it's a thousand to one there is no life at all in him. But if a man grow, though but in amiableness and self-denial, and more firmly in Christ, and more assured of God's grace and mercy, and more depend upon Christ for what he does, and can do nothing without Christ, and he knows it by experience that unless a man so grow, there is no life in him.

THE FOURTH EFFECT OF NATURAL LIFE: EXPULSION OF HARMFUL THINGS

Fourthly, another effect of the life of sanctification is this: life is such a thing as has an expulsive power to *expel* and drive out of the body that which is noisome and hurtful to it, and will cast and sweat it out. Nature cannot endure to be clogged with superfluity. Out it must, one way or other. Nature will ease itself, it cannot long subsist. Pain and sickness are grievous, and painful to nature. If anything trouble the stomach, or the body, out it must by vomit, or purge, it cannot stay if the man be living. So if grace be but living in the soul, there is an expulsive power in the soul that will purge away that which is contrary to it. It cannot endure superfluity, but away it must go. There it cannot stay, nothing will he keep, but that which is convenient for him.

A Christian, look whatsoever it be that a Christian finds superfluous, and finds contrary to the life of Christ in his soul, either too much, or contrary to his spirit, that he abandons it more or less by degrees, measure after measure, and time after time. So the Apostle exhorts in James 1:21, "Lay apart all filthiness and superfluity of naughtiness, *etc.*" If there be any thing which is superfluous or filthy, away with it. Let it not rest there; and if it be for no good purpose, let it have no rest in you.

There are many parts of knowledge that are not contrary to the life of sanctification, but are more than we shall have use of in our callings, and though they may be such things as others may make use of. Yet they are superfluous when they are of no use to us in our callings. Then put them away unless they be of use either for necessity, or expediency, then nature will cast them away, especially if they be naughty things. They are more than superfluous, then they are noisome and hurtful. And therefore a Christian man principally casts away that which is noisome and corrupt; both doubting and presumption is contrary to the life of faith, and therefore must be cast out, cast out all fears, and all self-confidence, "Perfect love casts out fear" (1 John 4:18). Faith strives against fear, and love strives against malice, and patience strives against frowardness, modesty against pride, and so every grace of God. Wonder to see how it will by degrees either sweat them out, or else set themselves by some serious duties of humiliation, and "so cleanse themselves from all filthiness of flesh and spirit, that he may grow to perfect holiness in the fear of God" (2 Cor. 7:1).

He is weary of it, and that life of grace casts out all the life of sin; he looks at the life of this world as something in it that is good. Yet so much of the world as he sees he cannot well manage, but with cumbrance to the Spirit of grace. He lays it aside and meddles not with it. He studies no more than to use in a practical life. He would live as David in Saul's armor, when he sees it troubles him he lays it aside. So shall you find it with a Christian, these things are unprofitable for him. Keep them out of your souls least they prove a snare to you. And whatever is superfluity cast it out, and whatever distracts you, and clogs you with cares, out with it; whatever is a burden to the life of grace, cast out all such things.

THE FIFTH EFFECT OF NATURAL LIFE: PROPAGATING ACCORDING TO ITS KIND

Fifthly, the last act of the life of sanctification is the begetting of the like and *propagating* according to their kind. It is the nature both of spiritual and natural life. It propagates its kind, though at the first it may be weak, yet it grows to that temper by which it may propagate. And the life of grace is most strong in this regard, it no sooner moves and feeds, or grows in any measure, or begins to expel any ill matter. But it will have a mind to be fruitful in begetting its kind. And that is above natural life, a Christian is most apt and ready to draw on others to be like himself.

As soon as ever, the woman of Samaria saw that Jesus was indeed the Messiah, and found true sweetness in Him. The very same hour she runs into the town and tells her neighbors, "Come see a man that has told me all that ever I did" (John 4:29), "Is not he the Christ?" And when they came and saw it they said, "We believe, not because of your word, but because we have heard Him ourselves, and we know that this is indeed the Christ." This is the proper nature of true life, as soon as they are truly begotten, they beget others of their own kind. Not but that sometimes a Christian soul hides himself long before he be well settled, but when he truly discerns that he lives, and is conscious to himself that God will be gracious to his soul. Then he desires to propagate the like grace unto others (John 1:41-46). When one had found Christ, they call others to come and see—"Then shall I teach transgressors Your ways, and sinners shall be converted to You" (Ps. 51:10); to show you that if God will but work a clean heart in David, and renew a right spirit within him; and his broken bones may be recovered, and if God shall be pleased to establish him with his free spirit, and he may be once again assured of the pardon his sins; then will he teach others the ways of God. If he be once converted himself, he will draw on as many others as he can. Thus you have five signs of spiritual life.

Discerning the Life by
Its Properties and Qualities

He that has the Son has life, and he that has not the Son has not life.
(1 John 5:12)

We are now in the next place to see how we may discern life by the properties and adjuncts of it. You heard before of the *effects* of life, now of the *properties and qualities* of this life by discerning of which we may know that we have life.

There be three properties or qualities of life.

THE FIRST PROPERTY OF LIFE: WARMTH

First, wherever there is life, there is some warmth. In 2 Kings 4:34, when the prophet had lain upon the child, and had done so seven times at length, the breath of the child began to wax warm, a sign that life was a restoring. And thereby the prophet discerned that life began to return into the body of the child because warmth returned. And so is the presence of the Spirit of grace, and the union of it with the soul and body of a man. It makes a man fervent and warm; "fervent in spirit"

(Rom. 12:11), and therefore it is that it is resembled unto fire (cf. Matt 3:11). "The Holy Ghost shall come down upon you, as it were with fiery tongues" (Acts 2), and shall warm and heat you. With whatever duties God shall call you to "quench not the Spirit" (1 Thes. 5:19). Now quenching belongs to fire; a sign therefore that the spirit is of a fervent nature, so far forth as it is capable of any quenching and destroying by the sons of men. And 2 Timothy 1:6, "Stir up the gifts of grace in you," as if you stirred up the embers of the fire, so stir up and kindle the gifts of God which is in you. Blow them up into a kindling flame, so that all these things express thus much; that since the Spirit of life which is in Christ Jesus and from Him, communicated to His members is a spirit of heat. Therefore wherever there is warmth, there is life. If no warmth, nor heat, there is no life. And as our spirits begin to wax warm, so we grow to life in Christianity.

Notable is that expression in Luke 24:32; "Did not our hearts burn within us, while He talked with us of the Scriptures?"—to show you that there is a power in the Word to convey such a measure of the Spirit of grace to the hearers, as that their hearts begin to glow within them, and to convey some heat and warmth into them when the Word is powerfully applied to the soul.

FOUR ASPECTS OF WARMTH

For the further opening of this point, you shall see it in some things principally, which are ever found in some measure in the spirits of Christian men that have any life in Christ.

Knowledge

First, that which is wonderful, and is indeed nowhere found but in them. Their very knowledge is warm, which in all other men is cold. Knowledge is but an empty speculation, brings forth no great matter of heat. But in a Christian, his knowledge is full of heat. "Zeal must be according to knowledge," knowledge is no knowledge without zeal, and zeal is but a wild-fire without knowledge (Rom. 10:2). So if Christians have a knowledge of God but no zeal, there is no saving life in that knowledge. It is not the knowledge of God's people.

Notable is that speech of our Savior in John 5:35 (speaking of John), "He was a burning and a shining light," not only "a shining light" to give clear instruction in the knowledge of the Messiah, and the true meaning of the Law; but withal "a burning light," so as that he had a notable power when hypocrites came before him to burn them up (Matt. 3:12). And so wherever he came he did not only show them what they should do, what shall we publicans do, and what shall we soldiers do? (Luke 3:3-15). But he did burn up not only those who were professed enemies to the ways of grace, but all those that he found in hypocrisy. He burnt them all up wherever he came, and if he did not find out their lusts, he would kindle a fire in them. He warmed Herod in such sort, as that he was constrained to do many things, according to John's ministry (Mark 6). And so shall you find it in all the servants of God that according to their life, if there be true life, there is true burning, though sometimes their burning is not so strong as their life. Yet there is heat and fervency of spirit mixed with their knowledge that, if they know the will of God they are inflamed, and their knowledge of Christ will not suffer them to "be barren and unfruitful" (2 Pet. 1:8).

So that the knowledge which a Christian man has is such, as by which he will do what he ought to do. If he see sin in his brother he will not suffer it to lie there (Lev. 19:17). If he see anything amiss in his brother that he sees not in himself, he will be helpful to him. Where the Spirit of grace is lively, they will not suffer their brethren to rest in sin, much less themselves. And therefore this is the warmth of this knowledge. It both burns up their own lusts like chaff, and all the sinful distempers that we see in the lives and ways of our brethren. This is one part of the heat of a Christian soul, that his knowledge is a warm knowledge. Look what he knows he thinks he must do, whereas another man knows many things, but he does them not. But a Christian, if he know it to be the will of God he must do it. And that is the reason why God's servants are many times counted very busy, as indeed the fire is ever very busily working. No creature in the house so busy as the fire is. And so the knowledge of God's people makes them to be so busy in doing, and therein they express the life of Christ.

Breath

Secondly, wherever is true life there is this warmth, a warmth in their breath, both in the natural and spiritual body. In this natural body, while we live, it is warm. And so long as we live we breathe more or less. It is but for a little time, if at all, breath be intercepted. It may be in some sudden fits, but ordinarily if it tarry long it is a sign of death. But if there be life, there is breathing. And that breathing is warm, some warm breath comes from him that is alive. And truly so shall you find it in your spiritual life.

If there be any true life in the heart of a Christian soul, there is always some kind of warm breathing. There is some measure of warmth in his prayers; the prayers of a hypocrite is always but lip-labor, and accordingly lust-labor. The words vanish away in the air, but there is ever more or less some kind of warmth in the prayers of God's servants. According to what the Apostle speaks, "even then when we know not what to pray for, nor how to pray as we ought then the Spirit helps our infirmities" (Rom. 8:26); that when we sometimes cannot bring out a word to God, the heart is full sometimes of anguish and discouragement in respect of inward desertions, or temptations, and outward afflictions. But yet though in such a case we be not able to tell what to pray for, yet there is ever in a Christian soul something that makes him seek to God, and the very sighs of such a soul come from some warmth of spirit within him. The scalding sighs and deep groans of the soul, they come from a spirit of life and warmth in Christ Jesus. Therefore though it be true, there be many cold prayers that God's servants do put up, yet there are some kind of sighs and groans that springs from them, which argues some heat and life in them.

And so is it, as they breathe thus to Godward, so do they breathe one to another. So that if they speak of the things of God, they speak not of God and His Word lightly and wantonly or loosely, as those that have no affection to them. But if they speak of the Word of God, of His threatenings, promises, or of any of His commandments, or any of the works of His providence, they speak not of them coldly, as those that took no pleasure in them. But if they speak of any of the things of God, they speak with some reverence, and desire after them, and settling a confirmation in them. They have love to the Word, and rejoice in it, and stand in awe, and in fear of it, and they exercise their hearts and wits about it. When at any time they speak of the things of God, so that there is some kind of warmth in the expression of a

Christian in some savory affection, whereby he esteems of the things of God above what is found in a hypocrite.

Soul

Thirdly, there is a certain kind of warmth by which the soul does not only affect the Ordinances of God, but by which it does in some measure digest them. There is no living man wanting some such measure of heat as makes him able to digest some kind of diet, though not always strong meat, especially if he be in any measure of health. And that is no small measure of heat, "the very longing desire, it always has to God's judgements" (Ps. 119:20); was it that even made his soul to break within him, and so to pant after God's Word, and His presence in His Ordinances (Psalm 42:1). There was a kind of panting, and longing, and eager desire after God by which it comes to pass that the soul of a Christian closes with God in His Ordinances, and turns them into nourishment within himself, and so is more strongly, and inwardly bent towards God in the ways of His grace. Whereas a dead spirit is flat, and has no affection to the Word, no affection to God's presence, no list to the things of this nature.

Mutual Kindling

Fourthly, things that are warm, put them together and they are the more warm. But put cold clogs and pieces of wood together, and they are never a whit the warmer. But if you take but two or three of them things that are well-kindled, and they will set all a fire that comes nigh them. Though ready before to go out for want of supply, if you lay two or three warm brands together, they will kindle one another. And truly so it is among Christians, take you a Christian that has this spiritual warmth in him, though almost benumbed for want of good company, and good conference, and breathing forth of God's Spirit and grace in the soul. Yet if he meet with two or three like himself, they presently begin to kindle one another. And the breath of such Christians is like bellows to blow up sparks one in another, and so in the end they breathe forth many savory and sweet expressions of their hearts, and edify themselves by their mutual fellowship one with another.

Yes, and sometimes they grow so warm by this means, as that they are fit to admonish one another, to exhort, and to comfort, and if need require, to rebuke one another, as occasion serves. "Have fervent love one to another, above all things have fervent love among yourselves" (1 Pet. 4:8). This is a special thing: love among Christians, by which love they so kindle one another to such deep respects to God, the ways of His grace, and so burn one out of another. Much sinful folly and frailty which will be in them that are so loose one to another, and raises them up to that power of godliness, which sometimes they had grown up unto, and now almost lost for want of often joining together. For by so doing, they do what they can to put out the fire.

When Satan means to put out the light and life of religion, out of both Church and Commonwealth, he lays one Christian in one corner, and another in another, that they shall, when they list, go to bed, and sleep. And then a lazy spirit shall come upon them, and so they lie, till they be dead in trespasses and sins. But above all things, have fervent love among yourselves, "forsake not the fellowship you have one with another, as the manner of some is" (Heb. 10:25, 26). Love covers a multitude of sins. So as that though there was much evil in Christians before, yet their very lying together does burn out all that superfluity of naughty stuff that hangs about the servants of God. "See that you love one another with a pure heart, and fervency of spirit" (1 Pet. 1:22).

This warmth in Christians, it is found in these four things. And thus you see the properties of this life.

THE PROBLEM OF COLDNESS

To pose a question: You say, but if this were always found in Christian men, how comes it to pass then, that the servants of God do many times find their hearts so cold in their prayers, and appetite so little to the Word, and so unprofitable under it? How should a man hear so much and profit so little, if a man did digest the Word? And is it not a common complaint of Christians? How much they hear and how little they profit? Yes, and will not some Christians say, he profits nothing at all; no, not anything? And is it so many times that Christians come together, and they are little edification one to another, very little profit? Sit together, and talk of matters that little edify, but rather corrupt the spirits one of another? How is it then that you say, wherever there is life there is heat? So such as makes them more lively in Christian duties?

And it might be objected that Luke 24:32; "Did not our hearts burn within us?"—A sign that till He came to them, and came into conference with them, and did rub them up, they were very cold hearted and dull spirited, and went on their way with much darkness of soul, without life and strength of soul until He came to put life into their spirits?

A First Answer: Distraction and Dulling of the Heart

It is true, many times God's servants are very cold and benumbed. And a cold spirit grows upon them exceedingly, so as that they scarce feel any life breathing in their knowledge, or prayers, or appetites to the Word, or love to their brethren—little warmth in any of these, partly through want of supplying the life of God's grace with fit nourishment, whereby the heart should grow warm. As natural fire, if it be not supplied with new fuel it will go out, and partly sometimes, by pouring cold water upon it; which is as much as in us lies to damp the fire. And we do pour cold water upon this life of grace when we admit of any sinful lusts in our souls. Those do marvelously eat out all that life and heat of spirit that sometimes we had in our hearts. And sometimes by an excessive use of worldly things, which without a very spiritual mind does clog the soul, as much as if you should throw cold water upon a fire, it will damp it very much.

So is this case, men sometimes walk in worldly business with worldly affections, and sometimes give leave to distempered lusts, and sometimes neglect to put any fuel to the fire of grace. But as soon as ever they find the heart well warmed with some good sermon, or a good prayer, or conference, or the like, they think this fire will never go out, and so they begin to neglect it. And so either the fire goes quite out, or else is so damped, as that you can discern no life, no favor or power of religion there. And therefore such a thing may befall God's servants, they may grow dull hearted one way or other as you have heard. But yet thus much let me say, though this sometimes do befall the spirits of God's people, yet even then when they want burning and chafing, and stirring up, there is something in them that argues some life. And where is some life, there is some heat. So much life as there is, so much heat is there. So much as you take away of your Christian heat, so much life you take away.

And therefore for these two disciples that went to Emmaus, it is said when they were talking one with another, they were talking of Jesus Christ, and upon all the things that befell Him in His passion. And said Christ to them, "What manner of communication is this," and what is the matter that you are thus sad? (Luke 24:17); what was it that made them sad? Was it not an affection of grief for all the evils done to their Savior that was life of grace? And some heat there was in them that their spirits should be so troubled to see their elders and princes, and all the people to cry out so bitterly against the Lord Jesus Christ, and not to leave Him till they had crucified Him. There was some sad expression came from them upon that occasion. And so, though it left the outward man sad, yet there was something in the heart. Though full of doubting through unbelief, what this Christ was and what this would come to, "we hoped this was He that should redeem Israel, &c." Then Christ began to put a little warmth into them by saying, "ought not Christ to suffer these things?" (vv. 24, 25); and so, "He opens to them the Scriptures spoken of Himself." And these words put new life into them, and did blow up the spirit and heat of that decaying life which was overwhelmed with grief and care, their hearts was heated yet. So that take you a Christian man, when he is even in the most disordered frame, look how much he has lost of his spiritual heat, so much of his true life; if he have left to be warm, so much life has he lost, and if his warmth be smothered, his life is smothered for the present.

And even as life will show itself in the very sad face of the heart, and dejection of spirit that they fall into, and sometimes in the deep sighs and groans of the heart, which in such a case it sometimes will break forth into. So a Christian soul, when his heat is most damped, there is a sad face in his spirit that he discerns all is not well with him. His spirit is benumbed and his heart in his own thoughts is frozen within him. It is a burden to him and a matter of sadness to his spirit. And therefore he does express himself sometimes with many sad and deep sighs and groans about his forlorn and lost estate. And yet sometimes you shall have his heart, even then when his heart is most cold (which is worse than the former). For you shall sometimes have a Christian soul, not only not affected with sadness when his life is smothered within him, but vanish away in much empty carnal delights, and contentments, and rejoicing in those comforts which have no life at all in them. A Christian man that has his life so deadened may come not only to have nothing left, but sadness of heart to behold it, but he may lose his sadness too. And even that vanish away in outward rejoicing, so as no life in his heart, in a manner, is left.

Peter, when he had denied his Master, his heart was much oppressed within him. He was pricked and wounded with anguish in his soul, but there was some life in that. But what was it with David after his committing of uncleanness nine or ten months together? He pleased himself in his pleasures, and delights, and contentments which his royalty put upon him, and made Uriah drunk, and did eat and drink himself liberally with him. And in the end put him to death, and that very sleightly, and when he hears of it, makes no matter of it. "But the sword devours one as well as another." And had not his pulse beating in him, no warm breath comes from him, but an empty flourish, and outward joyallity[6] as if he had sung all care away, and all fear of God out of his heart. As if there was no spiritual affection left in his heart of the estate of the whole Church of God. Whereas his poor servant could say unto him, "shall I go home and solace myself with my wife and children?"—the case standing with the Church so as it does, he would not do so. A word that one would have thought would have warmed a good man's heart, but he was not warmed with it, nor with any lively affection, not any beating of his pulse to Christianity, nothing stirring. But a swounding of the whole man that he that had seen David in such a case, and had never known him before. He might have written in his forehead, a man forsaken of God and void of all fear of his name, had he seen him in this case. Where was then David's life all this while? It was a fearful condition, and of all we read in the Scripture, none so far forsaken whose whole spirit was so far benumbed as David's then was? And yet truly life there was still in him; I doubt not though all this while you shall see that either David prayed not all this while.

---

[6] happiness, joviality

And that has been the case sometimes of right godly men that have sometimes not of three years together made a private prayer in their closets; have been content to come to duties in the family and cause others to perform duties. But for their own parts further than a form of religion, or shame, or satisfying of conscience forces them. They let all rest, no affection at all to the duty. They know God took no pleasure in such a soul while they lived in such a course, and so would they lie many months and years, and all that while not so much as lift up a private prayer to God. And this is a far worse case than the other, and yet even this sometimes befalls them. When as sinful lusts have so distempered the life of Christ in them, there is still a habit of grace in the soul, but yet scarce any life of religion putting forth itself. But still where warmth is removed, so much life from holy duties is taken away.

A Second Answer: The Venomous Power of Sin

And another answer to this point is that, even as you see it is by the Almighty power of God that there may be fire and not heat, as you see in the fiery furnace, where into the three children was cast though it was made exceeding hot, yet it had not power to hurt an hair of their heads, nor to singe a lap of their garments; the power of the fire was propended by the mighty power of God. As there is this power in God concerning material fire, so is there a marvelous hellish and devilish power in sin, though not an Almighty power. Yet very like to an Almighty power that that which has a mighty work of God by the Almighty power of His grace in the hearts of the servants of God the work of an Almighty power.

There is such a venomous power in sin as that it will suspend all acts of grace, not so much as show any act of grace in a Christian soul, but the soul and all the graces in it shall lie as the body of a man in a swound—not any breathing, or sight, or hearing, or motion, nothing to show of any spiritual life, that if he should continue so, you would conclude he were dead. Only this kind of life of grace is there, you shall have thus much life in him. There is a kind of unlistiness and heaviness of soul to act wickedness with all that strength and power, which sometimes a godly man, while he was carnal did reach forth his heart and hand unto a kind of frame of spirit in a Christian when it is at the worst, though it can solace itself very far in sin, and goes on hardening its heart in its own way, most desperately and frowardly. Yet notwithstanding there was always something in his heart that will not suffer his soul to break out with all that strength of the spirit of wickedness, as it did when it was carnal. And the reason of that is because of that speech in Galatians 5:17; there is *flesh* and *spirit* in that soul, so as neither can the spirit do what it would, nor the flesh what it would.

Take a Christian when he is most strong, and he cannot so glorify God, nor so edify his brethren as he would by reason of the body of sin. There is always in the best of a Christian something like the spots in the moon, some darkness in it, not a Christian man. But when he is most lively in grace, but he has some darkness in his best performances, so when corruption is most strong and grace most feeble and weak. As in the former corruption will weaken the best performances, so here corruption cannot carry a Christian man to do all that wickedness—which else he would break forth into, nor with that strength and vigor which else he would put forth in it. Though he do rejoice in his wickedness, and bear it out—yes, out-face his very conscience, and out-stare the very light of the graces of God within him, and go on pleasing himself in the hardness of his own heart, yet there is something in the bottom that keeps possession for God and makes him go about it bunglingly.[7] It becomes him not. He cannot set it forth with a grace. David in his worst comes not off with that full power of wickedness, which else his corrupt heart would willingly break forth into were it not for the Spirit of grace that moves slowly in such cases as there be, so that still the case stands clear. How much life, so much warmth, and that warmth will express itself if any life be there at all.

EXAMINE YOURSELF IN KNOWLEDGE

So that, take a survey of your own estates. By this means, you would know whether you have Christ or not; wheth-

---

[7] to carry out badly, to botch

er you have life or not? If you have the life of grace, there is some spiritual warmth in your soul, some heat in your soul. Do but consider then the knowledge that is within you. Is your knowledge such as lets you alone, and only puffs you up, and makes you to think goodly of yourself? If that be all the work of your knowledge, you are a dead-hearted Christian. If it cause you to vanish away in empty contemplation, and you therefore talk, that you may let others see that you have knowledge as well as others. And if it be dead, and cold, and empty, and vanish away in empty notion, and speculation, and dead conference, then your knowledge is barren in goodness. And that is an argument of no life in your soul.

But if there be any truth of life in your soul, your knowledge is warm and lively. Your knowledge that is in you has some zeal. And that sets an edge upon it, and makes it serviceable to God and your brethren. I know not better how to express it than in the description of our blessed Savior; "His eyes were as a flame of fire" (Rev. 1:14, 15). It is true, the eye is lightsome, but it does not burn. They are not hot, but the eyes of Christ is as a flaming heat. And the meaning is, Christ is described just according to the state of the Church to whom John was to write. As He had feet of brass when he writes to a Church that though burned in the fire, yet the more you burn it, the less it wastes. And the more pure it is, and by degrees the more bright. So when he speaks to a Church in persecution and it is not consumed, then Christ has feet like brass. But if he writes to a Church of Thyatira, a Church of a warm spirit, then "thus says He that has eyes like a flame of fire" (Rev. 2:19), meaning the knowledge that the Church had, which was full of zeal as well as of light, and according to the measure of its knowledge, so it grew more in grace. And therefore the works were more at the last than at the first. As their knowledge grows, so grows their zeal. So that if you have that life in Christ which accompanies salvation, your eyes are like a flame of fire, full of burning light, as well as brightsome knowledge.

Is your knowledge such as suffers you to sit down barren, and though you know that you ought to do this and that, yet you do it not? Then there is no heat and warmth in your knowledge. But if there be true life and warmth in your spirit, your knowledge stirs you up to be doing, and stirs up others to be doing also. And your knowledge will not suffer you to let them alone, just as Peter and John sometimes said to the high priests, "We cannot but speak that which we know, and have seen and heard" (Acts 4:18-20). And therefore though they threatened them in peril of life to speak no more in Christ's name, yet say they that which we know to be the Truth of God that we must needs speak. As Jeremiah speaks, "could not forbear" (20:9)—the light that was in him was a glowing and warm heat. And the Word of God in him was as a mighty fire. And it will not suffer him to rest and he must also stir up others. So then, examine whether there be any heat in your knowledge. If your knowledge be not according to zeal, it will but aggravate your condemnation.

Examine Yourself in Breath

Again, examine your breath, whether do you breathe or not? Do you smell a good savor in God's Word when you do read or hear it? And do you smell a sweet savor in the conference of Christian men? Or does it stink in your nostrils? If it be sweet to you, it is well. Do you pray to God with some kind of panting after Him? And your spirit is fit to faint within you? And you can sit down and bemoan yourself to God that you have so lost yourself when there is breath in you? Or can you bring out a word to edify your brethren? It is well.

But if there be no breath in you, it is an evident sign you are dead, or at least in a deep sleep. If you have no ability to pray, and can relish no Ordinance of God, and have no kind of aptness to edify another, then either there is no life in you, or else it is much benumbed, and therefore either no life, or none that is extant in you. And so, how do you find your warm affections stand to the Word? Have you a stomach to the Word? And have you not so much profit by it as to see you do not profit, and are ashamed of it? But if not, there is no life in you.

And if you love to be disjoined from your brethren and you are never better than when you are falling off and sitting loose from your brethren; if you love to be asunder, there is no life in you. No life of religion there, for religion desires to preserve itself. And love is a principal work of religion. "Above all things have fervent love among yourselves" (1 Pet. 4:8). A man had rather cover a multitude of wicked practices than lose the fervency of his love one towards another. And if therefore the devil throw brands among you and you fall asunder, one Christian hangs here and another there in the end while you lie so asunder the fire goes out; and men may bid one another good night, and then may you all take your pleasure in sin—the truth is then all the life of religion goes out, and every business in the family draws away, and so rests till all the life be lost. And therefore, if you see men are willing to sit loose and fall off one from another, then there is an end of the life and power of godliness; a bidding of religion good night. And no more profit to be had while such distempers of soul does last.

But if you see that men come together, as in that ancient famous vision in Ezekiel 37; every bone finds out his fellow and joins with him, and then there was a noise and a shaking, if you see bones gather, bone to his bone; then at the next prophesying flesh will come, and sinews, and the next prophesy, will breathe life into them—so if men begin to annex themselves one unto another as living brands; if one begin to seek out another, and to draw together, and to lie close together, if bone begin to gather to his bone, then there is hope of a host of armed men to stand up for God. In good ways, then there will be life, and strength, and power of godliness. Else make account of it, that in very truth there is no life; no power of religion. Where there is no relishing, no closing one with another, if therefore you see men closing together, and warming one another in the ways of God's grace, and there is some sense of your own unprofitableness under the Word, and if you can digest it, turn it into edification of yourself and others, then there is true life in you, and having life you have Christ, and in Him you have life in abundance.

There are two properties more of life.

The Second Property of Life: Pliableness

Where there is any life, there is some kind of pliableness. Whereas dead carcasses are cold and stiff and unsavory though never so sweet before; this is a certain truth, the more you keep a dead corpse above ground, the more it stinks and is unsavory. It shoots out at length, and you may sooner break him than bend him anyway. But while he is alive you may bend him which way you will. Now therefore consider thus much, if there be any truth of grace in you, "you are gentle and easy to be entreated" (Jas. 3:17). But if not, then you are of a stiff spirit, inflexible and implacable. For to be gentle and easy is the true nature of life. But if not, then have you lost your life. Then either you never had life or else it is in a swound, and so evapoured that there is no bending or bowing of it, but they are fit to be buried as a dead carcass.

Question: *What is this pliableness and easiness to be entreated, and on the contrary this stiffness?*

Answer: There are four things in easiness to be entreated.

First, easy to be pleased. Anything that you do about them is pleasing to them. That is a point of gentleness, and a gracious man in whom is the life and power of godliness, he is easy to be pleased. If you go about anything with any tolerable endeavor to give him content, he is not hard to be pleased. And if not easy to please, there is little grace. Or dangerous to be none at all if you have much ado to bow or bend them to comply with them that asks anything of them, there is a dead heart in such a spirit.

Secondly, a man that is easy to be entreated and gentle. If he be offended he is easy to be entreated (Rom. 1:31). It is a sign a man is of a reprobate sense when he is implacable and stiff; when life is gone, a man is stiff, not easy to be entreated.

Thirdly, if so be that he have offended another man, he is easy to yield and to acknowledge that he is in a wrong (Eccl. 10:4). There is in a living Christian an apt-ness to yield when he is in a wrong. If a man be in a wrong, and will not see his error, will not see the evil he has done in God's sight, his stiffness is a sign of his dead-heartedness. So much stiffness here, so much dead-ness in his heart, and so much nearness to the chambers of death. For a living Christian, if he have offended he is willing to yield, and will acknowledge himself a failure, and promise amendment.

Fourthly, he is willing to deny himself of his own right, even upon equal easy terms, to prevent an offense that may grow. And he stands upon equal terms, lest an offense should arise, he yields and denies himself (1 Thes. 2:6, 7). So Abraham yielded to Lot, though he had not offended him, yet he condescended to his inferior. And if any, Lot shall be the chooser (Gen. 13:8). This gentleness of spirit argues life of Christ in the holy servants of God. Abraham was not stiff, but gentle and easy to be pleased when he was offended.

Now therefore, are you easy to be pleased, easily en-treated to pass by a wrong? And if you have offended an-other, you will acknowledge it; and are easily willing to deny yourself to prevent offense, then you are not stiff, but are a living Christian. But if men be stiff in spirit, hard to be pleased, and froward, no man can give him content. As Nabal's servants said of him: "And if we have offended hard to be entreated, and will by no means see it, or acknowledge it; and by no means yield, but turn ourselves to endless devices, and if we stand upon our own ends, and we will have our own to the utmost farthing, and why should we bend; then truly we are cold, and little power and life breathing in us" (1 Sam. 25).

THE THIRD PROPERTY OF LIFE: SWEET & SAVORY AROMA

The last property of life is this: The body while it is alive is sweet and savory, but so soon as ever it begins to smell, it must be buried, it cannot be kept above ground. Every living Christian is a sweet savor to God (2 Cor. 2:15). And "let your speech be savory, seasoned as with salt" (Col. 4:6). And the Apostle says, "let no unsavory or corrupt communication proceed out of your mouths" (Eph. 4:29). How then do you find your own spirits? Do you breathe savory and sweet? And does your conference yield edification? And is it all well-pleasing to God whatever you do? Does it savor well in the nostrils of God and your brethren? If the duties you perform be so, it is a sign you are living in God's sight. But if your speeches be profane, conference unsavory and carnal, so much as we lose our sweetness, so much we lose our life. When a Christian carries himself serviceably and amiably, then we live, and in having life we have Christ.

~ *Sermon 11* ~
THE DANGEROUS AND UNCOMFORTABLE ESTATE OF EVERY SOUL WITHOUT CHRIST

He that has the Son has life, and he that has not the Son has not life.
(1 John 5:12)

Having handled a use of trial of life—and this depends upon our having of Christ—we come now to another use from this doctrine. It is to teach us the dangerous and uncomfortable estate of every such soul that has not Christ. For the text says, "he that has not the Son has not life." No life in us, if there be no Christ in us. This is that which the Apostle speaks often to, that "we are dead in trespasses and in sins" (Eph. 2:1, 5). This is the estate of them all, so far as we are without Christ, we are without life; no Christ, no life.

It is with the sons of men in this kind (that I may so speak) as it was with the soldiers in 2 Kings 19:35, "they were all dead corps." Truly, that is the case of us all by nature. Every soul of us, as long as we live in the world without Christ, so many men, so many dead corps, so many unsavory carcasses. And indeed all that work of life which you have heard opened, it is no spiritual motion, no feeding upon Christ, no growing in grace, no expelling of noisome lusts, no care nor endeavor to beget others to an estate of grace. In any men that are dead, no motion at all to any spiritual good. All our works, the best works we do in an estate of nature, they are all of them but "dead works" (Heb. 9:14), and so are we to any spiritual motion. As the Apostle tells you, we "none of us do good," and which is worse, we can do no good. Yes, and still, which is worse, we would do no good if we could; this is the estate of us all by nature. "The Lord looked down from heaven to see if any of them did good, but they are altogether become unprofitable, not one does good, no not one" (Rom. 3.12).

And he speaks of all men in an estate of nature without Christ. Not one does any good, no not one. "All the thoughts and imaginations of such men's hearts are evil, and only evil, and that continually" (Gen. 6:5) and Christ says as much of their words (Matt. 12:33, 34). And so in all our works; "A good tree brings forth good fruit, but a corrupt tree brings forth evil fruit" (Matt. 7:18). Wherein he shows you that as we do no good. So we can do no good, not a good thought, nor a good word, nor a good work comes from such a man all his days. And all our speeches are rotten and unsavory. Not any spiritual life in most seeming best duties, we are not able to speak unto any good purpose. Let it be truly moulded and it is a precious fruit of righteousness, but if spoke as comes from nature, be it never so well spoken, it is corrupt, either full of pride or self-conceit, or to please others, or the like.

Nor do we regulate our words by the language of Canaan, nor open our mouths from a spirit of faith. This is true in all natural men. We do not therefore speak because we believe, we speak not, because we believe God has commanded us so to speak (2 Cor. 4:13). As our Savior said in John 14, nor therefore work anything because God set us a work, or to aim at any service of God, or good to His people in it. So that as our thoughts be, so are our words: evil, and only, and continually evil. And much more all the works of our hands that require greater strength of grace than either our thoughts or our words do; so that without Christ there is no act of spiritual life comes from us, we would do no good if we could.

JEREMIAH 13 OPENED

If God should at any time assist us and supply us with something more than ordinary, yet we will not be made clean, that we might do well: "O Jerusalem, will you not be made clean, when will it once be?" (Jer. 13:27). As if it were a thing never to be looked for, God might wait upon a man from one end of the year to another, and sometimes be asking of him, "Will you be made clean?" And He may ask again, "Man, will you be made whole?" But if He but say, "Will you be made clean?" we have many devices to put off God. And we can never find that day wherein we will say, "This day we will hear God's voice, and be made clean; from this day forward I resolve never to think my own thoughts more, nor to do my own will more, but now I will give up myself to seek for life and salvation in Christ." That day is yet never pitched upon till we have found Christ, never since we were born until now.

But now it may be we are convinced that it is good to become a Christian, and we wish well to such as are Christians. But when it comes to the matter, we are but almost Christians, as was Agrippa; or if we be satisfied that we must become Christians indeed, then truly it must not be today. But tomorrow, and when we think to set God a day when indeed it shall be, as sometimes at our marriage, or when we come out of our apprenticeships, or when we fall sick, when left alone upon the deathbed. And if God say, "Yet, when will it once be?" we cannot yet set Him a day; only we will say, "We will consider of it," and we would be loath to disappoint God. As creditors will say to their debtors, "We would be loath to set you a day, because we know not whether we shall hold or no, and therefore spare us in that, but we will pay you as soon as we can." But when will it once be? Truly we are not yet persuaded, there is yet something or other to be done. And therefore you shall find this to be true, that we are so far from spiritual life in Christ, that none of us do any good. There is nothing you do whereof you may say, "This have I done because God has set me a work." And in respect of God's command, or that God may be sanctified thereby, never yet could we say so. And as we have not done any good, so neither are we able or capable of good.

And in truth this is a further want of spiritual action that if God should make us able to do it, yet we would not be willing to do it, but if He puts us to the question, "When shall it once be?" Read that chapter and the next, and see if ever they set God a time. They will by no means set God a time, least they over-much engage themselves. Indeed, sometimes it may be you shall see such men lying under some heavy hand of God, and near to death, resolve upon time. See our unwillingness to come off to God when we are in health, we think in sickness to be made clean, but in sickness, what will we say then? Some of you can tell what men are then wont to say; what do we then say? "Oh, if God would but restore me to health, you should see I would become a new man." Why, when he was in health he said, "If sickness or danger came, that should be the time wherein he would be made clean," but when sickness comes, then we put God off till health again?! As if a debtor should put off his creditor from summer to winter, and from thence to summer again, the answer will never be given. Why now it shall be this day say you in sickness, "it shall be when God shall bring me to health;" but why not today? You put off God from health to sickness, and from sickness to health again.

And when they do not so, and come and tell them of it, they will say, "Why it is true, God forgive them, they thought to have done such a thing, and they hoped to have done it." But when shall it once be? Why not today before tomorrow? What if you die of this sickness, will you go to hell immediately? Will you take no course for turning the wrath of God from you? Are not you now sick, why do you defer it any longer? And though he be not able to turn himself in his bed, yet he may turn to God. It is a vain thing to put off God to health, for in our sickness God will sooner visit us, and does expect that "in the day of our affliction we should seek Him diligently and early" (Hos. 5:15). When will it once be?

So that take notice of this desperate deadness of a man's heart out of Christ. He is dead in sin, so as that he neither does any good, nor is able to do any good, nor is willing to do any good. And as there is no spiritual motion in him, no act of grace, so it is another act of spiritual life, for a man to feed upon Christ; but do you think a dead man is able to feed upon Christ?

ISAIAH 44 EXPLAINED

You know what God said of the idolatrous people in old time in Isaiah 44:11-12. The same says He to every natural man; "He feeds upon what?"—upon Christ? No, no, "upon ashes." Why upon ashes? Ashes is far from feeding upon the living God, and yet truly a man feeds upon ashes. Every soul that feeds not upon Christ has some idol for his god, and so falls down to worship it, some god of profit or pleasure. And this is the estate of all wicked men, they "feed upon ashes." Upon ashes; it seems to me to be a borrowed speech, or similitude taken from children, or some women with child that being sometimes taken with some ill humor, and distemper of stomach, they have an eager desire to feed upon ashes. And such like dry unsavory meat. Children will be eating coals and ashes, and so will sometimes women with child. So truly it is with every natural man. He is a natural idolater. He worships something besides God. He feeds upon ashes, some dry and unsavory and unwholesome meat, which cannot profit him in the day of wrath; which gives not his soul any nourishment. For the soul of man is an immortal spirit, and we only feed it with profit, and pleasure, and credit, and these be but ashes, bodily food.

The good things of this life are no more suitable to a man's soul than ashes be to a man's body. And therefore Solomon so compares the estate of all the sons of nature. "Who knows the spirit of a man that goes upward, and the spirit of the beast that goes downward to the earth" (Eccl. 3:21)? His meaning is this; he complaining of the vanity that lies upon the sons of nature, he speaks not in the person of an Epicure (as some conceive) but his meaning is, "Who knows?" Which of all the sons of men considers, or takes it to heart that his soul goes up to any better place than the soul of a beast? Which of all the sons of nature feeds his soul upon better food than the soul a beast is fed upon? Do they not all feed, as if they all went to one place? And therefore upon the dust of the earth they feed.

Turn me out the man that is in an estate of nature, considers that his soul is to live forever, and therefore takes care to feed his soul to immortality. This is the woeful distemper of all the sons of nature that we feed not upon Christ, but upon the blessings of this world. So long as we are without Christ, all our food is upon earthly things here below. There is not any power in a man by nature, not any wisdom or strength in us to deliver our souls, and then is not this a false course? "A lying vanity." Is not my heart deceived with this and that? He is not able to ask his heart such a question, "Am I such a fool to forget all good to my soul thus long?" It would deliver his soul if he did but consider that there was a lie in the other way. And he flatters himself in his good estate before God, and considers not the truth of the thing; he thinks he is as fair a dealing man as any of them all, but "his heart is deceitful and desperately wicked" (Jer. 17:9), and so cannot see the falsehood of his way.

REHEARSAL OF THE THIRD AND FOURTH EFFECTS OF LIFE[8]

And for growing, which is a third act of spiritual life, a man is dead to any growth, never comes to any growth

---

[8] From Sermon 9

in grace. But he is apt to grow in evil and sin. "Evil men and deceivers shall wax worse and worse" (2 Tim. 3:13). Take you any natural man, and he is ever growing worse and worse, ever growing of the worse hand; he grows more and more unprofitable and more loose from God, and estranged from the ways of His grace, and settled in the ways of sin. And this is that which the prophet Jeremiah complains of in chapter 9:3, "they proceeded from evil to worse." And this is the estate of us all without Christ; we grow from prodigality to covetousness. And from wantonness to voluptuousness, and so go on till we come to take pleasure in all sin, though it be but for a season. This is all the growth and progress that such men make.

And in the fourth place, for cleansing ourselves from all superfluous and noisome lusts that we do not. Neither can we be freed from them: "O Jerusalem, wash your heart from your wickedness, how long shall your vain thoughts lodge within you?" (Jer. 4:14). Purge out all those sinful lusts, God knows the thoughts of the hearts of men are but vain (1 Cor. 3:18). And they being vain, God would have us to wash our hearts. How long shall it be that we suffer these lusts to lodge within us? We never cleanse ourselves from there, but such woeful cleansing it is, that if we go about to purge them out by the motions of the Spirit of grace, that He casts into our hearts; we think it's a troublesome work, and does cross the tranquility and peace of our estates. We think they are noisome, and therefore, if any good motion be darted into the heart in the ministry of the Word, or in the counsel of Christian friends, we are sick of it till we have cast out all those good motions again. And whatever good affection God has been pleased to cast into us, we are not well till we be shut of it.

As was the case of Abab. He comes sadly and mourning from Elijah's sharp reproof (1 Kings 21:28-29), but he could not be well at ease till he had cast it all off. With putting Naboth to death, and put it off with calling a counsel about going to war, and so damped all the sorrow that was in his heart. Let Cain have any good motion come in his heart, and he will put it off with building of cities. His sin and punishment is great (Gen. 4:13), and would he not now seek to God for mercy that his soul might live? No, he goes out from the presence of God, and from all good company and good counsel. And whither goes he then? Into the land of Nod, and there he builds cities, and calls them by such and such names, and so takes off his thoughts from any good motion, and extinguishes all the motions of grace. And truly so stood the case with Felix (Acts 24:25), when he trembled at Paul's sermon, he would not endure to hear him any further, but when he had convenient leisure he would hear him again; but he never sent for him.

INTRODUCTION TO THE USES OF OUR OWN WICKEDNESS AGAINST
OURSELVES

And so you shall ever find this frame in a natural man's heart,
those motions which the Spirit of God casts into his heart
that might induce him, and lead him on by the hand to better courses. We are not well till we have cast them all off.
Just as Paul complains of the Jews, "since you have put it
away from you, lo, we turn to the Gentiles" (Acts 13:46).
We purge and cast out the motions of God's Spirit and cannot endure that any Ordinance should bring us nearer to
Christ. "You have always resisted the Holy Ghost" (Acts
7:51); expelled the blessed of God that if the Holy Ghost
but dart any good counsel into their hearts. They cannot
endure to hear it, nor entertain any motion of it, but grieve
and vex the Holy Spirit of God. And they are not well till
they quench it (1 Thes. 5:19). We are alive to nothing but to
run away from God, alive to sin, "alive to do evil, but to do
well we have no understanding" (Jer. 4:22). Apt to purge
and cleanse ourselves from all good things, but wholly undisposed to do anything that is well. This is the true estate of
us all. Look at us as we are by nature, all of us without Christ
cannot put forth one act of spiritual life, not one good motion to be found in such a condition.

USE 1: TO EXPOSE THE BEGETTING OF CHILDREN OF HELL

And in the first place for begetting any unto grace, we
rather do the quite contrary. We addict ourselves to be-

get men to become "the children of hell," worse than ourselves, "two-fold more the children of hell" (Matt. 23:15). And because that may be more proper to corrupt teachers, Jeremiah speaks it of all the sons of nature, and those especially that had lived a while under the means. And were not thereby brought on to an estate of grace, those whom God had kindled some fire in their hearts, and whom he would have brought on to grace, even these; "They are all grievously revolted, walking with slanders, they are brass and iron, they are all corrupters" (Jer. 6:28). He does not say, they are all "corrupted," but all "*corrupters*," that is, such as are not only naught themselves, but they corrupt others also. They make others worse for their sakes. No man that sets his face to Godward, but if he come among them, he is the worse for them.

Every man is kept off the more from goodness by their means. They do not love that men should be too forward, or too precise, nor to keep such a puling, nor such a praying. We are all by nature corrupters. "All flesh had corrupted their way" (Gen. 6:11). Even every man had done it. Every one is the worse for us that has to do with us. If we see but any good disposition in them to be coming on in the ways of grace, we do as much as in us lies to quench, and damp, and smother them, and never rest by our good wills till we make them as ill as ourselves, and "harden their hearts from God's fear." This is the true carriage of all those who are out of Christ: "He that has not the Son, he has no life." No motion of spiritual life, no growing up in Christ, no purging out of sinful uncleanness; and therefore now to apply this, conceive thus much:

Further Application: Against Rome, the Begetters of Children of Hell

First, it applies itself against the Church of Rome who maintain that men in the state of nature have free will to lay hold upon Christ, and they conceive it is upon very fair terms. But I would only demand of you this question: Whether when they do lay hold on Christ (as they conceive) whether they have Him, or they have Him not? They will say they have not Christ till they have received Him; "for what have you that you have not received?" (1 Cor. 4:7). And till they have received Him, how shall they lay hold upon Him? And if not receive Him, they are dead men. And when a man is dead, what can he have by any benefit that is offered him? Offer him never so largely, and he can receive no benefit by it; and if that any do lay hold upon Christ, were they not living when they so laid hold upon Him. So that when they do lay hold upon Christ, whether is it an action of life or no? If not, how shall they lay hold on Christ?—and without Christ no life. A man in the state of nature neither does good, nor can he do any good, nor is he willing to do good; and therefore well does the Apostle say, "It is God that works in you both the will and the deed" (Phil. 2:12, 13). Anything that we do that is good is wholly from the grace of Christ, and this is just against the Papists.

USE 2: TO TEACH US TO BEMOAN OUR OWN ESTATES

Secondly, it serves to teach us all to bemoan our own estates, or the estates of any of ours, that we yet see in the gall of bitterness, lying in an estate of nature. Is it yourself, or your father, or mother, or your children or servants? Whatever he be; be he never so good a natured man, if he be yet without Christ, there is no life in him. I say, look upon him as your dead friend. If you did look upon your father, and mother, or children, and see them lie dead before you, you would mourn bitterly for them. You know what is said in Zechariah 12:10, "As a man mourns for his first born." If our first born, or any that is near to us die, we mourn bitterly for them, and refuse to be comforted. As was the case of Rachel's mourning for her children, and would not be comforted because they were not (Matt. 2:18). They were all dead, and therefore caused "a bitter mourning." It was the wounding and rending of her soul. And may not this be the case of many a fruitful mother, many children, and yet all of them dead in God's sight, not a soul living in the sight of God?

And is it not a far more bitter death to be dead in sin than to be dead in the body when it is a living soul in God's sight? Then "blessed are the dead that die in the

Lord, for even so says the Spirit" that never spoke words of falsehood (Rev. 14:13). I say therefore, if that our children live to God, and have the life of grace in their hearts, there is no danger of their death. Then your children shall come again to your hearing "at the resurrection of the just," and you shall embrace them with comfort, and fill your soul with unspeakable joy, and fullness of glory. If they die in the favor and grace of God, they shall "rise to glory." But if they be spiritually dead, no goodness in the world in them, no spiritual life at all, no life of righteousness or holiness, which are "the first fruits of the Spirit," and of glory in this world—then weep for these children, and those friends, that husband, or wife, or brother, or sister.

Weep for every soul that is in an estate of sin and death. They are as so many dead corps. You may sometimes see a whole house-full of dead creatures, not one of them living to God, not one of your acquaintance, not one of all your brothers and sisters. Weep and mourn bitterly for them that are thus wounded with sin, and bleed deadly, and gasp for their last breath, and it may be shall never find grace from God in this world. Their present condition is fearful. And mourn you for them in a godly manner that you may be the more earnest with God in that behalf. And never leave till you have got some grace from Christ for them. And in so doing you shall find that He that gave you children will give them life, and He that gave you brethren, and sisters, and friends, and acquaintance, He will put some life into them, and it shall do you good at the heart.

As in verse 16 of this chapter: "Let him ask, and He shall give him life." The promise is marvelous sweet and strong, you may handle the matter so that as you have instrumentally given them natural life. You may procure them spiritual life. They came out of your loins dead in sin, and they will grow in sin more and more, more unsavory, and more unprofitable, and worldly, and proud, and wanton. This is their natural condition. Well, if they be so born, then weep over them, and mourn bitterly for them. You would mourn for a child if stillborn, much more if you see it dying, and giving up the ghost, and lying in extreme and bitter pain, how much more for that soul that has no grace, nothing at all in them, in regard of which you can say, "This is a pledge to me of Jesus Christ in them"?

You know what a bitter mourning fell out in Exodus 12:30. "A great cry was heard in Egypt," and they all rose up at midnight. What was the matter? Why this was it: "There was not a house wherein there was not one dead," and upon this occasion they rose up at midnight, and filled their streets with bitter cries. And what then think you would they have done if in every family there had been but one alive? All dead but himself, neither one nor other, sometimes old, and sometimes young. All gone save only one to mourn for all the rest.

And this is sometimes the case of many a soul. He may rise every morning, and see not a soul in his family of which he can say, "This is not a dead corpse." If there were but one dead soul it might cause you to mourn, and that greatly just occasion to mourn bitterly. If there be but one in your house that comes not on to the ways of grace and salvation. This is it that God calls us to. Sadly to consider of it, bitterly to bemoan it, and to pray heartily for such poor souls to God, that He would be pleased to show mercy to them all, that you might have some living companions, some that might be wrapped up in life and peace, and bring them within the covenant of grace, and life, and salvation. If you have but the bowels of friends, if but the bowels of Christian men, take to heart your own, and others miserable condition, if they be dead, and without Christ.

USE 3: TO EXHORT US TO GET CHRIST

To teach us all that if so be that we, or any of ours be yet without Christ, let it exhort us not to give rest for our eyes, nor slumber to our eyelids, till we have procured Christ for ourselves and ours; that we may procure life for ourselves and others. What is it for a man to have a good wife, or a good husband, or beautiful children? What if he had rich kindred and acquaintance? What if he had all the world, and have not Christ, he have no life? Had we all the friends we have, and as much comfort as we could with, and want Christ, it were poor empty comfort, and therefore labor above all things to get Christ.

Motives to Get Christ

For motives hereunto:

First, it is taken from the sweetness of life; "skin for skin and all that a man has will he give for his life" (Job 2:4), and what is a life without grace? What is the natural life without a spiritual? This natural life is worth the giving and parting with for a spiritual. "What shall a man give in recompense for his soul?" (Matt. 16:26). You know what Christ said of Judas, and the same reason holds true in every man that wants life in Christ. "It had been good for that man he had never been born" (Matt. 26:24). So may we say of all our souls, it had been good for us we had never been born, if we die without grace. We shall then have our portion with hypocrites and unbelievers, and therefore let spiritual life be more sweet to you than natural.

Secondly, consider if you have Christ, "you have life," and that "in abundance." And you have all the blessings of God of all lives it is the most comfortable. If you have Christ, you have all the promises, "for in Him they are, yes, and in Him, amen" (2 Cor. 1:20). And they shall all be ratified and confirmed and established to you, and all the blessings of God are thine. "He has blessed you with all spiritual blessings in Christ Jesus" (Eph. 1:3). All blessings both spiritual and temporal too, all the blessings of this and another life (1 Tim. 4:8). All is yours; all the Ordinances of God is yours, and all the world is yours (1 Cor. 3:21-23).

Not a creature in the world but is at your service. Yes, your enemies is for your good and service. Esau was Jacob's servant even then when he calls him "Lord," and therefore make account of this. If you have Christ, make account of this, you have all things. And therefore read the promises and gather them up, and lay them up as a treasure. "All things are yours"—all the blessings you read or hear of, they are all some way or other for your benefit, and I want but faith to see and discern it, and a heart to acknowledge it. If I do feel it, and therefore if you want righteousness, or peace, or goods, or friends, or any blessing in this world, or for another, if you have Christ you have all that His is. "He that has given us His own Son, will not He with Him give us all things also?" (Rom. 8:32). So that there is a double motive, that every soul might be stirred up to look after Christ. And this is the season, stay not till tomorrow, and though the morrow be a Sabbath, a blessed day. Yet you know not what this day may bring forth. Some of us may fall sick, or die this night, or not sit to profit by to morrows means. As it is this day, and therefore while the day of grace lasts, take hold of Christ.

Objection: *But what shall I do to get Him? How may I come to have Him? You said, "we cannot reach Christ by nature, and though we could we will not; Are not exhortations then in vain?"*

Answer: No, they are not in vain, for though in nature we are neither willing, nor able to look after Christ, but look at Him as a vain refuse commodity. We would have lands, and goods, but no Christ, and therefore what must we do?

Though we be of that natural sinful distemper, that we would have all things but Christ, and let Him go. Yet while we are thus speaking to you, God many times conveys such a spirit of grace into us, as gives us power to receive Christ. What power had the cripple to stand, much less to walk (Acts 3:6, 7)? He had no power to walk; and it had been a vain speech to him if there had not been a power in it to convey strength into him by his breath. And the Lord Jesus working in it, which did convey such strength into him, as that presently he did walk. And truly so is it with the servants of God, those that shall be saved. We speak not in vain to them. The word that we speak conveys spirit and life into them. Then they begin to receive life in Him, and are glad that they may find Christ. And for other men, it leaves them without excuse, if they do not use the means, God appoints them to use.

The Means of Having Christ

And the means God prescribes to us are these:

First, as ever you would have Christ, labor wisely to ponder upon and consider how dead you are without Christ. For you shall never find life by Christ unless you find yourself lost without Him. "Christ came to seek and to save that which was lost" (Luke 19:10). If you see yourself lost, Christ will seek you up. Be fully satisfied of this in your judgement and mind, that unless you have Christ, you have no life. And therefore mourn and pray, "The whole need not the physician but them that are sick" (Matt. 9:12, 13). See yourself a sinner and a perishing creature unless Christ seek you up.

Secondly, take this means, as ever you desire to have life in Christ. If you know any sin by yourself, you are much to blame in yourself. If you do not by any means wash your hands of it, cleanse yourself from it. There are many sins which a man lives in which he might avoid by very common gifts which, would he renounce, God would not be wanting to lead him on to further grace. "This is condemnation that light is come into the world, and men love darkness rather than light" (John 3:18, 19). "Touch no unclean thing," meddle not with vain company (2 Cor. 6:17, 18). And have nothing to do with the "unfruitful works of darkness" (Eph. 5:11). And then I will "be a father to you, and you shall be my sons and daughters" (2 Cor. 6:18); if we would but abhor that which we know to be naught, God promises to receive us. And it is the same that you read in Isaiah 1:16-18, to show you that if men do begin to learn to be better, if they "cease to do evil, and learn to do well," if they acknowledge their sins in the sight of God, God will so sprinkle the blood of Christ upon them. As that their great sins shall be forgiven them, and upon the same terms men might feed upon the paschal lamb, they must "put all leaven out of their houses, purge out therefore the old leaven, and you shall become a new lump" (Ex. 12:15). Purge out the old, and you shall be new creature in Christ, purge out the "leaven of maliciousness and wickedness," and whatever is sinful before God, away with it, touch no unclean thing (1 Cor. 5:7, 8). And Isaiah 55:7, "Let the wicked forsake his wickedness, and the unrighteous his thoughts," and then, "I am a God ready to pardon, I will forgive all your iniquities."

Thirdly, "Seek the Lord while He may be found, call upon Him while He is nigh" (Isa. 55:6, 7). "Seek Him and your soul shall live; God is abundantly ready to pardon, *etc.*" How shall I seek Him? No man has a desire to seek but that which he has a desire to find. And therefore hunger and thirst after Him. As it is the first verse of that chapter, desire nothing so much as your part in Christ, and besides, endeavor to find Him in the means (v. 3). "Hear, and your souls shall live." Hearken diligently to the Word of God. It is a notable promise that in Proverbs

8:34, "Blessed is the man that hears me, watching daily at the posts of my gates, for he that finds me, finds life." Consider, there is no man that hears Christ but he finds Him; and if he find Him, he shall have life by Him.

And therefore how much cause have men to straighten themselves a little in their worldly business to hear daily? "For whosoever finds Me finds life," and he that hears Me finds Me. Hear therefore diligently, and your souls shall live. Shake off all drowsiness of flesh and spirit, and be desirous to receive Christ in His Word that is spoken to you, and so seek Him in calling upon Him (vv. 6, 7, 8): "Call upon Him while He is nigh." And when is He nigh? Every day, if you stay longer than the present day, you have no further opportunity offered you. Call upon God now and wrestle with Him in your prayers, that that which you have heard may be life, and the length of your days.

USE 4: TO TEACH THE SOUL

To teach every soul that has already found Christ, and yet complains you have a dead heart and a dull mind; a heavy spirit, heavy affections, nothing lively cannot expel your corruptions, cannot beget others to God, and are not active in spiritual works. Then if you find a want or decay of life, then seek for Christ again. Labor for more Christ and you shall have more life. Rest not in having a good measure of grace, for you will find a world of deadness and weakness in beginnings of grace. But as you would have any further measures of life, so look for further measures of Christ. For Christ dispenses Himself to us in measure by little and little, and use the same means to increase Him. As you did to get Him at the first, see yourself lost without Him. And thirst after Him, and hear diligently, and call earnestly upon Him for more strength. Use Christ and have Christ. Use grace and have grace. Grow up in the use of Him, and you shall grow up in the possession of Him. "And therefore as you have received Christ so walk in Him" (Col. 2:7, 8), as if that were the way to get more rooting in Christ. Labor to "live by faith," and walk to the glory of Christ, and by the rules of Christ, and by that means you will be more built up, rooted, and established in Him.

Use 5: To Comfort Those Who Have Life in Him

Of comfort to every soul that has any part in Christ, you have life in Him. And that in abundance, and favor with God, having Him you have life (Prov. 8:34, 35). "They that hate Me love death;" if you seek not Christ, you seek death, and mischief, and destruction to your own souls and yours. And therefore as you desire to find Christ seek Him. And having found Him, rejoice in Him, that God has given you to find Him. And then walk as those that desire forever to have Him, as not to change your portion by any means. If you have Christ, you have enough, and if you sit loose to Christ for the enjoyment of earthly blessings, what will they advantage you? But chiefly labor to get Christ. And then, "he that has the Son has life, and he that has not the Son has not life."

PART IV

ASSURANCES

~ Sermon 12 ~

ASSURANCES OF LIFE & BELIEF

These things have I written unto you that believe on the name of the Son of God, that you may know that you have eternal life, and that you may believe on the name of the Son of God. (1 John 5:13)

We are now come to enter upon the beginning of the conclusion of this whole epistle, wherein the Apostle rehearses the intention and scope of the whole fore-past epistle. The persons and subjects to whom he writes, and the end and scope of his writing: "These things have I written unto you." To whom? "To you that believe on the name of the Son of God." And he intends a double end:

First, that you may know that you have eternal life.

Secondly, that you may believe on the name of the Son of God.

Now to encourage to this latter end that John aims at—believing on the name of the Son of God—he propounds three motives in verses 15, 16, and 17; amongst which the last of them is a promise of prevailing with God for pardon and a prevention of falling into the great sin. And so propounds certain encouragements to the end of the chapter.

Now at this time, we shall treat of the first part of this conclusion, which is an expression that John here makes, or a description of the persons here spoken to: "to them that believe on the name of the Son of God." From the persons to whom John dedicates this epistle, to them that believe on the name of the Son of God; observe:

Doctrine 1: *This Epistle of John was written, or directed, to believers on the name of Jesus Christ.*

This is evident in the text, which may be gathered from the beginning of the epistle in chapter 1:4. He writes to such who by reading this epistle might attain to "fullness of joy." And those are only believers who are capable of that mercy and blessing. You may gather the same from the three sorts of Christians to whom he writes in particular in chapter 2, verse 12, "I write unto you, little children, because your sins are forgiven you," and these little children are divided into three sorts: "fathers, young men, and babes" (v. 13). So that look at all that John writes to; they are such as make a faithful acknowledgement of God the Father, as chapter 4, verse 4.

And look at his second epistle, and that is to the "Elect Lady." And look at his third epistle, and that is first to the beloved Gaius. And he shows you what a notable Christian he was. He wishes no further prosperity to his body and outward estate than his soul had attained unto. His soul was in great prosperity, only his body and estate was weak, for he was "the host of the whole Church of God."

So that look at all John's writings, and they are all written to them that believe on the name of the Son of God. And in very deed look at all the epistles of all the rest of the apostles, and they are all written to *believers*. If you sum them all up from first to last, look at the prothesis of every epistle. In the first, second, and third verses of every epistle, and they are written sometimes to saints by calling, sometimes to faithful brethren, sometimes to the churches of Christ, natural sons, partakers of the common salvation. In a word, only to those that were faithful believers in Christ Jesus. And when our blessed Savior Himself writes, He writes to the seven Churches of Asia, all of them such as sometime had been eminent, and glorious, and gracious. And amongst the weakest he had a few names, even in Sardis, "that had not defiled their garments" (Rev. 3:4). Now when a man shall consider that all the apostles do dedicate all their writings to believers and saints, it gives us just occasion of inquiry. Wherefore he writes to these, and to these only?

BENEFITS FOR BELIEVERS

Now the answer to which, to these he writes in regard of the special benefit and help that these writings might yield to believers, both to those that then lived, and to all other believers that should succeed them to the end of the world. And those benefits are many and diverse.

As first, *teaching*. That is one benefit the churches receive by these epistles. "Brethren, stand fast, and hold the traditions which you have been taught, whether by word, or by our epistle" (2 Thes. 2:15). This was one end of the apostles writing their epistles, to the intent they might teach the Church of God sundry things which else they had not known.

Another benefit the Churches received from these epistles was *admonition* and putting them in remembrance of the things they had heard; things which they did know before, and which happily they had forgotten. "I thought it necessary to put you in remembrance" (2 Pet. 1:12, 13).

And in verse 13, there is a third benefit of them. To stir them up to do such things, which though they well knew should be done, yet they were dull, and slow of heart, and stood in need to be *stirred up* to them.

Another end of their writings was this; that sometimes they might *humble and bring low* the spirits of those that were puffed up, and had not repented of the sin which they had committed. "I was sorry at the first that I made you sorry," but now I am not sorry, for it was a godly sorrow (2 Cor. 7:8). So that it seems the writings of the apostles did much prevail with the faithful people of God, and wrought in them such godly sorrow, that it was a comfort to the Apostle, that he had sometimes grieved them.

Another end was, that so by this means they might "*be strengthened* in the faith," according to what you read in the words of the text. To them that did believe, he wrote that they might believe, meaning that they might be confirmed and established in believing.

Also, to the intent that they might *fill the hearts* of God's people "with joy in believing" (Rom. 15:13); according to what you read was affected (Acts 15:31). So that, see how much help the Church of God has had by these writings, so that they have found much comfort in them. And these writings have been the foundation of the faith of God's people from that time to the world's end. They have ever yielded matter to the ministers of the gospel to preach and expound to the people, that by preaching they might bring on men to salvation, so that the Holy Ghost would not have ministers nor any other to be "wise above what is written" (2 Tim. 4:16, 17). That when these are put into the hand of a faithful scribe, taught unto the Kingdom of God, he may be able to use this two-edged sword of the Spirit, to all those ends by which we come to be made perfect unto salvation, and this is the scope of the Spirit of God in Scripture.

WHY THEY ARE WRITTEN TO SUCH AS BELIEVE

As they serve for those benefits, so also for those ends. It is taken from the little use which unbelievers will make of these writings till they come on to believing so little, that were it not for some believers among them, whom God had respect unto, none of all the apostles would have vouchsafed to have written any one epistle to any unbeliever of any town or assembly. None of them all writes to any but to such "as believe on the name of the son of God." Had there been any benefit likely to be expected from unbelieving nations, some or other would have written to them. But from first to last, look over them all, and observe them, whether they be written to particular persons, or to particular congregations, or to churches or nations, they are all written to such as believe on the name of the Lord Jesus. For it is with the apostles writings, as the Apostle sometimes speaks of prophecy or miracles. "Miracles are for them that believe not, but prophecy for them that believe" (1 Cor. 14:22). He does not deny, but prophecy is for them that believe not, but he speaks by way of opposition to miracles. Miracles are rather for them that believe not. And he would have believers know, it is rather for them to attend unto prophecy than unto miracles. So that this is the point: observe it as a just ground of the apostles dealing in these writings, because of the little use that unbelievers will make of them.

Take you men that believe not, and let them read the Word of God over again and again, and yet they receive little instruction from what they read, little admonition, little stirred up to any goodness, and you shall not at all find any blessing, no saving gift of God, can be wrought in the heart without faith, and because faith comes not by reading, but by hearing. Therefore, the Apostle writes not to them that believe not, but to such as are believers. If ever God had intended that the reading of these writings had been effectual to the begetting of faith, surely He would have followed them with mighty works as He blessed the preaching of the gospel in the primitive times, with miraculous works. But you shall not read in any Scripture that ever God so far blessed the Word read to any man, or that He ever wrought a miracle to confirm the Word read, where the Word has been taught. God magnified it much in the first publishers of it till the whole world was convicted.

And had God been pleased at any time to think that these writings should be effectual to convert men to grace. Surely, it had been a notable means for the apostles to have sent sundry epistles to many churches, to whom they should never personally come. But this was their care, to go all over the world, to preach here and there, round about the world, as much as in them lay, which they needed not to have done, in case the sending of an epistle would have served the turn. Notable is that speech, and famous in this kind: "Faith comes by hearing, *etc.*" (Rom. 10:14-17). So that in very truth, because the apostles did not see of what use their writings might be to any unbelievers, because all the work that reading could reach unto could not reach to beget and work saving faith, which is the principal scope of preaching. Therefore they did never address themselves to write any of their epistles to any unbeliever, but only to such as believe on the name of the Lord Jesus.

Objection: *You say, "But sometimes God has been pleased to bless in old time the reading of the Word to the conversion of souls; and therefore why may we not expect the like blessing upon the reading of the Gospel in these days, as well as the Law in former times? In Deuteronomy 31:11-13, (A place much stood upon in this case) it was commanded there that the people* should come up to Jerusalem, and there the Law should be read before them *(v. 11)*, that they may hear, and learn, and fear (v. 12), and their children that knew not the Lord, may learn to fear the Lord their God. *Where you see God blessed the reading of the Law, not only for the benefit of them that knew it before, but their children also that knew not anything, may learn to fear the Lord. And if God did so bless the reading of the Law in former times as a notable instrument to bring on them to believe that never knew anything of God's Word before, surely one would expect that the gospel, which of the two, if rather the ministration of the Spirit than of the letter, or than the Law, that it should be as mighty this way for the begetting of God's fear in men, as ever the Law was."*

Answer: You shall not read that this was the benefit or blessing that God did accompany the Law withal in ordinary reading of the same. But this was a solemn reading, once in seven years, and no oftener, or once in fifty years. It was a reading at the Feast of Tabernacles, in the year of solemnity in verses 10 and 11-13. In a time of solemn release, that was once every seven years. And what was the reason that then it should have such a more than ordinary blessing? Why, this year of release was the acceptable year of the Lord, which typed out to them the year of release by the Lord Jesus Christ. For He was crucified in one of these seventh years—in the year of Jubilee. And to make it a type and shadow of what benefit we should have by reading the Word, when we should be released from our sins by faith in His blood.

In that solemn reading, God gave a more than ordinary blessing to little children those poor ignorant things that usually come to the Congregation and hear much, but learn little. Yet even they in the year of release, when the time comes that God would shadow out to them their release by Christ; even then little children that know not anything shall get some knowledge, and fear of God by hearing of those words than read. So that it was such a reading as was upon such a solemn year of release as typed out Christ's redemption; to show you that men that are come to a year of release from all their sins by Christ. They shall hear and know, and though they know nothing before, now they shall never read but with some profit, and some growth in God's fear.

And another answer may be this; that when he there speaks of reading he speaks not of bare reading, reading is sometimes put for all that expounding and applying that did ordinarily accompany their reading at such a time. For it was at the same feast that Nehemiah speaks in chapter 8. It is said (Neh. 8:4-8), there was a pulpit of wood; and in verse 8, it is said, "They did read distinctly in the Law, and caused the people to understand the meaning of it." So that it was not a mere outward and bare reading of the letter, but an opening of the sense. And such a kind of applying it to the hearts of the people that the people went away much rejoicing, because they understood the Law that was read unto them. And many of them could not but joy and rejoice in it, as you see from verses 8 through 12, and when they had so done, the people went away rejoicing, and he said to them, "Go your way home, eat the fat, and drink the sweet, *etc.*" (v. 10). So that, this you shall find to be true, that God has either never so far forth blessed the reading of the Word as to bring on unbelievers to Christ, either never. Or if He have, it is at some solemn extraordinary feast, once in seven, or once in fifty years, which was their great Jubilee to make known to His Church what in after times it should be, when they knew Christ.

USE: THE PREVAILING OF SCRIPTURE OVER THE HEARERS

It may serve first to let us see a reason why so many writings of godly men to so good purpose, and by such holy men, and so effectually by many, have so little prevailed against the Papists and heretics in any kind. A man would wonder to read so many writings of so many holy men, and to see so few of the Church of God brought on to God by this means. Why, what's the reason? Surely it is no wonder the apostles themselves, though they should never prosper in writing to men that believed not. But to such as believed that they might have joy in believing, they knew reading would not prevail. It is true, it may be some means of conviction, and leaving men without excuse. And their writings have not been in vain, to establish them in the truth that believed it before, and for satisfying the judgements of them that are studious in the truth, to seek out the truth of God's will.

But for men that are unbelievers, and settled in the dregs thereof, never any writer in England, France, or Germany did any good, some have come over that have pretended that this and that man's learned writings has been of much help to them. But those who have professed such conviction have been but mere counterfeits and deluders of the State, and did it only to provide for their honor and credit here in this country. And as little has been done by the writings of godly men against the adversaries in this kind. So in very deed, if you shall look at all the good that has been done by reading in poor congregations that have had no means of preaching, the people are as ignorant as those that never heard of the name of Christ; as empty of faith, and of the knowledge of Christ, and of every grace of His, as those that never heard of them.

Objection: *But you say, "This is marvelous uncharitable to say that they who have but reading fall short of faith in Christ, and of the fruits of faith that accompany salvation?"*

Answer: Whether is it more uncharitable to let such as live under such means know their danger that they might come to salvation than to flatter them with a false opinion of their own safety; to speak peace to them, and yet they to live without God in the world. God's people are in an unsafe condition without God while they are without a teaching priest (2 Chron. 15:3). A long time they had been without God. Why had they not the Word of God read in their synagogues? Do you think Jeroboam's priests did not read the Law? Was there no mention of the Law of God among them? Had they not so much form of godliness, as to read the writings of the Law? Yes sure, their Civil Law in which their Civil Government stood, and by which they executed justice, was the Law of Moses. And did they not then understand the letter of the Law? Doubtless these books being their Law, they were known among the body of the people. And what did the priests, if they did not read the books of the Law, were they only to offer sacrifice to the calves? I doubt not the people did not do it. Neither was it usual to offer any of their oblations in their synagogues, but at Dan and Bethel only. And therefore they were not wanting to hear the Prophets read. And yet notwithstanding all that reading, it is said Israel has a long time been without God. They had a priest to read, but not a priest to teach. And so were without God, and without the Law; that is, the sentence God gives of the people at that time. And think not that God was uncharitable in so speaking of them, for God expresses His love in showing the people their dangerous estate (John 15:14, 15).

Question: *But is it not said (Acts 15:21), Moses of old time had in every city them that preach him, being read in the synagogues every Sabbath day; and is not then the reading of him preaching?*

Answer: It implies that when he is read, he is preached. For every Sabbath day when they read the Law, they gave the sense and meaning of it. That shows what diligence the priests did use when they did read they gave the sense and wisely applied it to the edification of the people. And not that reading was all the preaching they had, or that this was any preaching, that they only read the Word of God. For if they had but Moses read, and not preached, they were then without the Law, and without God in the world. And you know what God Himself threatens, "that He would send a famine of hearing the Word"

(Amos 8:11, 12, 13). Never was there a famine of *reading* the Word, since there was any face of a church at all; but "a famine of *hearing* the Word of the Lord," that men should go far from sea to sea, and from place to place to hear it, but should not hear it.

And by that means, the young men and the fair virgins should perish for thirst, and none to satisfy them with the Word. And those who were able to stir, would go far and near to hear the Word, and yet should not find it. And so shall perish for want of that knowledge of it, which does accompany salvation. So then, marvel not that the Holy Ghost says these things, "I write unto you that believe," to believers only was this written. Wonder not then if so little good be done among the Papists, or in any other churches where there is only bare reading. Make account of it, as the Lord says, "My people are then destroyed for want of knowledge" (Hos. 4:6). Was there ever any soul so desperately ignorant think you, as to take the place of a minister, and not have skill to read? No, but these had no knowledge to teach the people the meaning of the Law of God, "whose lips should preserve knowledge, and at whose mouth the people should seek the Law" (Mal. 2:7, 8).

USE: TO TEACH BELIEVERS

To teach all that believe on the name of the Lord Jesus Christ diligently to be conversant in the writings of John and of the apostles. Shall the Holy Ghost have a pen to write unto us, and shall not we have a hand to receive these writings, and by faith to behold and believe them? Shall He take care to write us letters from heaven from the Lord Jesus Christ, indicted by the blessed Spirit, and written by the hands of faithful scribes, who were carried to all truth? And shall they write them to us to continue to the end of the world, and shall not we attend to them? "These be written to every soul that believes in Christ." For if written to them that believe in Christ, then every believer may say, "These writings are written to me, to you and to me." And therefore let us carefully read, and attend to them.

And therefore do not neglect a letter written by such precious scribes and from the hand of a gracious God that directed them to us. But if written to us, and for our instruction and learning, let us hear, and read, and obey, and look at them as the chiefest blessings, and ornaments of God vouchsafed to us. Among all the means of grace, put up these writings as the Oracles of God, for our instruction. "Whatever was written aforetime was written for our instruction and edification" (Rom. 15:4), as well as for them that lived in ancient times. How much are the Church of Rome to blame that lock up these epistles from the common people in strange languages? And if they understand not Latin, they must not read, unless with license, or in a strange tongue. Heavy will the curse of God fall upon them; they may as well read a fable to them as the Scripture! Yes, many times the priests themselves understood not the Latin that they read. It was given to them as a clasped book. They were not able to expound it, but say that ignorance in the people is the mother of devotion, and therefore both fall into the ditch together.

Use 4: Unto the Unbeliever

Serves to be some direction to every carnal man, you say, if these Scriptures be written but to believers, will you not allow ignorant carnal men to read this part of the Word of God?

Answer: Even they have thus much benefit by the Word. First, whatever is expounded to them from this Word may be effectual to bring them on to salvation; but faith comes by hearing.

Secondly, these Scriptures when they are read, they are a profitable and helpful means to get knowledge, though that knowledge I believe reach not to salvation.

Thirdly, it is a means to put people in remembrance of what they know, though it be not to salvation.

And lastly, it kindles in them some desires to know these things that they might understand them, though that be rare. I dare not reckon the eunuch among the ignorant and unbelievers (Acts 8:30, 31). And that were a blessed use if men shall read the Scripture, and complain for that they cannot understand them, and shall be stirred up to desire a guide to help them to see and understand what they before understood not, and so be brought on to some knowledge, it were a blessed use of the Scriptures.

And besides, they are of this use: they are of singular benefit to discover to people what sin is, and open to men what moral and common virtues be. And so are a means to preserve people in a form of godliness whereby they know that magistrates are to be obeyed, ministers reverenced, parents honored, murder not to be committed, the Sabbath not to be profaned, God only to be worshipped. The body of these things they see are to be done, and these evils eschewed; they are a means to keep people in good order, and to prepare them to a better understanding of the ministry of the gospel that shall at any time be blessed to them. So that some profit there is hence to them that want faith.

But the principal thing the Apostle aims at is this; "I write unto you that believe on the name of the Son of God." But further, I say to you that are not yet brought on to believe, let this be your instruction, diligently to attend to what you hear from these words. For you may say, and truly you may read every day a chapter or two, and read them over again and again, and spend many hours about them, and in prayer too, and yet no nearer salvation then at the first, I say not. Not nearer salvation, for you are stirred up to many duties, but when you see you have read much, and prayed much, and yet get little hold of the saving grace of Christ, how should this provoke all that live without means of grace, to give diligent heed to that Ordinance of God, in which faith to salvation is wont to be conveyed? And that is a use that may be of notable efficacy to stir them up to hear diligently those who are destitute of the knowledge of God. Let them be the more diligent to seek after more means in the Ordinances of God.

USE LAST: ADDITIONAL BENEFITS

It is a use to all those that do indeed believe on the name of the Lord Jesus to be not only careful to read, but to read these Scriptures in hope of finding those very blessings for which these Scriptures were written and sent us. Were they written that you might be taught? Truly you make an ill use of reading if you know no more at last than at the first. You may well say, you are unprofitable if you do not observe something from your reading. And if they were written to stir us up to be doing good, you make an ill use of reading if it bring not forth some profitable fruits.

Yes, if by reading these epistles you might believe and be humbled and comforted, and your joy might be full in reading, then truly you should not rest till by reading you find some measure of faith strengthened in you to a holy fear of God, in whose presence you stand, and whose word you take in hand. And find your hearts take comfort from what you do read, since they were written for your sakes that believe, and for your sakes only if you shall be negligent to read them, shall you not take this blessed Ordinance of God in vain? And therefore read them, and read them diligently, and profitably, for the blessed ends for which God has written them, that you may find the blessed fruits of them.

Now we come to speak of the end for which he wrote them, that you might believe on the name of the Son of God, and to know eternal life, only now to speak of it so far as it is pertinent to this place.

Doctrine 2: *Such as do believe on the name of the Lord Jesus Christ by these epistles of John may know that they have everlasting life.*

So it is in the text; why by these epistles? First, because John, in this epistle, does set before you where eternal life is to be had. As the verse before the text, he in sundry places sets forth the Lord Jesus Christ as the life which we are to receive from the Father. He shows where it is to be had, and where forgiveness of sin is to be had, and by whom we have propitiation (1 John 2:2).

Secondly, these epistles set before us, and gives us certain means whereby we may obtain eternal life. As first, "If we confess our sins, He is faithful and just to forgive us our sins" (1 John 1:9). That is one means; and secondly, he calls upon us to look unto Him as our Advocate, and propitiation.

Thirdly, he does likewise give you certain signs by observing of which you may know whether you have the Lord Jesus Christ or not. This for one sign; "If we say, we have no sin, we make God a liar" (1 John 1:8); If we keep His commandments, we know that we know Him. If God give us a conscionable care to keep His commandments, we know that we know Him. And some other signs, as chapter 3:3, if God give us hearts to "purge and cleanse ourselves from all such sins" as hang about us, and if God give us hearts to love the brethren, *etc.* these and many more such signs of grace he gives us in this epistle.

USE 1: FOR THE REFUTING OF FALSE DOCTRINE

If God having thus written and given us these epistles, then first, it will be a just refutation of that Popish doctrine that think it impossible for a man to know that he is in an estate of grace. If John did write these epistles for this end, "that we might know we have eternal life," then sure we may know it, else John fails of his end. And for John to be disappointed were less matter, but the Holy Ghost Himself, for John being the pen-man of the Holy Ghost, the holy end he aims at not being attainable is to put a defiance upon the Almighty, and therefore the knowledge that we have eternal life may be attained.

And whereas they tell us, we may have a conjectural knowledge, but no certain knowledge. But to say we have a knowledge, and yet but conjectural is as much as to eat up a man's words he had formerly said. For a conjectural knowledge is no knowledge at all. Knowledge is the judgement or discerning a man has of a certain thing. If a man ask you whether he know if such a man have possession of such a place, and he say first, yes, and afterwards says he conjectures so; his knowledge is no knowledge, it is a false intelligence. If you ask a man if he knows whether such a man have such a portion of such a value, and he say he has, he conjectures so, it is no knowledge; but if he know it, then he speaks of a certainty.

And therefore, if the Holy Ghost says we may know it, then surely we may have more than a conjectural knowledge, even a certain knowledge of our happy estates. And were there no more arguments in the world to discourage a man from Popery, this were sufficient; even this very doctrine of doubting and conjectural assurance of a man's eternal estate, which leaves a man's conscience destitute of any peace. Consider therefore that the Church of Rome is a harlot, and brings up strange children. When she does not teach her children to know God to be their Father, it argues she is no lawful spouse of Christ. But do but hope such a one is your Father, but count it presumption to say, you know it. That Church that trains not up her children to know God to be their

Father is a false Church, and a sign that the Church of Rome has mixed herself with so many idols and abominations that she cannot teach the children of her Church to know that they are the sons and children of God, but condemns them to the death, if they dare presume to say that God is their Father.

Use 2: For the Knowledge and Comfort of Salvation

May refute that opinion of the Papists that will not suffer the common people to hear this Scripture. Take notice here how injurious they are to the faith of God's people, and to the knowledge of their chiefest comfort, to debar them of the knowledge and means of their salvation. Take away these Scriptures, and take away the principal means of the knowledge of our salvation.

Use 3: For the Teaching of the Doctrine of the Assurance of Salvation

To teach such as are in any doubtful temptation at any time about their first estate and condition, who are not able to apply with comfort assuredly their grounded knowledge, that Christ and eternal life is theirs. It may teach them among other Scriptures to be diligent in inquiring into this epistle, the Holy Ghost says it was the main scope of His writing unto all those that trust upon the name of Christ, that they might know their blessedness to lie upon Him. And those that did not certainly know they had found Him, he writes to them to look after Christ, to long for Him, and to desire after Him. Do you then desire not only to believe eternal salvation belongs to you, but to know it? For to know is something more than to believe.

A man may believe a thing, and upon good ground he may look for salvation there, and wait for it, and desire that he may be more assured of it. But to know that you have eternal life, and the certainty of it, that God has sealed it up to your soul and conscience, of which you need doubt no more—this is a far more greater blessing than to believe in Christ, though by believing we have eternal life. And therefore, if you so believe in Him as to look for salvation in Him, and not elsewhere, though as yet you be doubtful of your estate. Yet you may learn much by reading these Scriptures. Read them again and again, and leave not reading and searching into them, till you find even from this epistle ground of assurance.

USE 4: FOR THE DILIGENCE OF KNOWING GOD'S WORD

May serve to teach the children of God to know when you have made a good use of reading these Scriptures. You read much and often, and you think when you have done, you have done God good service. A usual vanity among Christians if they have prayed in the morning, and read a piece of a chapter, they think they are better blessed all the day after for it. And we are unquiet all that day when we have not had time to read and pray. But if that be done, we think we have quit ourselves well. But a man may read and never consider what he has gotten by it. A man may pray and never observe what answer God makes to his prayers all the day long. But God requires that you should get knowledge by reading, and that not of small matters, but of your possession of everlasting life. And therefore you read to purpose, when you thereby come to know that you have eternal life, and your joy is increased, and you are brought on to believe and trust in the name of Christ more and more, and unless you so read you have taken this blessed Ordinance of God in vain. And therefore be diligent and conversant in reading these epistles, and as you would search for treasure, so be diligent and laborious herein, that you may know you have eternal life.

BELIEVING ON THE NAME
OF THE SON OF GOD

That you may believe on the name of the Son of God.
(1 John 5:13)

Now we come to speak of the other end of the apostles writing of these epistles, and that is, that you may believe on the name of the Son of God.

Doctrine: *It is a holy end of the Holy Scriptures that believers may believe.*

John, when he writes the Gospel, he speaks as well to believers, as to others, but chiefly to believers. "These things are written that you may believe" (John 20:31). Say not what is this, but to make the work that is already wrought, for though faith and believing be wrought in the hearts of God's people. Yet such as do believe had need to be helped to believe more and better. It is not only the power of God to work faith in such as believe (Rom. 1:17), but to lead them on from faith to faith, from one measure of faith to another. And the gospel is revealed from heaven for that end, that such as believe not might be brought on to believe.

And such as do believe, may be carried an end in believing, such as are faithful, had need be yet more faithful.

You read also in Philippians 1:25, "I shall abide with you, for your furtherance and joy of faith," such a furtherance as is for the increasing and augmentation of your faith, so that there is not only faith but increase and growth of faith, too. As furthered by the gospel, "that I might supply the defects of your faith" (1 Thes. 3:10), to supply what is wanting in your faith. There is not any of the servants of God, no, not those that receive the Word with much joy in the Holy Ghost, in much affliction and tribulation, no, not those that give good pledges and evidences of their grace, as in 1 Thessalonians 1:4-7. Yet there is something wanting or lacking in your faith, not any, no, not the most exemplary Christians (v. 7), but there is something wanting in their faith. And therefore to this end he desires to come to them (v. 10), he is pressed exceedingly night and day, stirred up unto that duty with much vehemency and in earnestness of spirit desires exceedingly to see your faith, and to perfect what is wanting in it. A marvelous thing that the best Christians should yet have something wanting in their faith, so that this is not a needless work he undertakes in writing to them that believe on Christ, that yet they may believe better.

Question: *Now what is that which they had need grow unto?*

Answer: First, they had need to grow unto the belief of some further principles of God's truth some further articles of faith, which yet they know not. Some have need to grow in the object of their faith to believe more than they yet do believe. Some of the apostles did not believe the resurrection of Christ. Thomas said he would not believe unless he might see and feel (John 20:25). He was wanting in the belief of one article of faith, the resurrection of the dead. And 1 Corinthians 15, the whole Church was wanting in this, and in many other articles of their Christian faith. They doubted not but that their bodies should rise, but they wanted that before. And the Thessalonians, they wanted this in their faith. They could not tell what to make of the long delay of the second coming of Christ. They did expect a sudden coming, and therefore many of them were troubled in their minds, so as that they neglected their callings, and minded not their outward business in the world, expecting a sudden dissolution of all. And therefore the Apostle supplies what was wanting in their faith by acquainting them further of the counsel of God—that Christ must not come "to judgement till Antichrist have first come, with all deceiveableness and lying wonders," and till the Church have made an apostasy (2 Thes. 2:1-12). And the Galatians, they were ignorant of the doctrine of justification, for supply of which, and satisfying them therein that whole epistle is spent. So in all other churches the apostles' labors to supply what was wanting in the object of their faith.

Secondly, there is something wanting in their approvedness of the habit of faith, something wanting in the gift and grace of faith. The Apostle prays for the Colossians, "that as they have received Christ they would so walk, and that they might be rooted and established in Him" (Col 2:6-7). Many of them were not so rooted and established in Christ as they stood in need to be; not able to exclude and banish those doubts, and fears, and cares of spirit, that sometimes accompany believers, even those that believe already on the name of Christ. Yet there is something wanting in the root of their faith. For look as you see it is with a plant that is grafted into a stock, it does not forthwith take root, but a little matter will soon unsettle it. So is it in this case, a man may in some measure be implanted into Christ, and yet for a time be marvelously unsettled, and far off from that rootedness which God looks our faith should grow unto. And so in a building, it at the first framing may be so green, as that yet it is not settled upon the foundation. But it would have a time to be dried and withered that it may stand the firmer on the foundation without shrinking, and be more fit for a man's dwelling. So is it sometimes with the faith of a Christian man. He may be knit to Christ and may have a place in Christ, but his mortar may yet be green, and may be easily shaken with wind and weather of temptation, and not be yet rooted and established. There may want such holy confidence and assured persuasion of fellowship with the Lord Jesus Christ, as we had need to be lifted up unto a further increase of faith, which this epistle and such other doctrines as these be, are wont to work in them.

Thirdly, it may be increased in the comfort of it, in the sense and feeling of it. For it may so fall out that many a good soul may come to a large measure of a lively faith in the Lord Jesus Christ, as that they may cleave to Him, and seek Him early, and do and suffer anything for the name of Christ. And yet sometimes doubt whether their faith be sound-hearted or no. In such a case he doubts whether his faith be true or no, he wants the sense of his faith. For he believes not that he has faith. Now this faith of his had need to be increased in the sense and feeling of it, that he may plainly see the faith he has is no fancy, or presumption, or delusion—as he has very much suspected—but that he may see the faith he has is the faith of God's elect. He had need be built up in his faith more and more: "Lord I believe, help my unbelief" (Mark 9:24). He could not tell whether he might call his faith, faith or unbelief. He could not tell what to call it. He was willing to believe, but it was with so much difficulty, and so much impotency of faith that he prays for the removal of his unbelief. So that, in regard of the doubts that a man has many times of his own faith, he had need grow up in faith, that he may believe that he does believe. And this is that you read, "For the joy of your faith" (Phil. 1:25). This was something in which they were to be furthered. It was the joy and comfort of their faith, so to rise up in believing, as that they might have comfort in it. For so far as a man believes, and yet is doubtful of it, he has little comfort and joy in his faith. And therefore the Apostle would have them furthered in their joy, that their faith might be a joyful faith. Such as wherein they might have comfort, and might be joyful for that they had received faith.

And fourthly, faith had need be increased in respect of the acts—the proper acts of faith—which are chiefly persuasion and trust upon the name of Christ. And those heavenly truths in which the Lord Jesus Christ is revealed and graciously dispensed unto the hearts of His people, even these also had need to be marvelously enlarged in Christian men, above what at the first they do arise unto, see them both put together. Peter, when he walked upon the water, he was fully persuaded and did trust upon Christ for protection in a very doubtful and dangerous case. He did trust upon Him, but when the wind began to blow and the storm to arise, then Peter's faith began to shrink, and his body to sink, and then he cries out, "O Master, save me, else I perish" (Matt. 14:30, 31)! "O you of little faith," says our Savior, to show you that a man's faith had need be further increased. So you see our Savior rebukes him for his little faith, not only weak in the habit of it, but little in the proper act of it. He begins to shrink in his persuasion, and in his trust, and that was thought the littleness of his faith.

And so the two disciples that went to Emmaus. They looked sadly to think of the death of Christ, and complain of it to Jesus, and when He asked them why they looked so sadly, they tell Him the cause, concerning the death of Christ, and say they, "we trusted this had been He that should have delivered Israel" (Luke 24:21-24). "O fools, and slow of heart!" Ought not Christ to have suffered these things? It is to show you that there is, even in God's own servants, that are true believers, something to be supplied in the acts of their faith. Their persuasion and trust is many times very much overwhelmed, so as that many times they call in question the main principles and foundations of their faith. "'We trusted this was He,' but we are doubtful whether we be not deceived or not, God knows whether it was He or not; but we have just occasion of doubting." For they thought the Messiah should have lived forever. "And now this is the third day since He was crucified, and we trusted this was He, but now He is dead, and has lain so long in the grave, and we are therefore doubtful whether this was He or not." And therefore in this regard faith had need be increased.

Fifthly, faith had need to grow, even that faith which accompanies salvation, by which we believe on the name of Christ. Not only thus far as has been said, but had need to grow in the fruits of it. For many times though faith may have some strength and comfort, and put forth itself in some acts, yet notwithstanding it may sometimes fall out, and often does, that even the faith of God's people is much intercepted from putting forth itself, in those lively fruits of faith which redound to the praise and glory of God: "Faith works by love" (Gal. 5:6). Now you know what you have heard of the love of God's people that they may depart from their first love. Yes, so far depart from it as that he may fall short of the performance of his first works of his faith and love together (Rev. 2:4, 5). Faith at the first was more abundantly fruitful than now it is, and so their first love was more abundantly fruitful unto good works than now they are able to reach unto, but it is said of the Thyatirans, "their works was more at the last than they were at the first" (Rev. 2:19). It is a sign their faith was as much growing in fruitfulness as the other was decayed, so that something may be supplied to the faith of God's people, their faith and love, and the fruits thereof had need to be increased. So that, this is not a vain end of John's writing to them that believe on His name that they may believe, though they now believe, yet they had need to believe yet more, though it may seem to be a tautology, yet it is an evident truth.

Now then for further opening of this point, first to show you that all which at this time has been said, may be one reason of the point why John writes thus to them, which is taken from the defects that are found in the faith of all believers, which it were meet and necessary should be supplied.

THE MIGHTY POWER OF THE SCRIPTURES

It is taken from the marvelous power that is in this epistle, and so in other Scriptures, to supply these defects that are thus wanting in our faith, whether in the object of it, or in whatever else. There is a marvelous power in the Holy Scriptures to supply it all, and indeed the Scriptures are so carved out and so dispensed. And when dispensed aright there is a mighty power in them to supply faith, and the defects of it in every believer. The Scriptures are mighty through God, whether "preached, or read, or heard," or "conferred upon," or "meditated upon." For to my remembrance, the Scriptures are sanctified of God to none other use but to one of these five. The Word of God is mighty, and mighty to this end, that believing in the Word, whether preached, or heard, or read, or examining what you have heard, or meditating, or conferring upon it, there is a mighty power in the Holy Scriptures to supply the faith of God's people.

Preaching

There is a mighty power in the Scriptures preached. For He writes these things that they may be preached, and to be read, and to make use of them in conference, and meditation, and in them all there is a mighty power. But first for preaching: "The gospel is the power of God to salvation, for therein is the righteousness of God revealed from faith to faith" (Rom. 1:16, 17). By the gospel of God preached, the righteousness of God is revealed from faith to faith to lead on believers to believe. And not to rest growing in believing till they reach unto salvation; "It is the mighty power of God to salvation to everyone that believes." Such a one, while he lives shall be of the thriving hand of faith. And when the Apostle prayed so earnestly, night and day to come again to the Thessalonians, does he not therein imply, though there may be a mighty power in the Word read to increase faith where it is already wrought, yet his personal presence would help it much more, whether by conference or by preaching? And therefore he prays much to see them again. An evident argument, though the Word read may be of much use to establish us, yet much more the personal presence, and conference and preaching of the gospel of Christ, else that prayer of his had been something impertinent.

Conference

And so secondly, for conferring of the Scriptures. You know when the two disciples were doubtful whether that was the Christ or not; our Savior does not only reprove them for that doubtfulness, but He begins at Moses, "and opened to them the things written in the Prophets," till in the end "their hearts glowed and burned within them" (Luke 24:27, 32). And that was a furtherance of their faith, for then they presently ran to Jerusalem, and then they do not say, "We trusted this was He," but they say, "The Lord is risen indeed." In very truth without any further dissension, never distrusted it more, "He is risen indeed." So that there is a mighty power in the Word conferred upon in private conference. And therefore they doubt no more of it. So that the Word opened by way of conference made their hearts to burn within them. They do not call it preaching, but rather a private conference—an applying the Scripture to this point they stood need to be instructed in. And they go away with full resolution, "the Lord is risen indeed."

And you know the mighty power and use of the conference of Philip with the Eunuch upon that conference. The Eunuch believed and was baptized (Acts 8:37). So that take the Word preached, and there is a mighty power of God in it to lead a Christian man from faith to faith. And take the gospel of God and confer about it, and it is a mighty power to increase faith, that believers may believe.

Reading the Word

Thirdly, and so it is for the Word read. Another kind of dispensing this Word that is a special end of it, that "by reading you might believe on the name of the Son of God." That is the next use of the Scripture. They which do read, shall by reading find their hearts confirmed, and established in the faith (John 20:30, 31). There is a mighty power of God that accompanies the Word of God read to strengthen men in the faith, that such as believe already, may believe more, and be established in their persuasion of the truth of God.

Examination of Things Heard

Fourthly, if you shall examine the things that you have heard. That is another use of the Scriptures. An examination of what you hear; go home and consider whether the things that have been taught were true or not; whether agreeable to the Holy Scriptures or not. For a preacher speaks not the express words of the Scripture, but comments and explications of the Scriptures, and therefore examine whether that which is delivered be agreeable to the Scriptures which are alleged for to prove the doctrine. We must make use of the Scripture as a rule to measure all the sermon by we hear, whether it be of just length and breadth of God's Word or no, as the balance of the sanctuary, the two Testaments be, and when you weigh what is said, then you are confirmed and established in it.

Now, this kind of making use of the Scriptures to examine what you hear, it is of special use to help forward the faith of such as do believe. Yes, (and which is more) it may bring on men to believe, which it may be never did believe before, mightily stirred before, but believed not, till they go home and searched the Scriptures, seeing that which is spoken to be fully agreeable to the Word of God, they have been brought on wonderfully to believe. Famous is that of the Bereans: "They heard the Word, and what he spoke they received it gladly," they thought he spoke well, but "they searched daily to see whether those times which were spoken were so or not" (Acts 17:11, 12). Therefore see the blessing of God upon it, "many of them believed" (v. 12). They received the Word with reverence and did not cavil at it, but heard it patiently. And when they came at home conferred about it. And when upon examination, they saw it was according to the Scriptures of the holy prophets. When they saw that what Paul preached was suitable to Moses and the Prophets, the blessing of God was great upon them. For the number of them that believed was not a few.

To show you that a man that has heard the Word, and has been stirred with what he heard, if he shall go home and consider and weigh well, and see how one thing bears witness to another. So as that the Word preached, opens the Word written, and the Word written, confirms the Word preached. Then though before he was doubtful, as sometimes a godly man's heart may fail him in applying the Word to himself, as Jacob's heart failed and he believed not. Yet when he considered it, and saw what tokens of love was sent him, and laid circumstances together, then his spirit revived. So a man hears much, and something pertinent to him. Yet his heart may fail him, and may have much ado to gather any comfort out of it. But when he considers things more privately and searches the Scriptures, upon examination many a man believes the Word, which before he was doubtful of. Repetition and examination of the Word is marvelously blessed by God to this end to help forward our faith. It is of good use both to begin, and to increase faith; sometimes to work it, where it was heretofore wanting, much more to increase it where it was begun before, and therefore as we were begotten by the immortal Word of God. So, no Word of God being dispensed in any Ordinance of God, none of them but are of mighty use for the supplying our defects of faith, and to make us believe more.

Meditation on the Word

Fifthly, the Word also mediated upon. When a man has heard it, and searched it, and believed it, read and conferred about it, or say none of these for the present, but whether these have gone before or not. For the present the very meditation of God's Word, which a man now takes into his mind as he is riding or working. There is a mighty power in the Word, pondering upon it, and chewing of it, to make a man more rooted in it, more fruitful, and more comfortable in believing. This truth you see in Psalm 1:1-3. When a man "meditates upon the Law of God day and night," he grows to more delight in it. One of these helps another, and what will be the fruit of it? "He shall be like a tree planted by the rivers of waters," planted and rooted, and well-watered there, and "he brings forth his fruit in due season," and whatsoever he does shall prosper; not as planted in a dry wilderness, but by the rivers of water. And that makes him not only well-rooted and grown tall, but it enables him to bring forth fruit in due season. And as for his leaf it withers not, neither summer's heat, nor winter's frosts makes it to fall. But he still holds his greenness, and his fruitfulness, and he grows in all the graces God which tend to the praise, and glory of His grace. And this is by reason of his delighting and meditating in the Word of God, and thus you see the point opened.

USE 1: PROPIETY OF A FAITHFUL MINISTER

First then, you may from hence gather a sign of trial of your own faith. For if this be the spirit of a godly teacher to draw on those that are believers to believe, it is a good sign as of a faithful minister; so of a faithful hearer, when he desires to supply the defects of his own and others faith. You see John, a faithful minister to those Christians to whom he writes. He, when he had brought them on to believe and found faith wrought in their hearts, it was his care not there to leave them. He does not say as some would, "Well, there is now truth of grace in them, and truth of faith, such faith as accompanies salvation." And now he that begun this work in them will finish it, and so leave them. And you say, "Now you need take no further care about them, but now they will do well enough." No, this is not the spirit of a faithful minister of Jesus Christ, and it will be but uncomfortable to such ministers, as think now they may be left to the wide world, they will shift anywhere. But where we see any seeds of faith begun, we must be desirous to increase it in ourselves and ours. The apostles themselves pray, "Lord increase our faith" (Luke 17:5). And so they desire to increase other men's faith.

We had need grow fast this way if we would have a true sign of a lively faith, true and lively faith always desires to grow in itself. And it would cause the like faith also to grow in others, and therefore as you see faithful ministers are thus desirous to grow themselves, and to cause others to grow, as Paul prays "exceedingly night and day, to come to those" whom he had taken pains withal, "that he might make a supply of what was wanting in their faith" (1 Thes. 3:10). And as faithful ministers must clothe themselves with this earnest desire to be calling yet more and more upon believers. That such as do believe may believe yet more, and grow from faith to faith. Truly so godly Christians look, as ministers are desirous to grow in their own faith, and to help on others. So in Christians, it is a true sign of faith, not to content ourselves in truth of faith, but to desire earnestly after growth in faith. Had not they cause to pray that

Paul might come among them again and help them? And therefore, doubtless this is that which every true believer has respect unto.

Every faithful Christian prays for himself, "Lord increase my faith, Lord help my unbelief." This is the prayer of every soul that comes to Christ that though we have some measure of faith already, yet mixed with so much unfruitfulness, and unsettledness, and so many defects, that every Christian has cause to pray, "Lord help my unbelief." Sometimes a man is hindered with offenses and they are to be avoided. In which a man will not be able to put forth love unless he have a strong faith, and that was the reason why the apostles prayed so earnestly "Lord increase our faith" (Luke 17:5). For it was upon this occasion our Savior had been exhorting them, how to carry themselves in respect of offenses: "If your brother trespass against you rebuke him, and if he repent forgive him, *etc.*" (Luke 17:3). Now they apprehended it was a great work. They saw it was a great work to rebuke him. He had need have much faith before he can do that. But suppose upon that a man do humble himself and repent, then for a man to forgive him, it requires a great faith to forgive a wrong, or an injury offered to us.

But what if he come and offend me again and again, seventy times seven times? why if he do, and say it repents me, "you shall forgive him?" Now when they hear this, that a man must be so freehearted in forgiving wrongs and injuries done to themselves, they had need have a strong love, and strong love stands in need of a strong faith—to show you that a man that shall have occasion to trade with his faith, and to live and walk by him in faith, he shall have much need of the growth and increase of it. If it be but for the healing of offenses, many occasions and temptations may meet with us in the world, temptations from Satan, as well as from the world (1 John 2:14). And if a man have strong enemies, he will stand in need of a strong faith, to cut asunder all the "fiery darts of the devil" (Eph. 6:16); "above all take the shield of faith." There is no man willing to go to the field with weak armor. He would if he could have armor of proof, such as might repulse a weapon or a dart cast against him. So a Christian has to fight against many enemies. And a shield covers his whole body, and so differs from a buckler that covers but one part. But a shield covers the whole man stands upon the ground and covers him all over. And now faith being such a shield, it is of mighty force, and is able to repulse all the "fiery darts of the devil," and all the rest of the enemies of their salvation, so that the servants of God that know what use they have of their faith, they know they have need of the growth and increase of it.

And so again, in regard of their daily employments, "the just man lives by his faith" (Rom. 1:17; Gal. 2:20). A man does nothing Christianly and spiritually, but by his faith. Now when faith must be the instrument to help us to work all our works spiritually, we had need to grow to some life and fruitfulness in faith. And if our faith be not fruitful, we shall make but hard work of our daily employments. How shall we depend upon God, and do all in the name of Christ, and do all in obedience to a commandment, and live by a promise, for God's presence and blessing in it? How shall a man do this if he have not faith, yea, if he have not some dexterity of faith? A weak faith will then slug it, when a man stands in most need to use it. And therefore that a man may be ready to show his faith upon every occasion—in prayer in conference, in everything both concerning this life and another. A man had need of a great deal of faith, and therefore this is an evident sign that a man's faith is well wrought, a sound, and a lively faith, if it be a growing faith. But if you hear men saying they thank God they have a strong faith, and they always believed on Christ, and fie upon them that do not, let me say, this is a presumption of faith, but is no faith. Yes, it is the badge of the want of faith. When therefore you see the Apostle writes to them that believe, that they may believe more certainly, and more strongly, that is a true faith, and it will grow.

USE 2: INFIDEL PRACTICE OF PAPISTS

It serves to reprove the most sacrilegious and uncharitable faith of the Papists that take away these writings from the people. John writes this epistle to the intent that *believers* may *believe*. You heard that the word dispensed in any

Ordinance is of mighty power to increase faith. Where it is begun, and to beget it, where it is wanting. Take away reading of the Scriptures, and conference about them, and you take away all. And therefore an infidel practice to go about to take away the faith of God's elect. God sent us the Scriptures to the end that we might believe. And if this be the nature of faith, to desire that themselves and others might grow in faith, what are they but infidels in truth, who as much as in them lies lock up the Scriptures in a strange tongue that the people may not understand what is read unto them, and as much as in them lies drives the Bibles out of their houses. And it is heretical presumption for such and such men to use the Scriptures. This is infidelity and most sacrilegious to God. And it is likewise uncharitable and injurious to the faith of God's people.

An evident argument of infidelity, how can you charge the wisdom of God of more folly and lightness? God sends His Word to His servants that they might be reading, and hearing, and conferring of it; and that by believing they might believe. These men to cast an imputation of folly upon God. They are afraid that God did not consider the danger of it. If believers should fall a reading, and poor tradesmen a conferring about the Scriptures, they are afraid they will be distempered with heresy, and so trouble the whole Church. Do not they by so doing set the wisdom of God at naught, and show themselves sacrilegious again the truth of God?

USE 3: MIGHTY POWER IN MEDITATING UPON THE WORD

It may serve to exhort us all, since the Holy Ghost did write these things, to the intent "that you that believe on the name of the Son of God might believe."

First, "to you that believe," and then to you that believe not. You that have been diligent in hearing and reading the Word, be diligent in it still, and make it a point of your Christian practice, not to fail to read some part of it every day, unless you be necessarily hindered. Or if you have been necessarily hindered by business from reading, yet be sure nothing hinder you from meditating upon it, "the blessed man meditates on God's Word every night and every day," and though he takes the shorter time to it. Yet he must have some time for meditation upon the Word upon something he heard this day, or something he had sometimes read. And you shall find a mighty power in it to fructify,[9] as if you were "planted by the rivers of waters." For the Spirit of God breathing in the Word, and your hearts sucking it up, and by meditating upon it, you grow in more knowledge in the object of your faith, in the rootedness in the sense, and in the acts and fruits of your faith, and this by hearing, and reading, and meditating. Read therefore, "The king himself must do it daily," who has more business than any man (Deut. 17:19). And if he do so, God will learn him the fear of His name.

---

[9] to make something fruitful or productive

Now if God will not excuse kings, much less private men, who have less affairs than kings have; and therefore be reading every day, and when you cannot read, be sure you meditate upon some part of God's Word, every day and every night.

As ever you desire to believe, use the means that you may believe. This being sanctified of God to that end than be not you wanting to use it, and do not only so. But hear it likewise, and confer upon it, and search it daily whether it be true or not. Use the means that God has sanctified His Word to be dispensed in, and by which He will bless it to His people, and then you shall find this: "In believing you shall believe," you shall grow from faith to faith, and from sense to sense, and in the fruits of faith till you be perfect in Christ Jesus. Be diligent in hearing God's Word, for "it is the mighty power of God unto salvation," and confer of it. There is a mighty power in the Word being conferred upon. Take heed you neglect not occasions in this kind, and search the Scriptures, and examine what you hear, and you will find a mighty power in it to increase faith.

Since therefore God has given you His Word, and shed abroad the water of His Spirit to run through every line of the Scriptures. So that the more you shall read, and hear, confer, and meditate, and search the Scripture, the more you shall find the life of faith increased in you. And therefore you must not wonder if you see Christian men that neglect these duties, complain of the deadness of their hearts. Do you doubt in your persuasion is your confidence mixed with much diffidence? Then ask your heart this question: Whether have you used the Scriptures for those ends God has appointed them, and have you been diligent in conferring about them, and searching of them, whether what is delivered be suitable to them or not, and meditated of them, and brought them home to your house, and compared them together, and meditated upon them day and night, and taken times to chew and digest them? If you have done thus, then you would have believed more assuredly. But if we be negligent in any of these kinds, then wonder not. If we take away bodily food, we take away bodily heat, take away the fuel that nourishes faith, and then it must needs grow weak and infirm. And therefore as you desire to grow in believing, be diligent in these duties, that you may believe on the name of Christ, and in believing may believe much more.

And for you that do not believe savingly: Whose faith will not put you in possession of eternal life? Though this Scripture was not so much written for your use and benefit, as for them that already believe, yet since there is no means to come to faith but by the Word. Be not you wanting, as ever you desire to come to that faith which accompanies salvation. Be not wanting diligently to hear the Word of God, and confer about it with those that believe already, "Faith comes by hearing" (Rom. 10:17). And it is the mighty power of God to salvation. Be glad of any opportunity to hear the Word, and wait at the "posts of wisdoms gates" (Prov. 8:34, 35). "He that finds Me finds life," the promise is very plain, "waiting daily at My gates." Implying that in hearing we shall find Him, and in finding Christ we shall find life. Be diligent therefore to hear, and when you have heard it go home, and search whether it be true or not. And if you have liberty be doing this often, be conferring about it, as you can have any opportunity. God has sanctified these Ordinances to this end. Be diligent in inquiring after wisdom, after Christ in the Scripture. There is a treasure lies, dig for it and you shall have it, especially if with all these you join humble and hearty prayer to God for a blessing upon all these Ordinances. For 1 Timothy 4:5, they are all "sanctified by the Word and prayer" (cf. Prov. 2:2, 3). God would have you to use prayer, entreat Him to open your eyes and hearts that you may believe and obey, and that no Ordinance might be in vain to you, but might profit by them all, and might grow up in believing.

EMBRACING BELIEF IN THE SON OF GOD

And this is the confidence that we have in Him, that if we ask any thing according to His will, He hears us. And if we know that He hears us whatsoever we ask, we know that we have the petitions that we desired of Him (1 John 5:14,15)

In the former verse, the Apostle described to us the main scope of his writing this epistle, which was partly that believers might know that they did believe, and partly that they might "believe on the name of the Son of God." Now, in this latter end John aims at in writing this epistle, he exhorts believers to embrace it by three several motives in the verses following (vv. 14, 15, & 16).

The first motive is taken from the confidence of such as believe on Him for salvation, for the obtaining of their petitions: "This is the confidence that we have in Him," meaning, we that believe on His name, that if we ask anything according to His will, He hears us.

Secondly, another motive or benefit that flows from this is this: "That if we know He hears us, we know we have the things that we asked of Him."

Thirdly, here is likewise added another motive taken

from the prevalency of his prayers with God in such a point, as wherein of all others we may find this comfort. And that is, look as by believing on the name of Christ, we shall find comfort in respect of our everlasting estate. So we shall find this further benefit, that if we "see any brother, which has sinned a sin that is not unto death," not a deadly sin, that is, not the sin against the Holy Ghost. So mighty and prevalent shall our prayers be with God that in case we believe on the name of Christ, and ask pardon of sin for our brother's offense, "God will give him life." So that if we believe on His name, our prayers shall be heard, and they have a prevailing power with God to obtain at his hands the pardon of all our brother's sins that have not sinned unto death.

The Doctrines hence are these:

First, that a prayer that is made well, never speeds ill. Or thus: A prayer that is made according to God's will is ever granted according to our will. Or, as the Apostle says, according to our desire (v. 15). Secondly, such as believe on the name of Christ for salvation may be confident, and certain of the hearing and granting their petitions.[10]

Doctrine 1: *A prayer made according to God's will shall be granted according to our will.*

For so says the words of the text, "If we ask anything according to His will, He hears us." We praying accord-

---

[10] This doctrine will be addressed in the next chapter.

ing to God's will shall find acceptance according to our will. Notable is that speech of encouragement and acceptance of our Savior to the woman of Syropheonicia, "O woman great is your faith, be it unto you even as you will" (Matt. 15:28). She had prayed as Christ would, according to God's will, and she received answer according to her desire. As if a man that did believe, and had a spirit of prayer, and had learning to pray according to God's will, he might be able to carve for himself in the treasures of God's goodness, as if God would let him into the chamber of His presence of His grace and favor, and bid him take what he will, take for himself and his friends, and for his brethren as he will.

To Pray According to God's Will in Two Things

For opening of this point observe thus much. First, let us see what it is to pray according to God's will. And then secondly, what is the ground of the point. For the first, to pray according to God's will, two things are contained in that phrase, and yet diverse things besides those are comprehended in it.

First, when he says, "according to His will," it implies first that we pray for such things as God wills. Such things as are not according to His secret will, for so we cannot guide our actions for "secret things belong to the Lord our God" (Deut. 29:29), but of things revealed. It is according to His revealed will, and it implies that we should ask Him nothing but what He gives us commandment to ask. All that He commands us to do, as to ask that we may ask, and for that we are to pray for expressly—as for the glory of His Name, the coming of His Kingdom, and the building up of His grace in any, the doing of God's will, for our daily bread, &c.—These are the things He has given us warrant to pray for.

Secondly, according to God's will. This is evident that whatsoever we ask, we should ask it with submission to the will of God. So our Savior says in Matthew 26:39; He asked that which was a lawful thing, and yet because He would not trench upon that which might cross the will of His Father, He would not put forth any the least affection of His soul to the overruling the counsel of God, and therefore He expresses Himself thus: "Nevertheless not My will, but Your will be done." So that whenever we ask anything that is lawful, it must be with subjection of our own wills to the will of God. But for more full clearing of this point see it thus enlarged.

First, a man is said to pray according to God's will, either partly as His will is expressed in His Word, and partly the will of God, expressing the work of the Spirit in the heart of a child of God. For both these are effectual in every prayer that is made according to God's will.

First, according to His will expressed in His Word. Therein God requires that we should pray only for such things as are lawful, and such as therein He has commanded us to ask, that we may do them. Notable is that example in Psalm 119:4-5, "You have commanded us to keep Your commandments diligently." And in the next verse see what is his request, "O that my ways were directed to keep Your statutes." Look whatsoever God commands us to do. We have warrant to pray for that, we must pray for things lawful, and only for such.

Secondly, whatsoever we pray for, we must pray in the name of Christ (John 16:22, 23). He makes a large promise to such as so ask in His name, "Whatsoever you shall ask the Father in My name He will give it you" (vv. 23-24). This God requires, that we should put up all our petitions in the name of Christ.

Asking in the Name of Christ Requires the Exercise of Two Graces

Now, to ask in the name of Christ requires the exercise of two graces. First, he that shall ask in the name of Christ, implies the asking of it in humility—whatsoever we ask in humility and lowliness of spirit; that is, to ask in the name of Christ; and that will evidence and put forth itself in three or four several acts in every prayer that is made according to God's will, and put up in the name of Christ.

First, a prayer made in the name of Christ is made with this humility, whereby we acknowledge ourselves less than the least of all God's mercies. As Jacob does acknowledge in Genesis 32:10, he was less than the least of all the mercies he had already received. And therefore, if

God should never grant him more mercy, he could not but acknowledge He had done abundantly more for him already than he had deserved. He prays not in his own name, but in the name of another. And no man can pray in the name of Christ, but he must pray in humility. He must have no confidence in his own worth.

Secondly, he must pray in the sense of his own insufficiency, so much as to think a good thought, much less to make a good prayer (2 Cor. 3:5; Rom. 8:26). This is humility and self-denial, when a man comes before God and acknowledges his own unworthiness to ask any mercy of God, and confesses his own unableness to ask any blessing according to God's will.

Thirdly, a man asks in humility. When he puts up his petitions with submission to God's will, he desires not that God would satisfy him in any lust, but only grant him the things that are expedient for him, so far as may stand with the good pleasure of his heavenly Father, and no further (cf. Matt. 26:39).

Fourthly, there is another act of humility—to bend the heart of a man to make use of no mediation in prayer, but only the mediation of the Lord Jesus Christ. You read of a pretended humility, a voluntary humility, consisting in the worship of angels (Col. 2:18). They thought themselves not worthy immediately to rush into Christ's presence, but rather entreat the angels to intercede the Father for them. But it is counterfeit humility, and such men are puffed up with a fleshly mind in their voluntary humility. It shows that it is a vain pride of heart to express more baseness and meanness of spirit than God requires, and is but a counterfeit humility.

Praying Faithfully

Now, to pray in the name of Christ is not only to pray in humility, but also to pray in faith. And these acts of faith you have in all the prayers that you put up to God according to His will.

First, faith directs you to pray only unto Him, upon whom you have believed (Rom. 10:14). We only believe on God the Father, and on His Son Jesus Christ, and the blessed Spirit, and therefore upon the Lord. Faith only directs us to call. He teaches us not to pray to our mother (as the Papists do), nor to our brethren and sisters (as the Papists do to the saints and angels), but only to the Father. That is the voice of faith: "The Spirit helps us to cry, Abba Father!" (Rom. 8:15; cf. Gal. 4:5, 6).

Secondly, it is the nature and work of faith in every prayer. It does guide the heart of a man to look unto God with some kind of child-like confidence, repairing to Him as a Father. Such as by faith believe on the name of the Son of God, they come to God in their prayers, as to their Father (John 20:17). And it is the nature of faith to cry out as Thomas did, "My Lord, and my God" (John 20:28)! So that this is another work of faith, that whenever you come into God's presence to ask anything at His hand, you come to Him as to your Father. He knows what you want better than you can ask, and is more willing to grant whatever is meet for you. Then you can desire to come to God as our heavenly Father through Jesus Christ as an act of faith. He is so well acquainted with us in Him, that Himself loves us (John 16:26, 27). So that, to pray in faith is to come to God as the Father of our Lord Jesus Christ, and through Him a Father also to us, abundant in goodness and in truth; a Father that is great in counsel, and excellent in work; that has compassion of His own children, and will therefore perform that which seems good in His sight.

Thirdly, another act of faith, and that is for a man to come truly cleaving to the Lord Jesus Christ. Not to stand upon demurs and disputes, whether we had best cleave to God, and whether we had best do such or such things, and so be almost Christians. For if we so come, we cannot receive anything at the hands of God: "A wavering minded man is unstable, *etc.*" (Jas. 1:5-8). This is one, and a principal part of the meaning of it. He speaks of such a kind of wavering faith, as whereby a man is a ἀνὴρ δίψυχος[11] —"a heart, and a heart." He has a mind

---

[11] Greek: lit. "another heart," also rendered "double-souled"

to draw near to Christ, and to become a servant of Christ, and yet withal a mind to be hankering after some sinful lust or other which takes up his mind, and which his soul lusts after. And therefore, he is unstable in all his ways. Sometimes he is for God, and sometimes for himself, ever halting between God and the world. But let such men think they shall not receive anything at the hands of God, this should have been in the second place.

Fourthly, faith has respect unto this: to believe that what we have asked according to God's will, He will undoubtedly give it us. "Believe that you shall receive, and you shall receive it" (Mark 11:24); meaning, so far as you have commended your petitions to God in the name of Christ with subjection to the will of your heavenly Father. Believe it—that God has respect to your poor estate, and He will do for you what you desire. Yes, even in those things wherein He seems to delay an answer. But in the meantime, for your part make account your prayers are heard in that very blessing you desire. For God does wisely ponder, not only the hearts of the sons of men, but all the words of their lips, and He knows the meaning of the spirit in the hearts of His children.

And though we must express ourselves in words, in our desire of this and that blessing, yet God looks principally at the grounds of our desires, and wherefore we desire to obtain the blessing. What it is that moves us to have a desire after such and such a mercy, and observing well the bias of our hearts in such requests, He does in this respect constantly hearken to His servants and fails not to grant us the things we ask, even when He seems to deny us. In Hebrews 5:7, He speaks of the prayer of Christ: "He was heard in what He desired."

What was He heard in? Why, He prayed that "if it were possible the cup might pass from Him." And was He heard in this? Did not He drink it to the very dregs? Did He not taste of God's deepest displeasure? And how is He then said to be heard? Why, the Father did consider what it was that His Son did desire, which was principally that God's will might be done, and not His own.

And God's will being done, Christ's desire, being that God's will might be done, He was heard in the thing He desired. And again, He was heard in the thing so far as it concerned Himself, as to be saved from that which He feared. That though He did drink of the cup, yet He should be saved from being overwhelmed by those fears, which His soul trembled at, and groaned under, and pressed Him heavily, even unto the very death. Though not from tasting of them, yet from being overwhelmed of them, and He was supported in them. So that Christ's main end being the doing of His Father's will, and the redemption of mankind, in these things, He was graciously heard.

And so, Moses prayed that if it might be God's will, he might go over Jordan and see that good land. His end was to see that good land. Well, God said in displeasure, he should not go over, and yet in mercy He answers his request. For his desire was to see that good land. Now God could make him see that good land, and never carry him over Jordan. And He shows him all the land of Canaan—all the coasts of Israel from the one end thereof to another. God so strengthened his sight this way, as one would not have thought it credible. But that God was able to grant him his desire, and strengthened him beyond what he desired, so shall you observe God's manner of dealing with His servants. If we be content to pray according to the will of God, and bow our spirits to ask nothing but what is lawful, and with submission to God's will, and run to God as our heavenly Father in the name of Jesus Christ; and look at Him as one more ready to give. Then we to ask. Then make account God will ponder all the petitions of your souls and weigh well what you have said. And He knows what you aim at in asking this and that blessing. And though He may seem to defer it, He better knows your need of it than yourselves do, and when He seems most to cross it, then does He most abundantly answer it.

Moses said the Lord was angry with him, and would not hear him, and yet He did hear him. He limited God to a means to show him that good land, but he need not appoint God a course. Moses knew not how he should see it, unless he went over, but God knew how he should see it. So that even those prayers with which God seems to be angry, in regard of some infirmity that God may see in our prayers. Yet this we are to make account of, that even then, when God is displeased with our poor petitions, even then does He answer them most graciously. "God was wroth with me, and would not hear me, and He said speak no more to me of that matter" (Deut. 3:23, 25-26). It was a marvelous strange kind of expression of God's fatherly counsel to Moses, that when He is angry with some weakness in our prayers, and some unworthiness in us to desire, or have this or that; see His carriage. Moses, his words provoked God, and therefore, because he desires to go over Jordan to see that good land, God was wroth. And God would not have him go. And yet he should see it. He should have as much as he desired, but into the land he should not go. So that come with that confidence in prayer, that though our prayers be such as for which God may be angry with us, yet many times God hears those prayers, and answers them in mercy, far beyond what we could have thought. For Moses saw as much of it as could be seen, and he could not have seen so much of it if he had gone over Jordan, as he did then see.

Consider therefore, God marks the very bent of my soul and desire in every petition I put up. And therefore observing what I desire, He will accordingly grant either the thing I desire according to my desire, or that which I aim at in my desire. And this is a glory to the name of

Christ, whatsoever we should ask in our own names would be thrust out of heaven. Yet this magnifies the name of Christ, that a Christian soul believing on His name, and laying hold upon Him, and cleaving to Him, and shall come to God as believing that God is more ready and able and willing to grant than we to ask, and that He will grant us the very petition that we desire. This does magnify the name of the Lord Jesus Christ, and this is to pray according to God's will, as expressed in His Word.

But now in the second place, there is something in our prayers made according to the will of God as is expressed in the spirit of him that prays. For this you shall find ordinarily in Scripture, that men that pray, pray in the Spirit; "Praying in the Holy Ghost" (Jude 20) and "pray in the Spirit" (Eph. 6:18). And you know what the Apostle says in that well known place, in Romans 8:26, 27; "We know not what to pray for, nor how to pray as we ought, but the Spirit helps us, *etc.*" God searches the heart especially in prayer. He knows the meaning of the Spirit, for He makes requests according to the will of God. That is the words of the text, so that, if you would ask, how we may pray according to the will of God? Look what is revealed in the breathings of the Spirit, which marvelously declares itself in the wrestling, and longing desires that it puts up to God. "My soul longs and breathes after You" (Ps. 119:20, 81, 131); and it lets us know what the will of God is, and for that the Spirit helps us to pray.

Praying in the Spirit: Feelingly

Now to open this a little. First, you shall discern the will of God by the breathing of the spirit. When the Spirit helps us to pray feelingly and sensibly for those blessings that we stand in need of, when the Spirit does lift up our hearts, and reach after those mercies we stand in need of, in some feeling and sensible manner. The will of God is revealed in the breathing of the spirit that stretches forth itself in such a humble and faithful manner, as that the soul is very sensible of its need of it. We pour out our souls before God, for what we stand in need of in feeling desires. And this good Hannah expressed in her prayers, "I am a woman of a sorrowful spirit, I have poured out my soul before the Lord" (1 Sam. 1:15). To show you, there was an inward sensible work of the Spirit of God in her heart that did enlarge her, not so much to pour out words, as sighs and groans. This feeling power of the Spirit does mightily express what the will of God is that we should ask. This is according to the will of God, according to what you read, "With my spirit within me will I seek You early" (Isa. 26:9); my spirit within me, that is to say, he speaks as if there were a spirit within his spirit; besides the inclination God had given and wrought in him to the ways of grace. And besides, his soul that did animate his body, "the Spirit of God within him." With that spirit will he seek God early in prayer. The Spirit will inwardly be working, and turning him towards God. So then, this is the first thing wherein God reveals His will to us. And we pray in the Spirit, which we do when we pray in the sense and feeling of our own wants of those blessings we want at God's hand. That is, by a certain strength, greater than any of our own spirits can reach forth themselves unto. The Spirit of God comes, and helps us to wrestle with God with sighs and groans that cannot be expressed; that we think more than we speak, and we speak more than we thought of.

Praying in the Spirit: Fervently

Secondly, besides this, this Spirit helps us to pray unto God with fervency and heat of spirit, so much as that in such a case as this we strive with God in our prayers and wrestle with Him. "The effectual fervent prayer of the righteous avails much" (Jas. 5:16). When the Spirit of God helps us to fervency, to cry to God, and to be earnest with Him in that regard, and not to give Him over, and comes from a sensible want of the blessings we stand in need of. And that makes us go out of ourselves to God for the mercy that is according to the will of God. And this in Scripture is called wrestling and striving with God (Rom. 15:30). When you grow sensible of your own danger, and you strive with him for the blessing. This is to express fervency of spirit, and this was commended in Jacob, that "he wrestled with God" (Gen. 32:24, 26), which is expounded in Hosea 12:4, that "he prayed and wept." His wrestling was chiefly in prayer with tears, that God would be merciful to him in this case.

Praying in the Spirit: Perseverantly

Thirdly, we pray then in the Spirit when we also persevere in prayer, for that is also requisite in all the petitions we put up. Our Savior put forth a parable for this very end that men "should pray constantly, and never be weary" (Luke 18:1). Pray upon all occasions for everything that you stand in need of, and never give over till you be heard and answered. And the parable teaches thus much from the unjust judge; shall a sinful mortal man be moved with importunity, and shall not God arise, and be moved for those poor souls that cry unto Him night and day? Yes, doubtless though you may think God is not sensible of your prayers. But He rests Himself quietly in heaven, and remains in fullness of glory, who is blessed forever in Himself, and will not trouble Himself with such poor requests as yours is. But let me tell you, this woman did not so much trouble the judge here, nor could be more troublesome to him than a poor Christian is to God that wrestles with Him in prayer. God cannot be quiet in heaven for such a soul, but in the end He must rise and satisfy its desire. So you have the like, in Luke 11:8-13, "If you continue knocking he will rise," and so will your heavenly Father do for you much more. So as that though God might seem to be asleep, and rest Himself satisfied in that blessed estate He enjoys in another world, and no more regard things below than men asleep. Yet if you continue knocking and begging, you will disturb His peace till He arise and show mercy to you.

And this He speaks after the manner of men, to show you that He does as unfeignedly, and as deeply take to heart the desires of your souls, as any of you can do one of another. And therefore be constant and persevering in prayer, and never give over. When we have a good petition in hand never give over, when we pray for pardon of sin, or for peace of conscience, or for strength of grace for ourselves or for others. When we pray for the healing of our souls, or our bodies, for the Church or Commonwealth. Whatsoever we have in hand, if the Spirit of God do but move us this way, it is for us never to give over until God show mercy to us in some one kind or other, that we may see our requests was not neglected. "Watch thereunto with perseverance" (Eph. 6:18, 19).

Where you see what course God would have His servants to take, take this course; ever follow God, watch night and day, and never give over till He bless you and yours, until He bless magistrates. Give ministers a door of utterance, that they may speak savingly, and powerfully to the souls of their hearers, so as that as it were you may weary God, and prevail with Him to arise, and give you your desire.

Wherefore is it think you that Christ calls prayer knocking? But for this very end, to manifest unto us that when we continue praying we continue knocking, and we make as a loud noise at heaven gates. As any man that knocks at your house doors, and God so esteems the nature of prayer, "For to him that knocks it shall be opened" (Matt. 7:7). So that if God do but give us hearts to knock, and to be instant and constant in prayer, for that is knocking. If we be fervent and persevering in prayer, and spring from our feeling and sense of want of the blessing, and what comfort it would be to us to obtain it, and give Him no rest until we receive at His hands what we ask of Him; to him that thus knocks it shall be opened.

So did the woman of Syropheonicia. She knocked hard at our Savior's door of mercy, "have pity, have mercy upon me." And when at the first Christ answers her not a word, she then cries out again, "Lord, help me!" And when thereupon He tells her He was not sent to her, but to the lost sheep of the house of Israel, did she then leave off? No, she would not be put off. When He then told her, it was not "meet to take the children's bread and to cast it to dogs," she said, "Truth Lord, but yet the dogs eat the crumbs that fall from the table." Why then says our Savior, "be it unto you even as you will"? Like as a man that is weary of a petitioner. As if He should say, "Why, if you be so importunate that you will have no denial, if it must be so, why go your way, and be it unto you even as you will?" And when God gives us so to pray as not to give over, we may know for a certain, God intends to give us a gracious answer in all the desires of our souls, and this is to pray according to God's will.

Reasons Why Prayer is Answered

Now to speak of the second part of the doctrine. And that is the reason why a prayer thus made is ever granted, pray well, and speed well.

First, because in praying according to God's will, God does but fulfil His own will in fulfilling yours. As this is the will of God that all those things that are lawful for us to ask, and expedient for us, it is His will that we should pray for them. It is God's will that we should pray with submission to God's will; that we should pray humbly and feelingly and constantly. Now if we have prayed according to the will of God, then His will must needs be done. And His will is that now our wills should be fulfilled. This reason is taken from the faithfulness of God in the promise, and from the suitableness of God's will to ours, when we so pray.

Secondly, it is taken from the mighty power of the name of Christ. Whenever we use His name in prayer, not in lip labor; but when we pray in sense of our own unworthiness, and in some measure of childlike confidence, the prayers that we now make is the prayer of Christ, and "Him the Father hears always" (John 11:42). Now if Christ give us to use His name, look whatever petition we put up, and use His name in it, it is now the prayer of Christ. For look as if any of you should send your child or servant to any of your neighbors to desire such or such a favor from them, you send them, but the petition is yours. They desire it in your name, and if you send him, and bid him use your name, and then you are sure it will be granted. And if he should deny your child or servant of such a petition that he asks in your name, in denying him he denies you. So that God cannot deny the petition you ask in Christ's name; for Him He hears always, and all such petitions He has promised to hear.

The word of promise you heard before and it is full to this purpose, "Verily, verily, I say unto you"—He takes His own truth to witness it, as a solemn asseveration: "Whatsoever you shall ask the Father in My name He will give it you." And therefore, "Ask in My name that you may receive" (John 16:23). If therefore the Lord Jesus Christ do but give us this encouragement, that we faithfully give up ourselves to become His, and in sense of our own unworthiness to ask anything at God's hands. And we come to the Father as being set a work by Christ, and beseech Him to answer us in this and that mercy, and cannot give over till He receive our prayers, and reach us an answer of them, then the promise stands good, "Ask and you shall receive."

Thirdly, it is taken from God's acceptance, not only of Christ, but of the Spirit—the Holy Ghost, also. For that is much to be considered. For there is no prayer that is so wrought in this sort, nor any prayer thus put up, in sense, and feeling, and breathing of the Spirit in the name of Christ; but it is the prayer of the Holy Ghost Himself. And God that knows the meaning of the Spirit, He hearkens to all the requests of the Spirit. "The Spirit itself makes intercession for us" (Rom. 8:26, 27), so that these prayers are not only received and gratified, because they are put up in the name of Christ. But also because "the Spirit itself makes intercession for us, according to the will of God." And God knows the meaning and voice of His own Spirit. God knows that without this we could never be fervent for any spiritual blessing according to the will of God. Our dead hearts would soon make dead work of it. If there were no spirit in our prayer but our own, if our flesh be weak we shall soon have done. And therefore when God sees us pray thus feelingly, and are not willing to leave Him till He answer us in our desires, then God knows there is a mighty power of a spirit that speaks in us, and God cannot deny the intercession of His Spirit.

And further to strengthen this point, Christ Himself tells us that He will pray in our behalves for us. For the Lord Jesus Christ Himself sits at God's right hand making intercession for us. "At that day you shall ask in My name, and I say not unto you that I will pray the Father for you, for the Father Himself loves you, because you have loved Me, *etc.*" (John 16:26). And the Apostle sweetly expresses how the Lord Jesus prays for us; "Who is he that condemned, it is Christ that died, yes, rather that is risen again, who is even at the right hand of God, who also makes intercession for us" (Rom. 8:34). So that the Lord Jesus Christ takes up our prayers as our Mediator, as the great Master of requests. And He dresses and perfumes them from all that sinful frailty and coldness that usually accompanies our prayers. He perfumes with the merits of His own sufferings, and so presents them before the Father with His own worth in His sight. And so they come to be accepted in the sight of God. So you read in Revelation 8:3, howsoever that may be verified in some type of Christ on earth, yet especially it is meant of Christ in heaven, He perfumes the prayers of the saints, and expresses His own will to the Father, as beseems the majesty of the Son of God. And as a Mediator, He perfumes our unsavory prayers and presents them to His Father, so as they become accepted in His sight.

As if an elder brother should set a child one of his younger brethren to get his father a posy of flowers, and the child out of ignorance should gather some weeds and put in it; and the elder brother gathers out of the weeds and sprinkles the flowers; and then presents them in the child's name to the father. So does Christ to us. While we gather up petitions here and there, and as we think for the best, and some truth and work of grace there is in them, yet some weeds of sinful folly. Then Christ takes them out of our hands, and pulls out the weeds, and sprinkles them with the blood of His cross, and the merit of His sufferings, what He has done and suffered for us. And so by this means it is not possible that our prayers should be rejected.

USE 1: TO PRAY WELL

It may serve to teach us all. As ever we desire, we or ours might speed well, so to learn to pray well. No one can speed ill, that can pray well.

If you can but pray, you need ask no more for you and yours. If you or yours can pray well, they have enough; let them but speak, and speed; pray, and have, seek, and find. "Oh woman, be it unto you even as you will!" In such a case, God will accept you so far as to carry you in among the treasures of His grace, the store-house of His mercy, and there for to fill you with what you would have. And bring but your desires large enough, and open your mouths wide enough and He will fill them. The woman was to blame she borrowed no more vessels, so long as you have but a mouth to pray. Especially, a heart open and enlarged to desire much at God's hands, you shall need no more mercies but this, you have enough. If God give you a heart to pray, you want nothing.

And therefore of all blessings, beg this blessing; that you may learn to pray. You shall need no more mercy for this nor another world. I pray you consider what I have said in this behalf. Do but observe,

First, take heed you be not of a double mind; of a wavering mind (Jas. 1:6). Take heed of wavering. That is when a man halts between two opinions. When he knows not whether he had better cleave to God or to the world—loath to deny himself, and yet would be somebody. But if a man be of a wavering mind, let not such a man think he shall obtain anything at the hand of God. He must be of such a mind and heart as by which he must cleave fast to the Lord.

As Barnabas exhorted them with "full purpose of heart to cleave to the Lord" (Acts 11:23), and if so with full purpose of heart you cleave to the Lord, you do pray in some measure of faith. And then may you sooner learn what God has commanded you to do (Ps. 119:4, 5). And this you shall find of much consequence, that according as we hearken to God's commandments, so God hearkens to our requests. Look with what care you listen to Him, with the same care He listens to us. If He see that we give up ourselves to observe every word of God, then shall we never be confounded. If God see you have a tender heart to all His commandments, He will have as tender a respect to all your desires. And therefore be careful, as first to grow to a free-hearted giving up yourselves to Christ. So listen duly to what God commands, and then God will have a tender respect to every one of your petitions. When this is your first aim, then may you have respect to other things. God will then satisfy your souls in revealing to you His granting of all your petitions.

USE 2: COMFORT

Of comfort to every soul that has given up itself to Christ, and do thus call upon His name. This is the confidence all such have. They shall be satisfied according to their wills. Many a soul that has received a spirit of prayer is many times much discouraged. And what is the matter? "Why, this and that I have prayed for, but my faith is faint within me for want of the thing I desire." Why, but be not discouraged, heaven and earth shall fail, but the Word of God shall never fail. Do but consider what it is you have asked, and know there is no prayer of yours but it stands upon record in heaven. And God waits and stays but for a fit and seasonable time.

Notable is that speech in Daniel: "At the beginning of your supplication, the commandment went forth." It was sent forth to grant you your request but it was hindered so many days, that it could not be done till now, from the beginning the prayer was heard, and the answer was decreed, but it must have a time to be wrought. Look as you see a man that makes a petition to a king. The king grants the petition the same day it is asked, but it must pass from the privy seal to the great seal, and so be a good while before the business be gone through with. Truly so, the first day that any soul seeks to God in Christ for any blessing, God hears in heaven. Only it must pass through the hands of some angels. They must see it done, means and creatures must be wrought upon, something must be done before our petitions be granted, notwithstanding our prayers be accepted.

CONFIDENCE BEFORE GOD

And if we know that He hears us whatsoever we ask,
we know that we have the petitions we desire of Him.
(1 John 5:14-15)

Now to come to a second note.

Doctrine 2: *Such as believe on the name of Christ for salvation may be confident and certain of the hearing and granting of their petitions.*

There is a double act and a double object. The double act is confidence and knowledge. And the double object is first, hearing of our petitions. And secondly, the granting of our petitions, and both expressly distinguished in the text. And so the point will be evident, "Such as believe on the name of Jesus Christ for salvation" (for of them he speaks in verse 13), they may come to a confident, and certain knowledge of the hearing and granting of their petitions, and the having of them all fulfilled.

CONFIDENCE AND KNOWLEDGE

To open this point unto you. And because John does gather this from the end of his own writing. For he says he wrote these things only to them that believe in the name of the Son of God, for this end, that they might believe on His name.

Therefore, let me show you first how these two great benefits—confidence and certainty of hearing and having our petitions—does both spring and arise from what is here taught us.

First, which is the foundation of all the rest, speaking of adoption, says he, "Behold what manner of love the Father has showed on us, that we should be called the sons of God" (1 John 3:1). He does stand and wonder at the marvelous and incredible love of God that He should vouchsafe to stoop so low, and honor us so much; debase Himself, and lift us up. Not only stoop so low as to behold low things are on earth (Psalm 113), but so low as to take up such earthworms as we be from the dunghill, and set us among the princes of the people (vv. 5–8). He not only beholds them with an eye of providence, but His people with an eye of fatherly compassion, and lifts us up to become sons and daughters to Himself, and helps us to believe it that we are so.

This is the first ground of the certainty and confidence of the hearing of our petitions. If once we may come to be certain that we are the sons of God, upon which occasion a great part of this epistle is spent, this is the first ground. And these the Apostle is wont to join together, as the ground of all comfort in this kind (Gal. 4:5–6; Rom. 8:15). So that, to be persuaded or to grow confident that we are the children of God, will be a good foundation to the certainty of the hearing and granting of our petitions. To whom may a son come for any blessing but to a father? And what makes him more confident of speaking and acceptance than this principle that he knows he is the child of such a father as is willing and able to help him?

Secondly, another principle in this epistle tending to build up this certainty and confidence is not only our adoption, but likewise Christ's advocation: "If any man sin, we have an Advocate with the Father, Jesus Christ the righteous" (1 John 2:1-2).

What is it to be an Advocate? To be an Advocate is to plead on our behalves with the Father for the granting and answering of our petitions, for the pardoning and healing of all our transgressions, and the performing to us and giving of us all the good things we stand in need of—whether we ask them, or ask them not. But especially, there is no petition we put up, but Christ takes it at our hands, and puts it up in such form to His heavenly Father, as that by and through Him it is accepted. As a man retains an advocate in a court, he brings him his cause rudely drawn, so as it would be rejected in the court, but his advocate puts it into such a form, as is agreeable to the law, and suitable to the order of the court, so as it finds free acceptance. So we put up our petitions rudely, and many times, far short of that frame which God especially looks for from His servant's hands. But Christ takes them at our hands, and puts them into form, and so prefers them to His heavenly Father. And so as from thence we have good occasion, and good ground of confidence and certainty that whatever we put up in any measure according to God's will, being presented to our Advocate, to our heavenly Father, shall be accepted.

Thirdly, the Atonement, or *propitiation* that our Savior makes to our blessed Father, spoken of in the same place (1 John 2:2). Atonement, or propitiation—the thing is this: that whereas many a servant of God might fear his petitions would never be granted because he has been so sinful before God, and has so many ways dishonored God, that he knows not however God should hear such an unworthy creature as he is. Now the Apostle sets forth in this epistle the Lord Jesus Christ as our Atonement. That if we come to our Advocate, and say, "We have such suits and petitions to put up to our heavenly Father, but we have so displeased Him, that we think He will never regard us;" why, says the Apostle, "If any man sin, we have an Advocate with the Father, Jesus Christ the righteous, and He is the propitiation for our sins." And therefore for our own hearts, though we have just cause of discouragement in regard of our sins, yet we have a propitiation, an atonement. He makes intercession for us as an Advocate. But you say, "God will not hear Him for such sinners as we be?" Yes, He makes propitiation or atonement, that we perish not by our sins, nor that they should hinder God's acceptance of us, or granting our desires (1:7). And so here is a third groundwork of our confidence and certainty of our desires.

Fourthly, there is another, and that is the "anointment that we have received from Him, by which we know all things" (1 John 2:20), implying that though we be dark in our own minds, and dead, and straight in our own spirits, and do not know what the Lord or Christ has done for us. Why yet we have received an unction from the Lord Jesus, who will tell us what He has done for us. As a man's advocate will send his client word of all things how they go in the court about his business, that he may know how far he has proceeded, and where they stick. So the Lord Jesus Christ, He is the Holy One there spoken of: "You have received an unction from Him," He sends down His Holy Spirit into your hearts, and lets you see and know all the petitions and requests that God grants you. You shall no sooner have a petition granted, but you shall have it certified to you by this unction of the Holy One, whereby you know you have them granted, and for whose sake it is that they are granted by this unction. You know all things pertinent to life and godliness. And this is that which the Apostle Paul speaks (2 Cor. 1:21). God sends forth His own Spirit into our hearts to let us know so much, and this is a marvelous point that the Holy Ghost gives us to know all things that are done in heaven for us, and how far God has accepted us.

The Hearing and Granting of Petitions

Further, if you be inquisitive to know why the Spirit of God does certify the soul of this:

First, the Spirit certifies us of this that surely our petitions are heard and granted because He has given us a heart to pray. He has helped us to pray. We could never have prayed fervently and feelingly unless the Holy Ghost had helped us. We know we have straight hearts, and if we therefore come and pour out our souls to God in any spiritual affection, then we know we have this unction. The Holy Ghost came and opened our mouths, and healed our lips, and made us pray affectionately and feelingly. And that is a great light to the hearing of our petitions. For a prayer well-made is never ill heard, and therefore you know what is said, "You prepare the heart to pray and you have heard the desire of the poor" (Ps. 10:17). How shall a poor Christian know that his desire is heard? Why, you have prepared the heart to pray. If God prepare our hearts, then He will cause His ear to hear. These always accompany one another. That is something that this unction does; it works in all our hearts to pray according to God's will, and to pray in the name of Christ, and so satisfies us.

Secondly, this spirit of God that we receive from the Holy One, it is also a spirit of faith that inwardly persuades us that God has indeed heard us, and that He will do for us whatsoever we desire, and will sometimes evidently bear witness of it to the heart of a man. "What thing soever you desire when you pray, believe that you shall receive them, and you shall have them" (Mark 11:24). We must believe that what we have said to God, He will certainly do it, and the Spirit of faith will come, and say to the heart, "God in heaven says, 'Amen' to it, He gives out a fiat, let it be done."

David was in a grievous affliction, both in bodily affliction and spiritual desertion, as in the beginning of the Psalm. "He cried out day and night, God had forsaken him, and his soul was sore vexed; but you O Lord, how long, *etc*. And now away from me all you mine enemies, for the Lord has heard my petition," and He will accept me (Ps. 6:8). So that even while he is in bitter complaints and grievous mourning; while he is yet speaking, this unction comes and reveals to him God's acceptance of him. And therefore now he encourages himself, and casts a defiance upon all the troubles of his soul. He looks at them all as vanishing away like snow before the sun, and now he comforts himself therein.

And this oftentimes and usual when the soul makes use of God's Ordinances and privileges which Himself has granted, that surely God has heard our requests. He never refuses to grant that prayer which He stands to hear. For this purpose is that you read of the good woman Hannah in 1 Samuel 1:15-18. Eli suspected she was in some distemper, but says she, "I have poured out my soul before the Lord." She prayed feelingly, and fervently, and faithfully. Not words, but her soul before the Lord. She had prayed with her whole heart, and her soul did raise up itself heavenward. The strength of her desire was set upon that, and he then said, "The Lord give you favor in His eyes, and grant your request," which was as if this answer had come from heaven. For God does reveal Himself in His Ordinances. She looked at him as the high priest, and so a type of the Messiah and she took it as a voice from heaven. And the text says, "She went home, and looked no more sad." God had set it on, and spoken comfort to her heart, so as that her faith was established. She saw the voice of God in it, and went home resolved upon it, and takes such encouragement to herself from thence as to fear no more in that kind. When God's Spirit gives us to pray affectionately and to believe confidently, then we know we have our petitions, we are persuaded of it.

But besides this confident persuasion this follows, there is another work of faith. And that is a constant wrestling against all discouragements that falls between our requests and the accomplishment of our petitions. Famous is that story of the woman of Syropheonicia (Matt. 15:23-29). You know the manifold discouragements she met with. She prays, and at first God gives her no audience, "answers her not a word." She prays again, and then He gives her a denial to grant her any such request, and tells her plainly that it is not suitable to His calling, and therefore He may not apply Himself unto her. Yet she is not discouraged with this (which is very much) but she follows Him still. And though yet reproached and called a dog, yet she is not discouraged. But out of the word of reproach gathers some hope of comfort; if she be a dog, why then let her have that which belongs to dogs? Let her have but the crumbs that fall from the children's table? She is not discouraged with all the difficulties that lay in her way. Nothing shall cut her off from importunity. And when He could forbear no longer, He then tells her, "O woman, great is your faith, be it unto you even as you will." To show you that if the Holy Ghost do but give a Christian soul so much resolution and confidence, as not to give over praying, till God be pleased to give over answering; it is a good sign. This spirit of faith will certainly prevail at length. "All things are possible to them that believe," and not only possible but certain.

There is a third work of this spirit, and that is this: it works as it is a spirit of hope. And that moves a man to wait upon God that though God should tarry long, and he should pray heartily for such and such requests to be granted. In such a case as this our spirits would be sad and uncomfortable, and give over, and be ready to say, "Wherefore should I wait on the Lord any longer" (as that profane prince said in 1 Kings 6), having been long pressed with famine. He in the end burst forth with this, "This evil is of the Lord, why should we wait on him any longer?" Our foolish hearts soon grow impatient, and we cannot dance after attendance upon God. And therefore in this case though flesh and blood be short winded and soon weary, yet the truth is this unction when it works in us a spirit of hope, it still waits upon God. It sets itself to wait upon Him, and is very well contented to stay God's leisure, though He should tarry very long (Ps. 62:1; 130:4, 5). He sets both morning and evening watch for Him, and he is well contented to wait for Him; "Our eyes wait upon the Lord our God" (Ps. 123:1-3). So that when God gives us a spirit of waiting, then does He certainly seal up unto us the granting of our petitions. For when a man attends at the court for an answer upon his petition, if the king bid him attend, it is a good sign he means to grant him his request, else he would have rejected it. But a wise prince, if he see a man come in good sort and desire a reasonable request of him, that such a thing is according to his princely will, and he bids him to attend and stay there. A sign he means to take it into consideration, at least, and good hopes it will be ac-

CHRIST THE FOUNTAIN OF LIFE

cepted. Now God consults with nobody, but if He give us a heart to wait and stay, assure yourselves He means not to send you empty away. But it is an undoubted argument He will give us an answer, because you can thus wait upon Him.

There is a fourth work of this unction, and it tends marvelously to the speeding of our requests. And that is that which you read, "He will fulfill the desires of them that fear Him" (Ps. 145:19). Do you find that the Lord has wrought a spirit of fear in your heart, so as that you walks awfully before Him? And in the fear of His name goes about every duty? And in His fear depend upon Him? And endeavors to approve yourself before Him? Truly, He will assuredly fulfill the desires of them that fear Him. When we reverence Him in His Ordinances, pray with reverence, and in a holy fear (Ps. 2:11)—them that go about holy duties in a reverent and holy fear do all things in the fear of the Lord. He has a spirit of power to prevail with God. This is such a fear as whereby a man keeps covenant with God, and consequently prevails with God to keep covenant with them (Jer. 32:40). This fear is it which makes us keep covenant with God. This fear of God always keeps possession for God, so as that we dare not do that which is unlawful. We dare not sin against God, nor perform good duties carelessly and fearlessly. For the fear of God bows us to go about holy duties in a holy and reverent manner. And blessed is that man that so fears always.

If therefore God take from us a wanton and wild heart—a loose and unreverent heart— and work in us an awful reverent fear of His name in every duty of His service; and our own callings that keeps us from departing from God; and it keeps God from departing from us, that we always have Him near at hand to hear all the desires of them that fear Him. It is that spirit of which you read, spoken of concerning our Savior, in which He shall prosper in all the works of his hands. "The Spirit of the Lord shall rest upon him, *etc.*" (Isa. 11:2). A spirit of power, and of the fear of the Lord, and that shall make him quick of understanding, and so shall prosper, which is a blessing promised our Savior, "It pleased the Lord to bruise Him, and to put Him to grief, but the pleasure of the Lord shall prosper in His hand" (Isa. 53:10). This is the end of this blessing when God puts us to grief and humiliation, and so works in us the fear of His great name (which ever accompanies those dispensations). Then the work of the Lord prospers in our hands. If God give us a spirit of His holy fear in any duty we go about, then it will assure us that God will hear our desires.

Fifthly, but yet further, there is a spirit of obedience which does marvelously seal up unto us the hearing and granting of all our prayers and petitions; "Whatsoever we ask we receive of Him, because we keep His commandments, and do those things which are pleasing in His sight" (1 John 3:22). It is of necessary use that when God gives us hearts to listen to every word of His mouth, He will then listen to the desires of our souls. "The prayer of the wicked is an abomination to the Lord, but the desires of the righteous are his delight, and he that turns away his are from hearing the Law, his prayer shall be abominable" (Prov. 15:8; cf. 28:8-9). But if a man lend a listening to God's Law, it makes his prayer acceptable. Hearken to the Lord, and the Lord will hearken to you, else not. It is to this purpose what you read in Judges 9, latter end of the seventh verse, "Hearken unto me that God may hearken unto you." If God gave them hearts to hearken to what he spoke to them in God's name, then God will hearken to them. If we speak, and do as Eli taught Samuel to say, "Speak Lord, for Your servant hears" (1 Sam. 3:10). If we come before God with such a resolution that whatever God speaks to us we will hear it, and do it, we shall find this upon it; whatsoever we speak to God He will answer us and work it for us. So that an obedient Christian is a powerful petitioner, he is powerful in prayer. And this we may attain to by making use of this holy epistle of John that is written to all that believe on the name of Christ. This is a fourth direction that John gives us in this epistle, whereby you see how mighty this same epistle is to satisfy and fill our hearts with fullness of joy.

Reason: The reason of this confidence springs from the promises and the discerning of them clearly to belong to us. Now all these things discover to us many promises, confidence springs partly from God's nature, and partly from God's promise, and partly also from our own experience, and these are the staff of our confidence. And from hence it is that we grow to see many promises belong to us. We see the nature of God become fatherly to us. And we from hence in time gather many experiences of God's acceptance of us. And this strengthens our confidence in His hearing of our petitions. Our adoption assures us of God's nature to be ours, whereby God takes us to be His children. And He is one that is full of grace and goodness. Nothing is wanting on His part; He is a Father to us, and that is a great matter.

And in regard that Christ is our Advocate and Atonement, He brings all the promises to us, which in "Christ are all, yes and amen" (2 Cor. 1:20). And this Holy Spirit of God gives us experience of all that goodness that is in God, and the truth in His promises. Yes, and it gives us experience in this also; that He "that has given us His own Son, will not He give us all things else" (Rom. 8:32)? He gives us election, redemption, Fatherly adoption, and effectual vocation to the ways of His grace. And so He gives us experience of the greatest matters. And from hence we know that He will not deny us smaller things. As victory against the remnant of our corruptions, the greatest part of them is scattered before, the staff and strength of them already broken, and we now conflict but with remnants of corruption.

But now when the Holy Ghost says, "we know this," it goes far. For confidence and faith springs from the testimony of Him that speaks, or from the nature of Him upon whom we trust. But knowledge does not so much spring from the testimony of any, either God or man. But is commonly gathered from sense and experience. And experience is both a ground of confidence and knowledge. And hence comes the knowledge of all arts and sciences. Whence is their knowledge, but from their observation of many experiences? Physicians know it, and they therefore set it down in their books, they know it is so. Things that we gather from sense and experience, we are said to have the knowledge of.

Now this experience does not only give us confidence but knowledge. For by the unction that we have received, we do know the love of God that passes knowledge; Christ dwelling in our hearts by faith. We come to know the love of God towards us. There is not anything that concerns the love of God towards us, but the Spirit of God dwelling in our hearts by faith. It comes to pass that we are able to comprehend "the height, and depth, length, and breadth of the love of God" towards us (Eph. 3:18). This Spirit of God in our hearts gives us sensible experience and knowledge of God's love to us, of His atonement and grace to us, our consciences that had hells in them before. All such darksome evils are now vanished and scattered, and we know that sensibly we had power given us to pray, and to believe that our prayers are granted; and can wait upon God, and fear God, and make conscience of obeying His will.

Now this spirit of prayer that discovers these things plainly to our inward man, the sense and experience of it makes a Christian able to know what God has done for him, and makes him able to believe what God has promised him. And thus now when we ask anything according to God's will, He does not only say, "It is well said." But He takes a course to answer our requests. We have certain grounds to move us in what we ask, and the ends of our requests are right. Now God considers not always so much the letter of our prayers as the grounds, and ends of them, the scope we aim at, and God will so accordingly answer us.

USE 1: CONFIDENCE THROUGH FAITH IN JESUS CHRIST

Let it be first a ground of encouragement to every Christian soul that believes in the name of Jesus Christ. Trust not in your own good parts and good gifts. If any such things increase, set not your hearts upon them. Trust not in any worldly blessing, but believe on the name of Christ. And therefore that you may believe, humble your souls before Him in regard of your sins, and pray heartily in the faith of Christ. And why so? The ground is in the text, you shall not only be confident and assured of your salvation, which is a great mercy of God to my soul, and a greater than all the whole Church of Rome would grant. They may go to Rome, and from thence to Jerusalem, and from one place to another to have sought for pardon of sin. And yet not so much comfort promised them, that after all this they shall find it, but in the end to Purgatory they must go; and that is as ill as hellfire (say they) save only in durance. And this is all the help they have, they might whip and scourge themselves, and give all their goods away to the poor, and themselves go in sackcloth and ashes all their days. And when all comes to all, they must not be sure of any mercy or favor from God, which to believe would be heretical presumption. But they must notwithstanding all this rest in hellfire till the Day of Judgement, unless they will be at cost to purchase freedom from it. And (which is strange) though they would not suffer them to believe a release by Christ's pardon, yet upon the Pope's pardon they might have hope. And so they take more pains for an uncertainty than we for certainty and knowledge, but you shall not only attain certainty of salvation, but certainty of the granting of all your requests. No peace to the peace of a believer, and therefore lay aside all your confidence in the world, but be confident in the name of the Lord Jesus, and be certain of God's favor and goodness to you in Him, and then here is such blessings as will keep a man's heart warm in the worst hours.

Use 2: Confidence in Christ's Atonement

To teach such as believe on the name of the Lord Jesus, how you may come to be confident, and certain of the hearing and granting your petitions. How may we come to that? Have you good evidence to your soul of your adoption? that God is your Father? Then meditate well upon this point: that Christ is your Advocate to make intercession and atonement for you, in case you have displeased your heavenly Father. These two things will much prevail. They be strong helps to a weak faith. And then consider what unction you have received, and look up to God that he would give you a spirit of prayer; to pray feelingly and fervently and humbly before Him. And then labor for a spirit of faith, which if God give you so much faith as to persuade you, your requests are heard. And to wrestle against discouragements, and that the spirit of faith does work in your grace to hope and wait upon God, and withal a holy fear of His name. And obedience to walk obediently in doing His will. And patiently to suffer His will under His hand. And observe how the Spirit speaks evidently in this and that kind. And it will be a notable means to help you to grow confident, and certain that all your prayers are heard.

Now many a Christian soul falls short of this. He considers not the atonement of Christ in his prayer. But many times thus stands the case with them. There is much desoluteness in their lives, and looseness and fearlessness in their hearts before God. Rejoice not with trembling. God sees His servants loose in their obedience, and when disobedient they seek not to Christ for atonement. Whence it is that many times they are so full of doubts.

USE 3: CONFIDENCE TO PRAY WELL

Of much consolation to all those that believe on the name of the Lord Jesus, and make use of these blessed means: this is our confidence—that whatsoever petitions we ask, He hears us, and we know it. See how comfortable a Christian's estate is. He grows certain not only of his own salvation, but he is certain of the hearing and granting of all his petitions. If he can but pray well, he makes account all is well, let his distresses be what they will be.

Praying for the Blessing
of Life Upon Others

If any man see his brother sin a sin which is not unto death, he shall
ask, and He shall give him life; for them that sin not unto death.
There is a sin unto death, I do not say that he shall pray for it.
(1 John 5:16-17)

These words contain a third motive to encourage us unto that duty which is the main scope of this epistle (to wit) to believe on the name of the Son of God. Whereto the Apostle exhorts us (v. 13), and propounds first this motive, to wit—a blessed confidence of the hearing of all our petitions. Secondly, a certain knowledge verified that He not only hears, but grants our desires. Now he propounds a third motive in these words, taken from the benefit which by believing on Christ, we shall in some measure be enabled, and made capable of bestowing the like blessing upon our brethren, and that by our prayers. If such a man should see his "brother sin a sin which is not unto death, he shall ask, and he shall give him life." As an instrument, God at his request shall give him life. God will make him an instrument of conveying special favor to such a man.

The words contain three parts. First, a promise of obtaining life for such of our brethren as we shall see sin not unto death, and shall ask life for him.

Secondly, an exception from this general promise. He would have it understood of some special transgression, "of them that sin not unto death." He would be so understood, and would not enlarge this promise so far as that a faithful man by his prayers shall obtain pardon of sin for such as sin unto death, but not for that. That is the only caution that he gives, least this promise be taken to extend too far.

Thirdly, a prevention of an objection or doubt that might hence arise.

For might some man say, "All unrighteousness is sin," and every sin is a sin to death, and the wages of every sin is death (Rom. 6:23). And therefore, if the promise extend only thus far to procure peace and pardon for such as sin not unto death, then either you must grant some venial sins, or else this promise is of none effect. For if every sin be mortal, and you only promise pardon of sin to such as is not unto death. And no man sins but it is unto death, this promise is of none effect.

John answers to this objection in verse 17, and says, though "all unrighteousness be sin," yet there is a "sin that is not unto death." It is true the deserved wages of all unrighteousness is unto death, but there is a sin that is not unto death. Not that there is any sin which does not deserve death, but not that which does undoubtedly cut off a man from all hopes of life; but notwithstanding that sin he may be converted. As sometimes our Savior said of the sickness of Lazarus, he is sick, but not irrecoverable (John 11:4). So that the meaning of the Holy Ghost is that there is a sin unto death, which does not only kill the soul, but irrecoverably out of which there is no hope of recovery or salvation, and that sin they must forbear to pray for.

This promise thus opened will afford us three notes.

First, that a faithful Christian (or which is all one), a believer on the name of Christ is not to hide his eyes from observing and discerning the sins and slips of their brethren. If any man see his brother sin a sin which is not unto death, which he cannot see if he neglect to observe them.

Secondly, a faithful Christian discerning the sin of his brother is to pray for him. Let him ask when he sees him sin not unto death.

Thirdly, a faithful man praying unto Christ for the sin of his brother shall obtain life at God's hand for him, pardon and peace and grace for him.

THE BEHOLDING OF THE COMMITTAL OF SIN

For the first of these:

Doctrine: *A faithful believer is not to hide his eyes from observing the sins and failing of his brethren.*

If any man see his brother sin a sin, he must observe him, else he cannot see him. "When I saw that they walked not uprightly according to the truth of the Gospel, *etc.*" (Gal. 2:14), he observed them and discerned their course, he turned not his eyes from beholding it, but he did take notice of it. "Take heed lest there be in any of you an evil heart of unbelief, in departing from the living God, take heed" (Heb. 3:12-13). He does not speak of himself only, though that principally, but least there be in any of you an evil heart of unbelief. That is not only for every man to take heed to himself, but to his brethren also. As appears by the following verse, implying that a man should not only take heed to himself, but as much as in him lies, take heed to his brethren. And if you should ask how should I prevent another man from having an evil heart of unbelief? He tells you how; "by exhorting one another daily while it is called today," look to yourselves, and also to your brethren. And show your care of them by stirring them up daily. And this is that the Apostle speaks of in Hebrews 10:24, "Let us consider one another and provoke one another to love and good works." See therefore and observe one another, and see where anything is amiss, and stir up one another to every holy performance.

Reason 1: It is first taken from the love we owe them. Secondly, from the love we owe ourselves.

First, the love we owe to our brethren. God requires our love to our brethren. Yes, towards our enemies' ox or ass, we should not see one of them fall under their burden or go astray, and hide our face from them; "If you should see the beast of your enemy to sink down, you shall not pass by him and let him alone, but you shall raise him up from under his burden" (Deut. 22:4). Now if God require so much love to our beasts, and that to the beasts of our enemy, how much more does God require this love to our brethren, that if we see them going out of the way we should call them back again? If we see them to sink under the burden of sin, not there to let them lie. But though we could find in our hearts there to let them lie, yet we ought not so to satisfy ourselves, but to look unto our brethren in such a case, and do the best we can to recover them from going astray.

And in respect of ourselves, this benefit we ourselves shall have. We shall learn a more holy fear of the Lord, and have a more just jealousy over ourselves. We shall keep the better watch over ourselves when we see our brethren fall before us. See Romans 11:20; "Be not high-minded but fear," to show you that when we see other men through unbelief and corruption fall into any sin, we ought to benefit ourselves thereby not to be high-minded upon this occasion to bless ourselves. And we thank God it is not with us as it is with other men. We are not such and such as these publicans are wont to be. But fear we in such a case the sayings of others should be the fears of God's people. The more they see others fall, the more should they suspect their own aptness to fail in the like kind. If such things do befall the green tree, such as are full of the ointment of the Holy One. How easily may the dry stubble kindle, so that what out of respect to learn the more to watch ourselves, and out of compassion to our brethren to restore them, what by seasonable admonition (Lev. 19:17), and what through prayer in his behalf. It is a necessary duty of every faithful Christian man to observe the failings of his brethren.

For further clearing of this point, let me first show you with what an eye we should look upon their falls. Secondly, come to answer an objection, and then to make use.

First, when you look at the falls of your brethren, and have occasion to behold them, look not at them with a partial eye, or a hypocritical eye, as they in Matthew 7:3-5, but reflect we our eye upon ourselves. And conceive that there is either the same or a greater evil in our own bosoms, or at least there is a proneness in ourselves to do it if God should leave us to ourselves. A man should never see his brother fall into any sin, but if he know himself well, when he sees a moat in his brother's eye, he might see a beam in his own. For though God leave not all His servants alike to fall into scandalous evils, yet there is found in them all a root and aptness to all sin, that if God should not restrain them, they would fall into as great evils as the other have done. And hence a Christian man that is sensible of this, he knows there is not anything found in his brother that is singular, but he knows that both himself and all the rest of his brethren are subject to the like evils. And that is an eye of sincerity by which we should ever survey the falls of our brethren; an eye that does not so soon espy an evil in our brethren, but it sees the like, or a greater in itself.

Secondly, as we must not behold their falls with a partial eye, so neither must we observe them with a curious or censorious eye. For there is such an inbred vanity in the hearts of men, that we love to be prying into other men's frailties, and love to be busy in finding fault with other men, not out of a desire to amend them, but to reprove them, and to have something against them. "Be not many masters, for in many things we offend all" (Jas. 3:1-2). What is his meaning? His meaning is, be not of a masterly spirit, be not masters of many persons. To be every man's master is out of censoriousness. Our natures are ready to sift into every man's failings, and would ever be taxing of them. And that is the utmost end such men aim at, not so much the healing and cleansing of our brethren's sins, but to be masters over them. But my brethren, be not many masters; as if this were the frame of our spirit, to be busy as masters in an imperious manner.

Thirdly, neither with an envious and malicious eye. That is complained of by Jeremiah. He much complains of it, when a man opens his eyes to observe curiously, and to pry narrowly, that if they could but find him halting at any time, they would recompense it (Jer. 20:10). When a man observes his brother's halting to heal it, but for this very end that he may take advantage against him and overthrow him, they did stare in his face. And they thought to be even with him. They watched for his halting; this was an envious and malicious eye.

Fourthly, neither must I behold my brother's failings with a wanton eye. That is, when a man is not humbled for his brother's faults, but partly puffed up with it, and prides himself with beholding another man's failings, and thinks every man's fall is a refreshing to himself; he builds his comfort upon the remembrance of the failings of his brethren, and his own falling short of them. This is an in-bred vanity amongst men. This the Apostle taxed among the Corinthians, "You have not so sorrowed for it" (1 Cor. 5:2), you have not been so humbled for it as you should have been, but rather have been "puffed up." Puffed up, why so? What reason had they to be puffed up? Why only this, that they were not such as he was. They had carried themselves better than he had done. They compared themselves with him and in the balance found themselves better than he, and this puffed them up. And this is a wanton eye, for a man may behold it with a wanton eye, either when he prides himself in it, or is induced thereby to licentiousness, and are glad of the occasion, and will say, "If such and such men take such liberty, then they hope they may take the same liberty as well as such men do." And therefore they run into the same course with all greediness.

This is that which the Lord complained of in the whole Church of Judah in Jeremiah 3:7-8. "Her treacherous sister Judah saw it, and though for all the causes whereby back-sliding Israel committed adultery I had put her away, and given her a divorce, yet her treacherous sister Judah feared not, but went and played the harlot also." You heard one use that we ought to make of our brethren's failings was that we should thereby become to fear, but she saw the fall of Israel, and would not be reformed, she feared not. She was not humbled at such falls of her sister Church, but was wanton herself, and went and played the harlot also. As the Church of Israel had gone a whoring after false gods, Judah saw her sin, and saw me reprove and afflict her for it. Yet she feared not, but went and played the harlot; to show you that a man may see his brother's sin, priding himself in his better watching over himself, or with a wanton eye; and this kind of observing the falls of our brethren we ought not to make use of, he presupposes a man ought to observe and see his brothers sin, but not with any of these eyes.

USE 1: LEARN FROM THE SINS OF OTHERS

But for further use, learn we from hence not to neglect the falls of our brethren, and think it is good for us, neither to meddle nor make with them, let that be far from us. That was the spirit of Cain in Genesis 4:9; "Am I my brother's keeper?" As if he would neither meddle nor make with him. What had he to do with him? Now this is a churlish and an unnatural frame of spirit for a man not to be sensible of another's failings. We should look at every man's failing as things that behoove us to observe. And as much as in us lies rather to prevent them than not to take notice of them. Many a man thinks it is best to live quietly, and let every man say, and do as he will. But this is not that which the Apostle John would have to be in faithful Christians.

USE 2: BE WATCHFUL

Secondly, let it be our parts therefore to take a due observation not only of our own, but also of the steps of our brethren. We should not hide ourselves from the beholding of them. If we be occasioned to see it, we should not blind ourselves, and put out our eyes. You see that love to our brethren and enemies' beast would require it. If we find them out of the way, or fallen down under their burden; and you see God requires this love to ourselves, that we should make some use to ourselves of our brethren's fall.

As first, if you see a brother sin, whatever sin it be, learn we to fear God. And that is true Christian affection to be first affected with a holy fear of your own weakness. We should be jealous of the sinful frame of our own hearts that doubtless of themselves are as apt to start aside as any of our brethren's be. The want of this (as you heard) Jeremiah reproved in Judah. And this Paul required of the Romans; "Be not high-minded, but fear" (11:20); and what privileges has the Church of Rome above others? The Apostle knew that the Church of Rome had not received an impossibility of error in his time. He made account in his time. If that "Israel (which was the natural branch) were cut off, then be not you high minded, but fear." For if they be cut off, why may not you? First therefore lay we our hands upon our own hearts, and see if there be not the like folly in me, the same root of unbelief in me. Or if I be not led to the same, am not I led to as great, or a greater evil than theirs is? This use should we make ourselves.

Again, we should labor to make benefit to ourselves by it, look at your brethren in this case with such an eye as may stir you up the more to pity them. If they be gone out of the way, call him back again. If he lie under his burden, lift him up. Or if his estate and condition be such, as that you can by no means have opportunity to speak to him, or if you should, happily your labor would be in vain. And if you should fail here and cannot reach him, yet whether he will or no you may power out your souls to God in his behalf, and so may you do him good. We ought so to do, and not to fail therein. And that will be of special use to help us this way; to hear of the sins and falls of our brethren is much, but to see them is more. To see such heavy burdens lie upon his soul that he is not able to subsist in such a case as this, there will be a special compassion kindled in the heart of a living Christian. For living Christians are loving Christians, so far as living so far loving. For the whole life of Christianity is but faith towards God, and love towards our brethren.

Objection: *But say you, you would not have us to shut our eyes upon the failings of our brethren, but to see and observe them. But does not the Holy Ghost say, "Love covers a multitude of sins;" as if we should smother them, neither meddle nor make with them?*

Answer: But yet, though love cover a multitude of sins, yet how does it cover them? First, with a mantle of wisdom, then with a mantle of faithfulness, and then a mantle of compassion.

A mantle of wisdom. When a man so covers it as not to skin it over, but to cover it so effectually as that it may be covered from the eyes of God and man (Jas. 5:19, 20). This is a wise covering of a multitude of sins. When a man takes a course not only to cover them from the eyes of men, but principally from the conscience of the sinner himself, as that in time he be not over-pressed with them, and then when he is least able to bear them, and so endanger wholly to over-whelm him. For let a man go on in sin, he goes on from day to day and thinks himself whole; and yet it is neither covered from God's eye, nor from the conscience of such a soul. And in the end it cannot but see it, and then so bitterly bewail it, that it is much to be feared he will be quite overwhelmed with it. And therefore, this a man must have principal respect unto, principally to cover his sin from God's eye; and that it may likewise be so covered as not to be smothered and daubed, but cover it with an healing plaster, so as that in time it may be rooted out that no sprig of such a sin may remain there. Not a mantle of flattery, but healing; such as whereby they may be careful to take a course that such evils may be covered with some corrosive plaster.

Secondly, with a *mantle of faithfulness*. Not to discover the sins of others further than will be of necessity for the healing of them. If a man be fallen under his burden, or under his beast, and he is not able himself to help him up, he must then call them that are of strength, and may be of use to help a man in such a case. So that if in this case, if a man's integrity of heart tells him that he aims at no more in making known his brethren's failings, but to help his brother out of those falls (Prov. 11:13). When a man reveals a matter no further than to gather help to restore him, it is well. But because there is a snare in that, a man had need be wary. For a man may reveal it with derision and scorn, and then though a man should speak it to them that are able to help him, it would be a sin to him.

As you may read in Genesis 9:22– 23, Noah being drunk, and his nakedness discovered, Ham coming and seeing his father thus naked. He, in a deriding manner, goes forth and tells his other two brethren, when as he might himself have covered his nakedness, but he does it not, but goes forth and acquaints them. And they do what they can to cover it, they go backward, and draws a garment upon him. "And when he awoke," he by a spirit of prophesy knowing what was done, he said, "cursed be Ham forever." And he made him a servant to both his brethren. When it was in his power to have covered him but did not, but made a jest of it to his brethren, he was accursed for it. But because they in a modest reverent manner did cover him, a blessing fell upon them to this day.

To show you that God requires this faithfulness in us in this case. If we be able to do it ourselves, we must not discover it, but do it ourselves and let it go no further. But if the burden be too great that he cannot lift it up, it is too weighty a matter for him. Then he may call in those that are able to help him in such a work, so as that he do not speak by way of derision, but rather with trouble of mind to see him thus foiled.

Thirdly, so also a *mantle of compassion*. So as that if so be that a man's brother be brought at length to see his failing, and to acknowledge it, and shall express himself that it repents him he has so done, both in offending God and his brethren, then you shall forgive him. Our Savior said so in Luke 17:4. And the like you read (Eph. 4), so that when the Holy Ghost commends this as a property of love, "that it covers a multitude of sins," He means

CHRIST THE FOUNTAIN OF LIFE

not that it covers them in silence or forgetfulness or care-
lessness, as if we never meant to meddle nor make with
them, in a careless silence, and in an indifferent putting
of the matter from us, as if it nothing concerned us. But
cover them by wisdom, faithfulness and compassion,
even such as God for Christ's sake has showed to us.

Objection: *But you say again, but if a man be thus willing
to see and observe the failings of his brethren. It may be he shall be
counted a busy body in other men's matters, a bishop in another
man's diocese, meddling in matters that concerns him not, and
makes us to do there, where we have nothing to do?*

Answer: We may be so counted, but it is not to be doing where we have nothing to do. For God would have us
to take notice of one another's failings. God and Christian
love requires it. It is not out of our element and charge,
but God lays a charge upon us to keep and look to this and
that man's soul. As it was said to the king of Israel, "keep
this man, and if he be gone, your soul shall go for his soul."
It is for us to keep diligent watch, and to consider one
another, and to take heed. There be not an evil heart of
unbelief one in another. And therefore we must not only
have respect to the ways and words of our brethren, but to
the healing of their hearts to see there be no deceitfulness
in the bottom. God therefore requires that we should exhort one another daily, "while it is called today." If therefore you do but keep yourselves within these terms, not
meddling with other men's sins with a hypocritical eye to

condemn them and to justify ourselves; nor with a censorious, envious, malicious, wanton eye, but with an eye of wisdom, faithfulness, and compassion, in such a case you do not go beyond your commission.

Objection: *But you say, I shall be more busy, then I shall have thank for my labor, I may be worse, and they never the better?*

Answer: It may be they will be the worse for the while, and never the better, but "he that rebukes a man, afterwards shall find more favor, then he that flatters with his tongue" (Prov. 28:23). A man must sow this seed in patience. It may be a winter will follow upon it, but at length he shall find the fruits of his labors. Even as the husbandman waits with long patience till the season and time of harvest yield him a comfortable increase, he that deals plainly with his neighbor shall find more favor at the length than he that flatters him. If you lose his favor, it is but for a season. And if a man in this case have been more busy than for the present he gets thanks for, yet God will bless it, and recompense it, and God will not let such a man go without finding favor with himself, however he may from others.

Praying for the Sinning Brother

To open this a little further:

Doctrine: *Upon the sight of a man's brother's sin, a faithful man is to pray for him.*

"If any man see his brother sin, let him ask." So did holy Moses (Ex. 32:31–33). This was the first work he had to do upon their sin, and he spent forty days and forty nights about that work. When he saw it was a sin, and punished it as a magistrate, he satisfies not himself in so doing. But he gets to God, and wrestles with Him about it, and lays his own soul to pawn to God, either pardon that sin, or if he do condemn them, condemn him with them. The like did God direct Job to do. He bids his three friends go to Job, "and he shall pray for you, him will I accept" (Job 42:7–8). God would have it so, Job must pray for them when he sees them in a sin. And Jeremiah speaks to the same purpose, "My soul shall mourn and weep in secret for you" (13:17). And the pattern of our Savior is without exception. Happy was he that could do him a mischief, and all men cried, "Out away with Him, crucify Him! crucify Him!"—that when one would think a man's heart should burst with indignation, yet He prays to His Father, "Father, forgive them, they know not what they do" (Luke 23:34). He prays for pardon of their sin when they use Him most wickedly, one that had never done them wrong. And so you read of Stephen, the first Christian martyr in Acts 7:60, when they flung stones about his ears, "he kneeled down and cried with a loud voice; 'Lord, lay not this sin to their charge.'"

Reason 1: It is first taken from the compassion which we owe to our brethren. We ought to pray for them if they had been but sick. "When they were sick I mourned for them, my prayer shall be for them in their misery" (Ps. 35:13). Now if a man should pray for men in any calamity, how much more in this, the greatest of all the rest, we ought most to pray for our brethren when they sin.

Reason 2: Taken from the duty that lies upon a Christian to exhort his brethren (Heb. 3:12–13; Lev. 19:17), and neither of these can prevail without prayer. For this as well as anything else is sanctified "by the Word and prayer" (1 Tim. 4:5).

Reason 3: Taken from the desperate danger of sin, and the helplessness of a man under sin; unless God put in, and therefore in some case though if man be too weak, he may call in others to help. Yet however amongst the rest call for God's help. For unless we do so, all helps without Him are in vain. Though good helps are of special use, God blessing them to save and lift up a poor soul out of sin. But know this, that it is a work of an Almighty power to deliver a soul from sin no less than the redemption of the Lord Jesus Christ; "He redeems Israel from all his iniquities" (Ps. 130:8). Unless He put forth a redeeming hand, there will be no good done. There is such a deceitfulness in sin as that it will harden a man. Sin is of the nature of poison, it stiffens and hardens the body, puts out the eyes, and so inflames it with heat, that it is not possible to quench it. So when a man has once sinned against God, he presently loses his eyes. Satan and his lusts having gotten him into sin. They first put out his eyes that he shall see no danger nor hurt in it. And then he is so hardened with the sin he has committed, that no counsels or admonitions can recover him out of it, but only the mighty hand of God. And therefore prayer must be made to God for him.

Reason 4: Taken from the displeasure that God takes if He see that we do not pray for them. When we forget to remember them before the Lord, this is ill-taken. God is displeased when there is none to stand in the gap in such a case as this. "God does not afflict willingly" (Isa. 48:17; cf. Eccl. 3:33), and yet if he be stirred up He must destroy them. If there be none to stand in the gap, you then provoke the wrath of the Lord. And this displeases Him much, and God may justly leave us to the like sin for which we are not humbled in others.

Reason 5: Taken from the blessing that befalls God's servants. When we do so, as was upon Job (42:8–9), when Job begins to pray for his friends. Then God turned the captivity of Job, he had long time lain under many vexations, woeful calamities, but when he begins to pray for his friends that had sinned, then the Lord turned his captivity. And so it is expressly said, "I will restore comfort unto him, and to his mourners" (Isa. 57:18-19). To show you that God will restore comfort to us if we lament the falls of others, and mourn over them in that condition. We shall have comfort in their comfort because we did mourn in their grief. If God's people can mourn with their brethren in sin and misery, God will restore comfort to them, and to their mourners.

Before we make use of this point, come we to the next.

THE RECEIPT OF PEACE, PARDON, AND GRACE

To further open this:

Doctrine 3: *A faithful Christian praying for his brethren fallen into any sin shall obtain peace, and pardon, and grace for him.*

It is said so in the text. "If any man," that is, any man that believes in Jesus Christ, "he shall ask, and He shall give him life." So that you see here is the promise made to such. The promise is that upon asking, he shall give life to his sinful brother. Who shall "give him life?" Interpreters take it both ways, and both agreeable to the text, and the analogy of faith. For whether he that prays be as an instrument, or God—it is all one. For it must be God that does it, and he that prays is an instrument. He procures to his sinning brother great favor from God.

Life—that is, the life of justification, and of sanctification, consolation, and comfort to his soul notwithstanding his sin. The promise is evident, he shall prevail with God to bestow life upon his brother. This you shall see evident from Scripture. "I fell down before the Lord forty days and forty nights, *etc.*" (Deut. 9:25-26), and thereupon the Lord did show mercy, and pardoned their sin. Job prayed for his friends, and the Lord said He would accept him (Job 42:8, 9). And so our Savior, He prayed for His crucifiers. And it is generally thought that the powerful prevalency of Peter's sermon in converting three thousand souls at once did especially spring from our Savior's prayer, and the efficacy of it (Acts 2:37). And Stephen, he prayed for his persecutors, and Paul was one of them that had a hand in his death (Acts 7:6). And yet ere long God answered Stephen's prayer in converting Saul. So that let a man (a believing Christian) pray for his sinning brother, and He shall give him life.

Reason 1: It is taken from the pleasure that God takes to knit the members of the Body of His Son together, and no better means to join us together, and so fitly to make us useful members one to another than this. Those members of the Body that are most weak should be most helped this way: "Every member" should be of some use one to another, and it does better compact the body together (1 Cor. 12:21-22). God did not say to Job's friends, "Go you and pray for yourselves," but, "Go to My servant Job, and he shall pray for you." He would have them beholden to Job, of whom they had spoken the thing that was not right, else God would not accept them.

Reason 2: It is taken from the intercession of Christ who performs that office for every member of His Body. This honor have all His saints; though they do not merit this by their prayers, yet there is this efficacy in their prayers. Not of merit, but of grace—to prevail with the Father in their brethren's behalf (Rom. 8:34). Intercession is such a part and kind of prayer as a man makes for other men to procure favor from God to them, to be mediators for them, to pray for others in the name and mediation of Jesus Christ. And that for His sake they may be accepted, God will then hear us for Christ's sake in the behalf of our brethren.

Encouragement to Intercede for Others

It may be a ground of much encouragement to every Christian man to wrestle earnestly with God in the behalf of his brethren. When you see them "sin a sin that is not unto death," be it a man's wicked covetousness, and such as a man is froward in it, and will by no means be admonished, and go on resolutely in it, yet in this case God expects and requires we should mourn for him (Isa. 57:17–18), and therefore neglect not to pray for your brethren in this case.

First, it will displease God if you pray not for them. Is it nothing to you to pass by, and to see such a man lie in sin? Assure yourself of this, God's heart will sit loose towards you if your hearts sit loose to your brethren, and therefore neglect not to pray for them.

Secondly, if you pray for them you shall have comfort restored to them, and to yourselves with them. And though for the present you might seem to procure hurt to yourselves, and no good to them. Yet pray, and pray heartily, and use the best means you can, and you will surely find the comfort and benefit of it. May not this be a notable encouragement to you this way, that God should be pleased to make you an instrument of life to your brother. When he is a dead man in God's sight, a dead man will be stiff and cold and putrefied. And yet even such a man if you pray for him, you shall give him life to his soul.

Objection: *You say, But does not many a man pray for his brethren, and yet is not heard and accepted, did not Abraham pray for Ishmael? And what think you of Samuel's prayer for Saul, and yet says God, How long will you mourn for Saul (1 Sam. 16:1); I have cast him off, mourn no more for him; so that sometimes a man may pray for his brethren, and that earnestly, and yet his prayers fall to the ground in vain?*

Answer: First, it would be considered whether a man be a brother or not. Abraham did not pray for one that was already gracious that did belong to the election of grace. And the text does not reach to such a brother. But I understand it of such as are either called or belong to the election.

Secondly, suppose you do not know whether he belong to the election of grace or not, it may be you pray for them whom you have not used other means to heal them. I doubt not but David prayed for Absalom and Adonijah, but not using other means, his prayers are rejected. These are not prayers of faith, when other good means are not used.

Thirdly, it's possible that a man may pray without faith and without fervency (Jas. 5:15). And such requests should be faithful and fervent. And God requires you should come before Him and submit yourselves to Him, and acknowledge your own unworthiness to ask such a blessing. And yet, in the name of Christ, you press God with it. And you must walk close with God in a course of Christianity, else your prayers are to no purpose. And to wait on God through Christ for a gracious acceptance, and God will recompense your prayers and labor of love in due time.

FINIS.

RECOMMENDED RESOURCES:

Emerson, Everett. *John Cotton*. Boston: Twayne, 1990.

Ziff, Larzer. *The Career of John Cotton: Puritanism and the American Experience*. Princeton: Princeton University Press, 1962.

_____, ed. *John Cotton and the Churches of New England*. Cambridge: Belknap, 1968.

Quinta Press (www.quintapress.com/PDF_Books.html), for the works of John Cotton

23548623R00228

Made in the USA
San Bernardino, CA
27 January 2019